# ENHANCING SOCIAL COMPETENCE
# IN YOUNG STUDENTS

# Enhancing Social Competence in Young Students

■ ■ ■

*School-Based Approaches*

Joel Hundert

pro·ed

8700 Shoal Creek Boulevard
Austin, Texas 78757

**pro·ed**

© 1995 by PRO-ED, Inc.
8700 Shoal Creek Boulevard
Austin, Texas 78757-6897

Hundert, Joel.
    Enhancing social competence in young students : school-based approaches / Joel Hundert.
        p.    cm.
    Includes bibliographical references and indexes.
    ISBN 0-89079-620-3
    1. Problem children—Education (Elementary)    2. Adjustment disorders in children.    3. Social skills—Study and teaching (Elementary)    I. Title.
LC4801.H76    1995
371.96′7—dc20                                                    94-25217
                                                                        CIP

This book is designed in Weiss

Production Manager: Alan Grimes
Production Coordinator: Karen Swain
Art Director: Lori Kopp
Reprints Buyer: Alicia Woods
Editor: Debra Berman
Editorial Assistant: Claudette Landry

Publisher's Note: This book was a joint effort of PRO-ED and the National Association of School Psychologists (NASP). Many individuals contributed to the development of this book; the efforts of Leslie Hale, Susan Gorin, and the NASP Publications Board are greatly appreciated.

Printed in the United States of America

1   2   3   4   5   6   7   8   9   10    99   98   97   96   95

*To Debra and Derek, whose understanding and support allowed me to complete this book and to the children, families, and teachers who motivated me to begin it.*

# Contents

# Preface

One can get easily discouraged when contemplating the magnitude of the challenge of helping children with maladjustment and preventing maladjustment in others. A sizable portion of a generation of children is growing up without adequately developed interpersonal skills for coping with others, dealing with stress, or finding personal contentment. Adding to the magnitude of the problem is the lack of clear answers for solving this problem. Certainly, providing more treatment to those in need, by itself, may not reduce childhood maladjustment. The large number of children with established emotional disorders tend not to access clinical services, at least in the numbers needed to have impact for the entire child population. In part, professionals need to find ways of preventing causal factors leading to maladjustment, as well as blocking their deleterious effects when they do occur.

This book explores school-based strategies for promoting social competence in young children. Schools hold promise as a setting that may be able to deliver a range of social competence–enhancing interventions, including:

- Universal enhancement of social competence in all children

- Targeting programs for children who do not yet show signs of maladjustment but who are at heightened risk

- Programs for children with already developed maladjustment

The need to develop a comprehensive service system of social competence–enhancing interventions is one of the themes that runs throughout this book. Other themes include the following:

- One needs to understand and target the developmental pathways of both childhood maladjustment and children's social competence.

- Children's social behaviors must be understood and treated within the social contexts that occasion them.

- Generalized and durable improvements in children's adjustment require the involvement of multiple socializing agents, in multiple settings, over multiple years.

- The impact of social competence–enhancing interventions is determined by the likelihood that they will be implemented. Professionals need to design school-based interventions with an understanding of factors affecting teacher implementation as well as schools' ways of adapting to change efforts.

- An analysis of the benefits of a social competence–enhancing intervention should be based on consideration of its impact on the incidence of maladjustment and its consequences for a designated child population.

- Targets for interventions, assessment of social competence, and evaluation of intervention effectiveness need to be based on systematic and empirical information.

I attempt in this book to combine a theoretical and practical perspective on these themes that would be of interest to learners and practitioners alike. The book is divided into three sections. The first section focuses on developmental issues affecting childhood maladjustment, social skills deficits, and interventions. Chapter 1 addresses the developmental pathways to childhood maladjustment. Chapter 2 explores the connection between childhood maladjustment, developmental problems, and social skills deficits. Procedures for selecting appropriate targets of intervention are examined in the third chapter.

The second section considers social skills interventions for young children. Chapter 4 focuses on programs that have addressed the needs of preschool and kindergarten students. Programs that are based in schools but that target individual children at high risk are described in Chapter 5. Chapter 6 deals with school-based programs that focus entirely on classes and are universally available to all students. Chapter 7 describes one particular school-based class-focused intervention. The involvement of peers and parents in promoting social competence is described in Chapter 8.

The third section addresses assessment and implementation issues. Ways of assessing the effect of classroom setting variables on a student's social behaviors are described in Chapter 9. Chapter 10 discusses assessment methodology for judging students' social competence and evaluating program outcome. Chapter 11 discusses factors that affect teacher imple-

mentation of programs and consultative strategies for working with teachers. The final chapter explores issues of introducing social competence
interventions and change efforts in schools.

## Acknowledgments

I express my appreciation to several individuals who were especially helpful in the preparation of this book. First, I thank Penny Burlak for her
insights and practical programming ideas for social skills training in
schools. I also thank Benita Hopkins for guiding my thinking on planning
and consultation models for preschoolers with disabilities. Gratitude is
also extended to Jim DeRoy, Debra Hundert, and Lynn Taylor who provided technical support. I extend a special thanks to Chuck Cunningham
for his most helpful comments on drafts of this book and his long-standing
encouragement.

# Developmental Considerations

# ■ *chapter 1*

# Developmental Pathways to Childhood Maladjustment

## ISSUES IN PRACTICE

- ■ What is the prevalence and nature of childhood maladjustment?
- ■ Which children develop maladjustment?
- ■ What is the course of childhood maladjustment?
- ■ What is the relationship between childhood maladjustment and later adjustment problems?
- ■ How well do professional services address maladjustment in the child population?
- ■ What is the developmental pathway to childhood maladjustment?
- ■ How do we prevent maladjustment in children?

Today's newspapers are rife with accounts of both violent and morally offensive crimes committed by the youth of our society. We read of 10-year-olds brandishing dangerous weapons in school grounds, of a 13-year-old honor student planning to stab her teacher, of 11-year-old boys robbing a convenience store at gunpoint. In the United Kingdom, only weeks after a pair of 10-year-olds allegedly murdered a toddler, two 17-year-old girls were jailed for torturing and killing a 70-year-old woman.

These horrendous accounts elicit justifiable outrage from the general population. Increasingly, people are demanding answers to two basic questions: What is causing the high level of violence in our youth? What can be done about it? Outcries of public concern are reflected in popular attitudes toward educational priorities as well. Year after year, polls suggest that student behavior is commonly perceived by the public as the most serious single problem in our schools (Gallup, 1983).

Without question, childhood violence inflicts a great toll upon victims, perpetrators, and society alike. At school, about one in six children report being bullied in the playground (Olweus, 1991). Chronically aggressive children tend to become adolescent and adult offenders, with associated drug, alcohol, and mental health problems (Robins, 1983). Much of the taxpayers' money devoted to helping children is used to provide expensive services, either therapeutic or criminal justice, for children with fully developed behavior and emotional problems. In the United States, yearly incarceration exceeds $40,000 for each offender, and the number of incarcerated juveniles continues to increase (Zigler, Taussig, & Black, 1992). Unfortunately, the human cost is immeasurably greater. Over a 30-year period, the U.S. homicide rate has risen 30%, becoming second only to accidents as the leading cause of death in youths (Lore & Schultz, 1993).

Many factors associated with increased child violence perhaps reflect pervasive changes in the fabric of our society and life patterns. The breakdown of both traditional families and values, the effects of increased poverty, and the commonplace exposure of children to violence in the media have all been cited as contributors to weak social and moral development (Zigler et al., 1992). Chronic economic and social stressors may have rendered many parents in today's homes incapable of adequately guiding the healthy social development of their children. As a result, the schools, in the capacity of socializing agent, are increasingly forced to control, if not resolve, the problem of childhood maladjustment. In modern times, as Comer (1980) stated, "Schools are asked to solve social problems they did not create" (p. 16).

This chapter examines the prevalence of maladjustment in the child population and associated risk "markers." Also explored is the stability of childhood maladjustment and its relationship to indexes of adult adjustment and service utilization patterns. Finally, this chapter considers the developmental pathway toward childhood maladjustment.

## Childhood Maladjustment: Methodological Considerations

Any intervention aimed at reducing maladjustment in children must be based on consideration of both the number and the characteristics of children who display adjustment problems. Epidemiological studies examining these two factors differ in their (a) method of selecting a representative sample of children, (b) choice of instruments used to measure maladjustment, and (c) criteria for identifying a child as a "case."

### Sampling Strategies

One sampling strategy is to select a group of children within a relatively small, well-defined geographic boundary. For instance, in the Isle of

Wight study (Rutter, Cox, Tupling, Berger, & Yule, 1975), an estimated prevalence of childhood disorder was determined from measures of virtually every 8-year-old child on the island. Although this data collection strategy may reduce population sampling errors, the extent to which any particular geographic area is representative of a broader population base may be problematic. For example, Boyle and Offord (1990) suggested that the Isle of Wight sample does not reflect the typical urban–rural distribution of children in most areas of the Western world. Hence, because urban living has been associated with increased risk of maladjustment (Boyle & Offord, 1990), the results from the Isle of Wight study may underestimate the prevalence of childhood maladjustment in the general population.

A second sampling strategy is to obtain a stratified representative sample of children from a larger geographic area. For instance, the Ontario Child Health Study used a random sample of over 2,000 children (ages 4 to 18) from across the province, representative of age, sex, and, urban–rural distribution (Boyle et al., 1987). In a second example, 20% of children attending all New York City day care centers were monitored in a 7-year longitudinal study (Kohn, 1977).

## Measurement of Maladjustment

Determining the prevalence of childhood maladjustment requires both efficient procedures for measuring the behavior and emotional functioning of a large number of children and criteria for identifying instances of maladjustment. In the Isle of Wight study, a two-step process identified childhood maladjustment (Yule, 1981). In the first step, all children in the sample were individually screened by parent-report questionnaires, results of which were used to identify high-risk children. In the second step, identified children received detailed follow-up assessment, consisting of both direct clinical examination and administration of additional psychometric measures.

Another strategy for determining the prevalence of childhood maladjustment is to assess randomly selected children from a sample representative of the general population. Esser, Schmidt, and Woerner (1990) used a combination of strategies in their study of the prevalence of childhood emotional disorders. All parents of the 1,444 children born during a 6-month period in Monheim, Germany, were invited to complete behavior rating questionnaires describing their children's behavior. Of the 400 respondents, children scoring within the top quartile were individually assessed by clinicians on their degree of behavior and emotional disturbance.

In the Ontario Child Health Study, Offord et al. (1987) obtained ratings from both teachers and parents for children aged 4 to 11 and self-report measures for youths aged 12 to 16, in order to identify children

with one or more emotional disorders. The use of multiple raters to identify children at risk adds to the information base provided, but at the same
time raises the potential of rater disagreement. The interinformant agreement rates for conduct disorder found in the Ontario Child Health Study
are shown in Table 1.1. Only 6.5% of the 4- to 11-year-old boys rated by
teachers as having conduct disorder were also so identified by their parents (Offord, Alder, & Boyle, 1986). Likewise, agreement between teacher
and youth self-report ratings for male conduct disorder was only 17%.
The interinformant agreement rate for girls was even lower. Lack of agreement to such a degree may suggest that if emotional problems are identified by one rater of a child, then it is unlikely that others will also rate the
same child as maladjusted.

How could discrepancy among raters be so high for problem behaviors that, on the surface at least, would appear easy to identify? One possibility is that the self- or other-report measures were neither exact nor
consistent enough. For instance, differing standards of troublesome behavior combined with insufficiently exact definitions of problematic symptom
areas may account for low levels of interinformant correspondence.

A second possibility is that the discrepancies reflect instances of situation specificity of behavior. In other words, children's expression of maladjustment may differ at home and at school settings, depending on the
differential expectations in each situation. The behavior requirements for
children in a classroom to attend to structured lessons and to perform academic tasks differ substantially from the behavior expectations in most
occasions at home. Children's differing responses to the varying demand

TABLE 1.1. Prevalence (per 100) of Conduct Disorder by Informant for
Age and Sex Categories, Plus Interinformant Agreement

| | | | PREVALENCE | | | PERCENTAGE AGREEMENT |
| | | | PARENT | TEACHER/YOUTH | | PARENT AND |
| AGE | SEX | N | ALONE | ALONE | OVERALL | TEACHER/YOUTH |
|---|---|---|---|---|---|---|
| 4–11 | Boys | 710 | 1.4 | 4.9 | 6.5 | 6.5 |
| | Girls | 718 | 0.4 | 1.8 | 1.8 | 0.0 |
| 12–16 | Boys | 607 | 4.4 | 7.2 | 10.4 | 17.0 |
| | Girls | 624 | 1.9 | 2.9 | 4.1 | 11.1 |

Adapted from "Prevalence and Sociodemographic Correlates of Conduct Disorder" by D. R. Offord,
R. J. Alder, and M. H. Boyle, 1986, *American Journal of Social Psychiatry, 6*(4), pp. 272–278, and from
"Ontario Child Health Study: Correlates of Disorder" by D. R. Offord, M. H. Boyle, and Y. A.
Racine, 1982, *Journal of the American Academy of Child and Adolescent Psychiatry, 28,* pp. 856–860.

expectations in the two settings may produce discrepant views of their adjustment from parents and teachers.

## Case Selection

The situation specificity of children's behavior and emotional functioning impacts on strategies of case selection. A conservative strategy would be to identify maladjustment only in children about whom raters agree regarding its existence. Although this conservative approach reduces the rate of false positive identification of maladjusted children, it may also potentially exclude from attention other children in need of help.

# Prevalence of Childhood Maladjustment

Considerable agreement exists across internationally conducted epidemiological studies that the prevalence of maladjustment in children is approximately 12% to 15% (Office of Technology Assessment, 1986). Esser et al. (1990) found evidence of psychiatric disorder in 16.2% of a sample of 8-year-old German children; the probability of maladjustment was twice as high for boys as for girls. In Ontario, Canada, the prevalence rate of one or more childhood emotional disorders has been estimated at 18.1% (Offord et al., 1987). The Isle of Wight study revealed psychiatric disorder in 12% of 10-year-olds. For an inner London borough, the prevalence was identified at 25.4% (Rutter et al., 1975).

Conduct disorder has been identified as the most common problem of childhood maladjustment, constituting about half of all disorders that account for the prevalence rate of children's mental health problems (Esser et al., 1990). The estimated prevalence of conduct disorder ranges from 4.2% (Rutter, Tizard, & Whitmore, 1970) to 6.7% (Connell, Irvine, & Rodney, 1982) and differs according to children's developmental levels and gender, as reflected in results of the Ontario Child Health Study (Offord, Boyle, & Racine, 1991) reproduced in Table 1.1. As indicated in the table, the incidence of conduct disorder was found to be much greater in boys than in girls, the ratio being 3 to 1 for 4- to 11-year-olds and 2 to 1 for 12- to 16-year-olds.

The prevalence rate of childhood maladjustment represents the estimated percentage of children exhibiting emotional problems at a single point in time. Without repeated measurement of the same population of children, it would be difficult to determine accurately whether the rate of childhood maladjustment is on the rise. Over the past 10 years, however, reported increases in juvenile delinquency (Bruininks, 1991), incidence of violent crime (Lore & Schultz, 1993), and occurrences of childhood aggression (Olweus, 1979) suggest that childhood maladjustment is a growing phenomenon. Nonetheless, not all children are equally likely to develop maladjustment.

## Children Likely to Develop Maladjustment

The development of childhood behavior and emotional problems has been associated with a number of both child and family "markers." The presence of a marker identifies a child's increased risk of maladjustment, but does not necessarily constitute a cause of the problem. Boyle and Offord (1990) illustrated the distinction between a marker and a cause in their investigation of the increased risk of conduct disorder in children of single parents. They found the single-parent family to be a marker of childhood conduct disorder, but not always a causal factor in its development. In some cases, for instance, a child's antecedent maladjustment may have contributed to the marital breakdown; in others, both problems may have been triggered by a third variable, such as parental emotional disturbance.

One way of expressing the degree of risk predicted by a marker is the calculation of "relative odds." Relative odds (RO) identifies the extent to which a risk factor increases the probability of associated childhood disorder; a score of 1.0 indicates that the factor does not increase the likelihood of maladjustment beyond the population base rate of the disorder. The formula for calculating RO is as follows:

$$RO = P(D\backslash R)/P(D)$$

where $P(D\backslash R)$ is the conditional probability that a child characterized by the risk factor will exhibit a conduct disorder and $P(D)$ is the base rate (prevalence of the disorder in the general population).

Suppose, for example, that conduct disorder is found in 5% of the general child population $[P(D) = .05]$, but in 11% of the population of children in single-parent homes $[P(D\backslash R) = .11]$. Using the above formula to calculate relative odds, the result would be .11/.05, or 2.2, suggesting that children from single-parent homes would be 2.2 times more likely to display conduct disorder than children from two-parent homes. Based on results from the Ontario Child Health Study, the relative odds of conduct disorder in children aged 4 to 16 are shown in Table 1.2.

Some factors associated with increased risk of childhood maladjustment include low socioeconomic status (Rutter et al., 1975; Sameroff & Seifer, 1983), low family income (Boyle & Offord, 1990), large family size

TABLE 1.2.  Sociodemographic Correlates of Conduct Disorder for Children Aged 4 to 16

| CORRELATE | (N)[a] | RELATIVE ODDS | SIGNIFICANCE |
|---|---|---|---|
| On welfare | (171) | 3.1 | $p < .00001$ |
| Subsidized housing | (110) | 2.9 | $p < .001$ |
| Low income | (571) | 2.1 | $p < .00001$ |
| Unemployed | (261) | 2.1 | $p < .01$ |
| Overcrowding | (386) | 1.7 | $p < .01$ |
| Low mother's education | (368) | 1.6 | $p < .05$ |
| Single parent | (273) | 2.2 | $p < .001$ |
| Large sibship[b] | (381) | 1.5 | $p < .10$ |
| Urban residence | (1,668) | 1.2 | n.s. |

a. (N) refers to the number of children with the correlate.

b. Large sibship was defined as four or more children, aged 0 to 18 years, living in the household.

From "Prevalence and Sociodemographic Correlates of Conduct Disorder" by D. R. Offord, R. J. Alder, and M. H. Boyle, 1986, *The American Journal of Social Psychiatry, 6*(4), p. 277. Copyright 1986 by Brunner/Mazel. Reprinted with permission.

(Rutter et al., 1975), urban residence (Boyle & Offord, 1990), and a single-parent home (Boyle & Offord, 1990). Odds of developing maladjustment also are found to increase if one or both parents suffer from emotional disturbance. For instance, the odds of childhood conduct disorder escalates to 50% in cases where the history for both parents includes child neglect, abuse, crime, or drug addiction. Similarly, increased risk of childhood maladjustment has been associated with parental depression (Billings & Moos, 1983), domestic violence, family dysfunction, and parent criminal arrest or psychiatric disturbance (Sameroff & Seifer, 1983). Finally, child variables that increase the risk of maladjustment include a history of medical illness, an active temperament, and male gender (Boyle & Offord, 1990; Lewis, Dlugokinski, Caputo, & Griffin, 1988; Rutter & Quinton, 1984).

According to Rutter (1987), the identity of the specific risk factors present is not as important as their cumulative effect in contributing to maladjustment. Because children who succumb to emotional disorders tend to have experienced a combination of risk factors, cumulative odds predict child maladjustment better than does any single variable (Sameroff & Seifer, 1983).

## Stability of Childhood Maladjustment

Once maladjustment is fully developed, children tend to maintain their problems into adolescence and adulthood. Stability of the most prevalent disorders is described below.

## Aggression

Longitudinal studies report the stability of childhood aggression. From a sample of some of the most disruptive kindergarten students in Montreal schools, over half maintained high levels of aggression 4 years later (Tremblay, Loeber, et al., 1991). A similar maintenance rate was identified in a longitudinal study of aggression in third-grade students, followed over 3 years (Campbell, Breaux, Ewing, & Szumowski, 1986). More striking is evidence that aggression persists over even longer periods of time. Farrington (1991) found that half the students identified by teachers as aggressive at age 8 continued to show aggressive patterns at age 32.

## Antisocial Behavior

The antisocial behavior of children and adolescents who commit criminal acts tends to persist into adulthood. As high as 50% to 70% of juvenile offenders are later arrested as adults (McCord, 1979). Loeber (1982, 1991) suggested that the following markers are associated with increased stability of antisocial behavior in children:

- Frequency of antisocial acts
- Number of settings in which the acts occur
- Degree of variety in the types of antisocial acts displayed
- Age of onset of antisocial activity
- Co-presence of hyperactivity

## Conduct Disorder

Esser et al. (1990) followed to age 13 a sample of all 8-year-olds who were born during a 6-month period in Monheim, Germany. Over half of those characterized by psychiatric disturbance at age 8 continued to display maladjustment at age 13. The most stable of these disturbances was conduct disorder, which was maintained by almost all children characterized by this form of maladjustment at age 8.

## Peer Rejection

Children rejected by peers tend to remain so as they grow older. Coie and Dodge (1983) followed samples of students from third to fifth grade, over a 5-year period. Yearly social status scores revealed that, in any year, approximately 20% of students were rejected by their classmates. Forty-five percent of all children maintained their original social status (i.e., popular, neglected, average, controversial, rejected) over a 1-year period and 30% over a 4-year period, with the greatest stability in status displayed by the rejected students. Rejected children seldom changed social status; if they did, they rarely moved from rejected to popular.

Howes (1990) discovered a similar stability level for peer rejection from kindergarten to Grade 3. In this study, sociometric scores were obtained for a sample of 102 kindergarten students, 45 of whom were followed to Grade 3. More than one third of the students maintained their social status during the course of the study, with the rejected students showing the highest rates of stability.

Because peer rejection often co-occurs with aggression, it is important to separate the contributions of rejection and aggression to later childhood maladjustment. It is possible that aggression, rather than peer rejection, is the true indicator of disorder. In a 3-year study of Black third-grade children from low income families, Coie, Lochman, Terry, and Hyman (1992) provided evidence that, as separate factors, both childhood aggression and peer rejection predicted adolescent behavior and emotional disorder; in combination, moreover, they produced additive predictive impact. Table 1.3 reproduces results of their study, identifying the prediction factor of aggression and peer rejection in Grade 3 to serious adjustment problems in early adolescence.

As demonstrated in the table, 18% of students identified as neither aggressive nor rejected in Grade 3 later displayed serious maladjustment problems, whereas later disorder was reported for 62% of their aggressive

TABLE 1.3.  Percentage of Subjects Showing Serious
Adjustment Problems in Early Adolescence as Predicted by
Third-Grade Rejection or Aggression

| AGGRESSION STATUS IN 3RD GRADE | REJECTED IN 3RD GRADE | | NOT REJECTED IN 3RD GRADE | |
|---|---|---|---|---|
| | % | *N* | % | *N* |
| Aggressive | 62 | 21 | 40 | 20 |
| Nonaggressive | 34 | 41 | 18 | 139 |

From "Predicting Early Adolescent Disorder from Childhood Aggression and Peer Rejection" by J. D. Coie, J. E. Lochman, R. Terry, and C. Hyman, 1992, *Journal of Consulting and Clinical Psychology, 60,* p. 790. Copyright 1992 by The American Psychological Association. Reprinted by permission.

and/or rejected peers. Those identified in Grade 3 as either aggressive or rejected showed elevated incidence of later maladjustment, but not at the levels of children with both problems.

## Implications

Results of the Coie et al. (1992) study suggest that the 5% of children identified in third grade as both aggressive and rejected make up about 50% of those later labeled maladjusted. A similar ratio has been reported in investigations of adolescent crime (West & Farrington, 1977). The fact that aggression in young children tends to continue over time may imply not only that behavior disorder does not disappear on its own, but also that it becomes increasingly more resilient and less sensitive to treatment as a child matures (Loeber, 1991). Recognition of the stability of childhood aggression may encourage the pursuit of early prevention and intervention strategies. For example, early elimination of behavior problems in the 5% of children with the most serious adjustment problems may reduce by half the later prevalence of maladjustment in children.

# Relationship Between Childhood and Adult Adjustment

A high percentage of children suffer from one or more emotional problems, displayed as both antisocial behaviors and conduct disorders that persist over time, resulting later in crime, drug abuse, and mental health problems in both adolescence and adulthood. Studies examining the relationship between childhood and adult adjustment have been based on two different types of methodological design (Kupersmidt, Coie, & Dodge, 1990; Parker & Asher, 1987). The first of these, called "follow-back" or retrospective, determines the relationship between childhood risk and adult maladjustment by searching the available archival records of maladjusted adults to identify childhood factors distinguishing this group from a group of well-adjusted adults. Although relatively easy to conduct, the retrospective design is limited by its dependence on selective and biased archival information (e.g., school records) as indicators of childhood functioning (Parker & Asher, 1987).

In the second design, termed "follow-forward" or prospective, a sample of children is followed over time to identify factors associated with later maladjustment. This design features two advantages over the retrospective design. First, because it is not dependent on selective archival data, the follow-forward design provides more reliable information than its follow-backward counterpart. Second, this design enables researchers to determine the sequence by which events leading to maladjustment unfold, thus potentially tracing the developmental pathway of childhood disorder. The major disadvantages of the follow-forward design, however, are both the high expense and the complex logistics of mounting a study that tracks several children over a prolonged time span. Figure 1.1 illustrates the two designs.

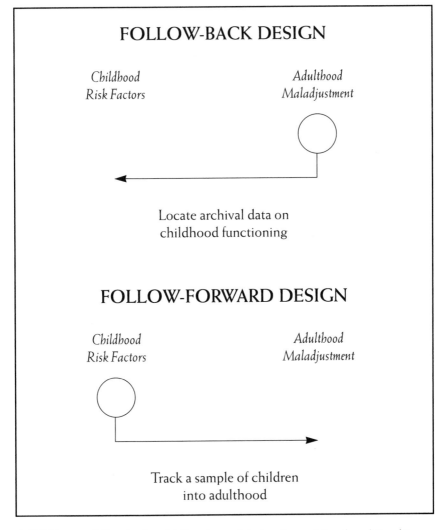

FIGURE 1.1.   Follow-back and follow-forward designs for studying the relationship between childhood risk factors and adult maladjustment.

Childhood maladjustment has been associated with such later diffi-culties as early school dropout, criminality, and adult psychopathology, each of which is discussed below.

## School Dropout

One sequela of childhood maladjustment is an increased probability of later dropping out of school. A follow-forward study tracking more than 1,000 sixth-grade students into high school (Gronland & Holmlund, 1958) reported that slightly more than half the students with low peer acceptance in elementary school failed to complete secondary school, representing a dropout rate 2.5 times greater than that of popular students. The relation-ship between peer acceptance and school dropout was most pronounced in female students; 35% of rejected elementary school girls later dropped out, compared to 4% of popular girls.

## Criminality

Determining the relationship between childhood maladjustment and later criminal behavior is complicated by the lack of a common definition of "criminal." If, for example, arrest and/or conviction are used as possible cri-teria for criminality, this approach may unwittingly bias results in favor of children from higher socioeconomic backgrounds because proportionally few of them may be arrested for criminal acts they may have committed (Kupersmidt et al., 1990).

Despite the problem of case selection, evidence does suggest a rela-tionship between childhood maladjustment and later criminality. An early follow-back study examined the military records of soldiers dismissed for either disciplinary or other conduct problems (Rolf, 1961). When records from child guidance clinics were examined to determine early differences between good and bad conduct soldiers, it was discovered that more than half the bad conduct soldiers were characterized by poor interpersonal relations as children, double the rate for good conduct soldiers.

In a follow-forward design, West and Farrington (1977) tracked 411 eight-year-old urban English children for 24 years. Initial levels of emo-tional adjustment were measured by teacher ratings, direct interviews with social workers, and sociometric ratings of classmates. Eleven years later, 25% of the total sample of children had been convicted of at least one criminal offense, with students initially rated as "troublesome" showing significantly higher rates of delinquency than their peers. By age 32, 57%

of the children rated as aggressive at age 8 had been convicted of crime, representing twice the conviction rate of nonaggressive children.

A child's social status may mitigate the connection between peer rejection and later delinquency. However, Rolf, Sells, and Golden (1972) suggested that the higher rates of delinquent crime associated with children who are rejected by peers is applicable only to children of middle and upper socioeconomic status. The delinquency rate for boys in the lowest level of socioeconomic status was found to be high regardless of whether the boys were popular or rejected. Thus, a background of poverty seems to override the lowered probability of delinquency associated with peer popularity.

## Adult Psychopathology

Considerable evidence demonstrates a link between childhood problems and later psychopathology. Follow-back studies suggest that schizophrenic adults tended to be antisocial, socially isolated, and immature children (Lewine, 1981). Of children screened for behavior and emotional problems on school entry, those listed on a psychiatric registry 11 to 13 years later had been distinguished by higher levels of peer rejection (Cowen, Pederson, Babigian, Izzo, & Trost, 1973). Moreover, peer ratings were identified as more sensitive indicators of later mental health problems than either grades, achievement scores, or teacher ratings. Yet, while the association between low peer status in elementary school and adult psychiatric disorder is persistent, it is not always strong (Rolf et al., 1972).

# Service Utilization of Maladjusted Children

Studies suggest that very few maladjusted children ever access professional mental health services. The Ontario Child Health Study (Offord et al., 1987) found that only 16% of children suffering from one or more emotional disorders had received either social or clinical service within the previous 6 months, although two thirds of those children were deemed in need of professional help. Other estimates of service utilization suggest that only between 6% and 30% of maladjusted children receive mental health services (Lewis et al., 1988).

A number of factors may explain the low utilization rate of professional help for this population. Certainly, the unavailability and/or inaccessibility of mental health treatment in the system may be one salient obstacle. A second problem may be lack of consensus among significant adults regarding the existence of maladjustment in any particular case. Referral of a child for treatment is usually initiated by one or more adults who perceive the presence of a behavior or emotional problem that warrants professional treatment. Parents of a child presenting behavior problems at school but not at home are unlikely to request professional assistance. In fact, most children rated by teachers as poorly adjusted are not so rated by their parents (Offord et al., 1986).

Child referral to mental health clinics is often determined by factors beyond the child's actual behaviors. In fact, many clinic-referred children display rates of deviant behavior similar to those of nonreferred children (Rickard, Graziano, & Forehand, 1984). One important factor related to parental referral of children for treatment is the parents' own emotional adjustment. In one study, maternal perception of child maladjustment was a better discriminant between groups of referred and nonreferred children than the actual occurrence of children's deviant behavior (Griest, Forehand, Wells, & McMahon, 1980). Moreover, maternal identification of maladjustment in referred children, in turn, was best predicted by maternal depression.

Child referral seems to reflect an interaction between the presence of behavior and emotional problems and the degree of adult tolerance for those problems within the setting of their occurrence. Parental tolerance of their children's behavior is, in turn, influenced by broader contextual factors that may be either temporally or spatially removed from the immediate situation. For example, Dumas (1989b) found that the number of positive contacts outside the home predicted how well socially isolated mothers managed their children each day.

Because few maladjusted children are referred for service, and because existing referrals are motivated by a complexity of variables beyond the particular behavior of the child, it is unlikely that a passive/receptive model of service will adequately serve the needs of the population of children requiring mental health care unless coupled with improved client recruitment strategies and/or ways of specifically targeting children at risk for maladjustment.

## Developmental Pathways

Kazdin (1993b) suggested that effective programs for maladjusted children must be derived from models that explain the influence of various factors in the development of maladjustment. An understanding of the variables leading to childhood dysfunction may suggest interventions for both treatment and prevention. An examination of developmental pathways to childhood maladjustment might also pinpoint critical ages at which children are most malleable to intervention.

## Factors Affecting Development

Most models of maladjustment agree that a combination of variables contribute to dysfunction in children. For instance, Rutter (1987) suggested that the development of maladjustment reflects a complex interaction of four variables: individual disposition, ecological disposition, current circumstances, and prevailing opportunities. A similar list of factors, reported by Olweus (1991), was found to determine an "aggressive personality" in boys.

The factors of predisposition, family variables, and stressful life events are each examined in the following paragraphs.

**Predisposition.** Individual differences in children's behavior styles can be discerned almost at birth (Kagan & Snidman, 1991; Thomas, Chess, & Birch, 1968). While some babies appear placid and happy, others are difficult and demanding, crying for long periods of time and resisting comfort. Such apparently innate differences in behavior style and mood continue for at least 5 years.

Children temperamentally predisposed to difficult behaviors are three times more likely than calmer children to develop later behavior problems (Graham, Rutter, & George, 1973). Abidin, Jenkins, and McGaughey (1992) followed a sample of 100 children, 6 to 12 months of age, over a 4½-year period. Infants who were initially judged by mothers to be moody and demanding were more likely to be later rated as poorly adjusted. A longer follow-up investigation of the relationship between temperamental predisposition and later maladjustment was completed in the *Bloomington Longitudinal Study* (Bates, Maslin, & Frankel, 1985). Although the predictive power was low, initial measures of temperament at age 6 months accurately predicted the emergence of externalizing problems at age 8 years.

Whether caused by a genetic link, by perinatal factors, or by other conditions, it is evident that some children develop early patterns that predispose them for higher risk of maladjustment and aggression. The possibility of a genetic base to aggression has been investigated by an examination of concordance rates for criminality in pairs of monozygotic and dizygotic twins. Christiansen (1977) discovered a 35.2% probability for criminal conviction of one monozygotic twin if the second twin had also been convicted; this concordance rate was about three times that of dizygotic twins.

Adoption studies are also able to address the genetic basis of aggression. Mednick, Gabrielli, and Hutchings (1984) examined the association between birth father criminality and conviction rates of their biological sons, all of whom had been adopted by noncriminal fathers. Adoptees of criminal biological fathers showed higher conviction rates than those whose fathers had been crime-free. Moreover, the likelihood of conviction for the adopted children increased in proportion to the number of crimes committed by the biological father.

Family variables. Both parenting style and other family variables have been linked to the development of emotional problems in children. Olweus (1991), for example, suggested that of the four factors contributing to the formation of an aggressive childhood personality, three pertained to parenting practices. Specifically, these practices included lack of parental warmth, overprotectiveness, and "power assertive" child rearing.

A considerable body of work examining the link between parenting styles and children's antisocial behavior has been described by Gerald Patterson and his colleagues (Patterson, 1986b; Reid & Patterson, 1991). They used naturalistic observations in the home to examine differences in interaction patterns between families with either "distressed" or "nondistressed" boys. Families of distressed boys were characterized by higher rates of violence for all family members. Interactions among these family members tended to be coercive in nature, with longer durations of negative exchanges. For instance, a mother's demand may be countered by a child's complaining, which is responded to by the mother's issuing a threat, and so on. Moreover, despite the higher rates of aversive reactions to their child's behaviors (about three times that of nondistressed families), the actions of parents of oppositional children were less likely to elicit child compliance than those of the parents of nondistressed children. These early patterns of negative exchange were associated with high incidence of aversive behavior in young children. Not only was the rate of these behaviors for distressed preschoolers twice that of their nondistressed peers, but also it did not diminish as the children reached elementary school age. In contrast, the rate of aversive behavior in nondistressed children decreased as they matured.

Other research has confirmed the link between parenting style and aversive child behavior. Patterson, Capaldi, and Bank (1991) assigned much of the cause of aversive behavior in children to negative and inconsistent disciplinary styles used by their parents. Loeber (1982) associated a lack of parent monitoring with the development of antisocial behavior in children. Similarly, Wilson (1980) discovered that parents who are chronically unable to either discipline or monitor their children tend to produce antisocial offspring. In a laboratory study measuring mothers' interactions with their 2- to 3-year-old children, conducted by Campbell et al. (1986), the incidence of negative maternal feedback and impulsive control strategies displayed in the laboratory setting predicted later maternal ratings of their children as aggressive and/or hyperactive at age 5.

Other family variables have also been associated with a heightened risk of childhood maladjustment. For instance, children are more vulnerable to emotional disorders if one or more parents have experienced a history of mental illness (Sameroff & Seifer, 1983), criminal conviction (West & Farrington, 1977), marital discord (Lewis et al., 1988), or economic disadvantage (Loeber, 1982). These variables appear to have an impact on parental provision of the care and stimulation necessary for successful child development (Farrington, 1991).

**Stressful life events.** Stressful life events that disrupt the nurturing and emotional security provided by parents have been linked with increased risk of childhood maladjustment. For instance, repeated hospitalization for medical ailments incurs increased risk of emotional disturbance in preschool children (Lewis et al., 1988). The birth of a sibling is a common stressful life event. In one study, more than half the sample of children 2 to 3 years old developed new toileting problems following sibling birth. Other studies have confirmed the emotional impact on children of family separation precipitated by parent illness, divorce, or death (Lewis et al., 1988; Rutter & Quinton, 1984).

Esser et al. (1990) used the number of stressful life events experienced by children as a significant predictor of the development of psychiatric disorders from age 8 to 13. The cumulative impact of stressful life events can be estimated by the *Life Events Record* (Coddington, 1972). Events considered to be highly stressful to children include:

- Death of a parent
- Divorce or marital separation of parents
- Acquisition of a visible deformity
- Death of a sibling or other close relative

Events considered less stressful include:

- New membership in a church/synagogue
- Decrease in number of arguments between parents
- Decrease in number of arguments with parents

■ Change in parents' financial status

■ Sibling's leaving home

Although children scoring high on the *Life Events Record* would be presumed to be at increased risk for later maladjustment, no *overwhelming* empirical evidence of a link between life stressors and maladjustment exists. Many studies examining the connection between stressful life events and behavior maladjustment in children have used a cross-sectional experimental design, which prevents an investigation of the impact of contemporary risk factors on adjustment at a later time. Some prospective studies have failed to determine significant links between stressful life events and adjustment either 5 months (Swearingen & Cohen, 1985), 2 years (Dubow, Tisak, Causey, Hryshko, & Reid, 1991), or 5 years (Gersten, Langner, Eisenberg, & Simcha-Fagan, 1977) later. Dubow et al. (1991) found that maladjustment levels in one sample of children related not to the number of stressful life events the children experienced, but rather to the amount of social support they received in dealing with these situations. In the same study, the children who maintained a number of close friends also rated themselves at low stress levels.

## Models of Developmental Pathways Toward Childhood Maladjustment

The complexity of factors that may contribute to childhood maladjustment is striking. Because it is unlikely that a single intervention can address all potentially existing variables contributing to maladjustment, it is necessary to pinpoint those variables that should be targeted for treatment. Patterson et al. (1991) argued that interventions should target those factors in the causal chain of disorder that are most "proximal" to the production of maladjustment. Risk factors more distally connected (e.g., parental depression or economic disadvantage) would be addressed only when they either interfere with developing parenting skills or diminish gains the parents may already have made. The relationship between proximal and distal family variables contributing to antisocial behavior in children is depicted in Figure 1.2.

Recent advances in statistical methodology make it possible to evaluate the progression of factors leading to child maladjustment. A path analysis can determine whether factors operate directly on the disorder or are moderated by other variables. Patterson described a method for both constructing and evaluating the developmental path of childhood antisocial behavior (Patterson, 1986a; Patterson & Dishion, 1985), results of which

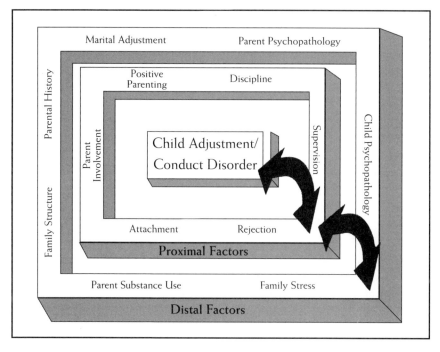

**FIGURE 1.2.** A conceptual model of proximal and distal factors contributing to child maladjustment. From "Early Prevention and Intervention with Conduct Problems: A Social Interaction Model for the Integration of Research and Practice" by J. B. Reid and G. R. Patterson, in *Interventions for Achievement and Behavior Problems* (p. 721) by G. Stoner, M. R. Shinn, & H. M. Walker (Eds.), 1991, Silver Spring, MD: The National Association of School Psychologists. Copyright 1991 by The National Association of School Psychologists. Reprinted with permission.

have been published (Patterson, 1986b; Patterson et al., 1991). Data for Patterson's path analysis were derived from the *Oregon Youth Study,* a longitudinal examination of fourth-grade boys and their parents. Thorough assessment packages consisting of home observations, questionnaires, interviews, teacher ratings, peer nominations, and intelligence tests were obtained for each family, first when the index child was in Grade 4 and later when in Grade 6. By using a path analysis, Reid and Patterson (1991) examined whether contextual risk factors, such as maternal depression or economic disadvantage, operate on childhood maladjustment through their effect on parental discipline and monitoring, or through direct impact on the child. Their analysis of data suggested that these factors influence children by the disruption of parenting behavior.

A second path examined by Patterson and his colleagues (Patterson & Dishion, 1985; Reid & Patterson, 1991) is the relative effect of parent monitoring, early childhood antisocial behaviors, academic achievement, and association with deviant peers on the development of delinquency in seventh-grade boys. Their analysis indicated that ineffectual parenting led to both antisocial behavior and academic failure in children. The added factor of association with deviant peers by Grade 6 accounted for 50% of the variance of delinquent behavior in Grade 7. Thus, bonding with other antisocial children seems to both strengthen and consolidate a child's progression toward delinquency.

Results of the work of Patterson and his colleagues highlight the important role of parental factors in the development of antisocial behavior and academic problems in children. They also point to the need for intervention prior to the development of deviant peer group bonds. The model illustrates that deviance may first be acquired in the home through a negative-reinforcement learning process, wherein the child's coercion successfully terminates the demands of other family members. Later, deviance is maintained by a positive-reinforcement learning paradigm, when it elicits approval and attention from deviant peers.

Patterson et al. (1991) described the possibility of two developmental paths to antisocial behaviors in children. An "early starter" path refers to children who enter school already affected by such factors as aggressive personality predisposition, lower socioeconomic status, and coercive family processes. Early starter children tend to develop pronounced antisocial behaviors by Grade 4, behaviors that are later strengthened by association with deviant peers.

"Late starters," however, while displaying no early signs of maladjustment, develop problem behaviors after they enter school. Reid and Patterson (1991) found no clear developmental pathway characterizing late starters. Loeber (1988) also differentiated between children who initiate antisocial tendencies early and late in childhood. He suggested that late starters are more likely to be females who display covert, nonaggressive conduct problems, such as stealing.

Similar path analysis of factors contributing to the development of delinquency has been reported by Tremblay, Masse, and colleagues (1992). They analyzed the results of a longitudinal study of 324 children in Montreal, following them for 7 years after initial assessment in Grade 1, to determine the degree to which poor school achievement was a necessary causal factor in the development of delinquency. They documented both school records for Grades 1 and 4 and disruptive behaviors reported in Grade 1. Results indicated a difference in causal pathway for boys and girls. In boys, there appeared to be a direct causal link between Grade 1 disruptive behavior and self-reported delinquency in Grade 7, with no causal contribution suggested by poor school achievement. In girls, however, none of the proposed causal models accounted for the development of delinquent behavior in Grade 7.

# Conclusion

## IMPLICATIONS FOR BEST PRACTICE

■ Resources for children's mental health services need to shift from expensive, one-on-one therapies to broad-reaching, early intervention initiatives.

■ Because of low interrater agreement, identification of children with maladjustment should be based on multiple sources of information.

■ Childhood aggression is situation dependent, and interventions should be planned setting by setting.

■ Children at risk for maladjustment need to receive help before their problems are consolidated by "bonding" with other deviant children.

■ Children's mental health services should lessen the prevalence of maladjustment and the burden of suffering in the population of children.

■ Services should be provided in schools and other community settings to remediate behavior and emotional problems of children who already have them, to prevent childhood maladjustment in at-risk children, and to promote social competence in all children.

■ Schools are not enough to bring about lasting change in the social development of children. More hope would come from a coordinated response with parents, community agents, and others, sustained over a number of years.

The bulk of resources for dealing with adjustment problems in children are consumed in the provision of treatment to "casualties" of the system (Cowen & Gesten, 1978), but are unavailable to the majority of children in need. Approximately one in every six children shows signs of clinically significant emotional disorder, which tends not to improve spontaneously. Professionals need to find new models of service provision that will result in a reduction in both the incidence and the severity of maladjustment in these children. (The role of peers in the maintenance of childhood maladjustment is discussed further in Chapter 2.)

The discovery of developmental pathways to maladjustment may be an important source of information for intervention model development. The work of Patterson and others suggests the importance of targeting interventions at coercive family processes that may cause children to develop antisocial behaviors before they enter school. A second possible goal is to equip children with social competencies to overcome behavior patterns that have already been developed. A third aim may be the prevention of bonding with other deviant children.

In addition to treatment strategies for already established clinical cases, professionals need also to contemplate interventions directed at reducing problems in the entire population of children. One option is to target any children at heightened risk for maladjustment. A potential service delivery model entails screening children in day care centers and schools to identify those at risk, who would then receive treatment. A second option is to target children living within geographic areas characterized by such risk factors as overcrowding, subsidized housing, or large proportions of single parents, all of which are associated with high rates of childhood maladjustment. For example, because a disproportionate number of children suffering from developmental delay were found in one economically depressed section of Milwaukee, an intervention project was introduced into this specific area of the city (Garber & Heber, 1977). Treatment consisted of a combination of programs targeting both the children and their single mothers over a 6-year period. From age 4 months, children attended subsidized day care while their mothers received remedial education and vocational training to improve both employment and parenting skills.

A third option is to provide intervention for all children within existing preschools and schools. As Cowen (1991) stated, "Virtually all children in modern society go through a formal education experience for many years. This reality challenges us to develop ways of engineering educational experiences that not only transmit knowledge but do so in ways to advance wellness" (p. 405). Children not responding to this "universal" approach then may be targeted for additional help. Interventions offered in collaboration with schools must both address the multiplicity of problems that affect children within the various contexts in which they occur and provide long-term interventions involving teachers, parents, and the community in focused efforts to reduce maladjustment in children (Kazdin, 1993b).

# chapter 2

# Childhood Maladjustment and Social Skills Deficits

## ISSUES IN PRACTICE

■ What social skills deficits characterize maladjusted children?

■ What social skills deficits are associated with children with learning disabilities, mild mental retardation, or attention-deficit/hyperactivity disorder?

■ What is the relationship between maladjustment and academic weakness?

■ What is the relationship between aggression and peer rejection?

■ What is the chain of environmental events that maintain childhood aggression?

■ What is social competence and how does it differ from social skills?

It has been suggested that both treatment and prevention of childhood maladjustment should evolve from an understanding of its development and nature (Coie et al., 1993; Kazdin, 1993b). This chapter focuses on social skills deficits common among children with adjustment problems, including those children who are complicated by such developmental disorders as attention-deficit/hyperactivity disorder, learning disabilities, or mild mental retardation. Also addressed is the relationship between childhood aggression and peer rejection. The discussion is synthesized into a working model of interactions that maintain aggressive behavior in order to propose targets for intervention. Finally, the goal of social skills training is discussed, along with concepts of social competence and psychological wellness.

## Response Domains of Social Skills Deficits

Maladjusted children are distinguished from their well-adjusted peers by higher levels of social skills deficits that can be clustered into the following three response domains (Ladd, 1985):

1. Behavior (doing)—for example, deficits in peer group entry skills, deficits in appropriate classroom behaviors

2. Cognition (thinking)—for example, deficits in social cue interpretation, deficits in solution generation, deficits in self-control

3. Affect (feeling)—for example, low self-esteem, depression and loneliness

## Behavior (Doing)

Children with maladjustment have difficulty initiating and maintaining friendships with peers. Because play is one of the most important ways in which children initiate and maintain relationships with one another, poorly developed skills to engage peers positively in play situations inevitably hamper a child's ability either to form friendships or to garner peer acceptance. Aggressive–rejected children commonly display hostile tendencies in play, including heightened frequencies of shoving, fighting, and teasing (Dodge, 1983). Their play has also been described as immature, and commonly directed toward either younger or unpopular children (Dodge, Coie, & Brakke, 1982; Ladd, 1983). Elevated rates of inappropriate play behaviors are furthermore accompanied by low rates of cooperative interaction and prosocial conversation (Dodge, 1983). For example, although aggressive–rejected children approach peers in play attempts as often as do nonaggressive children, they characteristically use briefer, less effective strategies to initiate these social exchanges (Dodge, 1983).

Findings cited above suggest that some behavior difficulties of maladjusted children may represent their misguided attempts to gain peer acceptance. In other words, in their unsuccessful efforts to be accepted by peers, maladjusted children may adopt poorly formed group entry strategies that affect peers in ways opposite to the intended acceptance.

Similar patterns of poorly formed peer-directed behavior occur in the classroom as well. Here, maladjusted children attempt social approaches toward peers more frequently than do popular children (Dodge et al., 1982; Kupersmidt, Coie, & Dodge, 1990). These contacts are inappropriate in the context but give further weight to the notion that some problem behaviors of aggressive–rejected children represent their inept attempts to gain peer acceptance.

## Cognition (Thinking)

The cognitive skills required both to interpret social situations accurately and to generate alternative social strategies are important components of effective social interaction. Dodge, Pettit, McClaskey, and Brown (1986) proposed that children's actions in interpersonal situations can be predicted by their ability to interpret the social cues of peers accurately. Rubin, Le Mare, and Lollis (1990) demonstrated that children who clearly understood the social expectations of a particular social situation (e.g., entering a play group) later handled these situations well when exposed to them. However, this relationship between social perception and later social behaviors pertained only when exposed to the same situations. Children who were proficient in identifying social expectations in one situation were no more proficient in dealing with a different social situation (e.g., responding to peer provocation).

Results of the study by Rubin et al. (1990) suggested that a child's ability to process social cues is situation specific, rather than reflective of a generalizable aptitude. In further illustration of this point, Rubin and Rose-Krasnor (1992) found that unpopular children experienced difficulty in generating alternative solutions to social situations that involved conflict, but not to nonstressful social situations. In response to stress inducement, unpopular children tended to pursue aggressive, vague solutions that were not carefully planned.

Rejected children tend to display poorly formed cognitive strategies, in terms of both the quality and the quantity of solutions proposed (Akhtar & Bradley, 1991; Lochman & Lenhart, 1993). Dodge (1993), and later Crick and Dodge (1994), suggested that socially competent children are able to interpret social cues and generate goals and behaviors in response to those cues. More specifically, according to this model, a child must (a) encode cues that are both internal (e.g., feelings) and external (e.g., observed actions of others); (b) interpret these cues (e.g., causal and intent inferences); (c) clarify goals; (d) decide on a response; and (e) enact the behavior. Children who are aggressive–rejected have difficulty at all five steps of processing social information. They commonly generate options for handling social situations that are not only fewer in number (Lochman & Lampron, 1986) but also of inferior quality to those of their peers (Guerra & Slaby, 1989). They seem to experience difficulty in enacting the behavioral options they select and evaluating the effects of those actions (Dodge & Feldman, 1990). Moreover, options generated tend to involve either direct action or aggression, rather than cooperation or prosocial activity (Parke & Slaby, 1983). Rubin, Bream, and Rose-Krasnor (1991) speculated that the tendency for maladjusted children to select antagonistic solutions may be related to deficits in their interpretation of social events. For instance, they tend to overinterpret hostile intent in the actions of others (Dodge & Frame, 1982), such that an accidental bump, for example, may be viewed as purposeful provocation. This erroneous perception of malevolent intent in others may precipitate the adoption of hostile solutions to social problems.

Moreover, aggressive–rejected children are less motivated by prosocial goals than are their peers (Renshaw & Asher, 1982). Instead, they tend to endorse dominance and revenge as motivational factors (Lochman, Wayland, & White, 1993), with less concern about the suffering of victims (Boldizar, Perry, & Perry, 1989).

## Affect (Feeling)

Until recently, most research on the social skills deficits of maladjusted children focused on behavioral and cognitive domains. However, growing evidence suggests that maladjusted children also suffer from elevated levels of loneliness, depression (Asher, Parkhurst, Hymel, & Williams, 1990; Bierman, 1989), anxiety (Wheeler & Ladd, 1982), and poor self-esteem (Lochman & Lampron, 1986). Harter (1982) suggested that aggressive–rejected children are more likely to label themselves as poorly skilled at making friends. Because they expect to fail in social situations, they tend to avoid trying. These expectations of failure reflect children's attribution of their social performance to events beyond their control. Maladjusted children tend to perceive themselves in passive social roles, manipulated by circumstances outside their influence (e.g., others are unfair).

# Social Skills Deficits and Developmental Disabilities

Social skills deficit is a feature common to a number of developmental disabilities, including learning disability, mild mental retardation, and attention-deficit/hyperactivity disorder. The association of social skills deficits and each of these developmental disabilities has been the subject of considerable study, as discussed in the following sections.

## Learning Disability

Children with learning disabilities have a high incidence of social skills deficits (Coleman & Minnett, 1992; McConaughty & Ritter, 1986; Oliva & La Greca, 1988; Rourke, 1988). It has been estimated that between 40% (Baum, Duffelmeyer, & Geelan, 1988) and 84% (Gresham, 1988) of children with learning disabilities have pronounced social skills weakness. Consistent with this range were results of a meta-analysis suggesting that nearly 80% of children with learning disabilities are less socially accepted than their normally achieving peers (Swanson & Malone, 1992).

Signs of adjustment problems in children with learning disabilities include:

■ Lower rates of peer interaction (Bryan, 1974)

■ Increased classroom off-task behavior (Feagans & McKinney, 1981; La Greca, 1981)

■ Higher teacher rating of maladjustment (McConaughty & Ritter, 1986)

■ Lower self-rating of self-esteem (Schumaker & Hazel, 1984)

■ Lower sociometric ratings of peer acceptance (Stone & La Greca, 1990)

■ Higher parental rating of maladjustment (McConaughty & Ritter, 1986)

It is interesting to note that children who show low academic achievement but are not identified as having a learning disability have been found to have social skills deficits indistinguishable from children with learning disabilities (McIntosh, Vaughn, & Zaragoza, 1991; Sater & French, 1989; Vaughn, Haager, Hogan, & Kouzekanani, 1992). Similarly, samples of children selected for behavior disorder (Scruggs & Mastropieri, 1986) or "not making a good adjustment" (McConnell et al., 1984) are characterized by academic weaknesses at levels comparable to those of children with learning disabilities.

The link between academic and behavioral problems is strong and may have a number of possible explanations. Four hypothetical causal models adapted from Hinshaw (1992b) to explain the link between social and academic deficits are illustrated in Figure 2.1. One possibility (the academic causal model) is that academic weakness both precedes and produces maladjustment. In this proposed sequence of events, a child's academic weakness results in negative school outcomes, which in turn contribute to the development of behavior difficulties. Deprived of most forms of positive attention in school, low achievers may adopt negative behaviors to receive recognition in class. Moreover, the frustration that is likely to develop from unsuccessful school performance may erupt in peer-directed aggression. Larson (1988) used a similar academic causal model to describe the link between learning disabilities and delinquency. In this

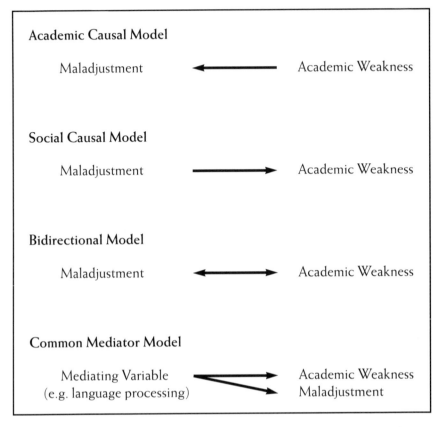

FIGURE 2.1. Four hypothetical causal models of the link between academic weakness and maladjustment.

model, school failure precipitated by learning disability was suggested as the cause of negative self-image, school dropout, and delinquency.

A second explanation of the link between academic weakness and maladjustment (the social causal model) contends that maladjustment precedes academic difficulties. In other words, inattentive, disruptive behavior in the classroom is said to impede learning and result in academic failure.

A third explanation (the bidirectional model) suggests that simultaneously academic deficits lead to maladjustment and maladjustment leads to academic deficits. Each area of deficit contributes to the other in a cyclic causal chain.

The fourth causal model (the common mediator model) suggests that both academic weakness and social maladjustment are products of a third variable that underlies dysfunction in both domains. In this model, the same deficits in cognitive processing, language, and perception that may be responsible for low academic performance may also have an impact on children's processing of information in social situations, resulting in behavioral maladjustment as well (Hinshaw, 1992b; Rourke, 1988; Strayhorn & Strain, 1986). One possible common mediator of academic weakness and maladjustment is low intellectual ability. The link between below-average intellectual ability and delinquent behavior has been well established (Hirschi & Hindelang, 1977; Lynam, Moffitt, & Stouthamer-Loeber, 1993). On average, delinquent youth score 8 points lower on standardized intelligence tests than nondelinquents (West & Farrington, 1973).

Weaknesses in "executive" areas of cognitive functioning (e.g., attention, concentration, planning, self-monitoring) may interfere with a child's ability to govern his or her actions in both academic and social situations. The association between IQ and delinquency was examined by Lynam et al. (1993) as part of a longitudinal study. They found a strong negative relationship between a youth's intelligence and the seriousness of the delinquent acts committed, with the direction of this relationship running from IQ to delinquency. Wentzel (1991) found that intelligence accounted for the single largest source of variance in the link between social competence and academic achievement for a sample of 12- and 13-year-olds.

## Mild Mental Retardation

Social skills deficits are also common in children with mild mental retardation. In fact, mental retardation is in part defined by deficits in adaptive behaviors, including social competence (Wallander & Hubert, 1987). Children with mental retardation experience difficulty in both making and maintaining peer relationships (Berry & Marshal, 1978). Studies have found that, compared with their nonhandicapped peer group, children with developmental disabilities play with peers less frequently (Guralnick & Groom, 1988; Kopp, Baker, & Brown, 1992), show higher rates of teacher intervention, are more often recipients of negative behaviors from classmates (Novak, Olley, & Kearney, 1980), and display fewer reciprocal patterns of play in both preschool (White, 1980) and elementary school playgrounds (Roberts, Pratt, & Leach, 1985).

With lower levels of social competence, children with mental retardation are less likely to be selected as playmates (Strain, Lambert, Kerr, Stagg, & Lenkner, 1983) and they receive lower peer ratings than developmentally matched children without disabilities (Guralnick & Groom, 1987). These patterns of social rejection and low peer interaction continue throughout elementary school (Roberts et al., 1985) and high school (Handen, Feldman, & Honigman, 1987), and into adulthood (Salzberg, Lignugaris-Kraft, & McCuller, 1988).

Given that developmental skill level is an important factor in determining both the quantity and the quality of interpersonal relationships, it is understandable that children with mental retardation display deficits in social interactions. Proficiency in such developmental areas as cognitive processing, interpersonal communication, and motor skills helps determine the degree to which a child is able to initiate and maintain play with other children, particularly during the preschool years (Kopp et al., 1992).

However, enhancement of social competence in children with disabilities does not evolve merely through physical integration in settings with nondisabled peers (Odom & McEvoy, 1988). Gresham (1982) argued that the faulty assumption that administrative placement of children with disabilities in integrative settings alone promotes normal behavior has misguided the educational mainstreaming movement. Promotion of social competence in these children requires careful programming targeted at both increasing specific social skills and developing structures within the school environment, to maximize the likelihood of these children's interactions with others.

## Children with Attention-Deficit/Hyperactivity Disorder

Ratings of parents, teachers, and children with attention-deficit/hyperactivity disorder (ADHD) themselves indicate that this population has difficulty developing positive peer relationships (Pelham & Milich, 1984). Similarly, sociometric measures of peer acceptance of children with ADHD indicate that they are consistently rejected by their peers (Hinshaw, 1987). In turn, peer rejection may be related to the excessive behaviors of these children in play situations. In one study, for example, hyperactive children placed in play groups with nonhyperactive peers scored higher than their peers in levels of physical aggression, but lower in popularity (Pelham & Bender, 1982). In a different study, King and Young (1981) demonstrated that hyperactive children tend not to modulate their play to fit changing cues for role-appropriate behavior and are rated more negatively by their peers than nonhyperactive children.

As is the case for children with learning disability, the reason for the link between ADHD and social maladjustment is unclear. However, impulsivity, inability to adjust behavior to fit situational demands, and problems in both comprehending and attending to social skills have all been raised as possible causal factors (Pelham & Milich, 1984).

## A Common Social Skills Program

The pervasiveness of maladjusted social patterns of children with learning disabilities, children with mild mental retardation, and children with ADHD has prompted the suggestion that difficulties in interpersonal relationships become a criterion for the identification of children in categories of both ADHD (Pelham & Milich, 1984) and learning disability (Interagency Committee on Learning Disabilities, 1987; Porter & Rourke, 1985), adding to its current inclusion in the diagnosis of mental retardation. Children in all three groups tend to display heightened levels of aggression in peer interaction, and are more likely to be labeled as having a behavior problem by teachers, parents, and peers.

If children with differing developmental disabilities share common social skills deficits, is it necessary to separate children into distinct diagnostic groupings (e.g., children with learning disabilities, behavior disorders, mild mental retardation, or ADHD) each to receive separate social skills intervention? Would strategies used to increase the social adjustment of one diagnostic group be effective for another group? Certainly, interventions used to promote social competence in children with learning disabilities (see McIntosh et al., 1991), mild mental retardation (see Wallander & Hubert, 1987), and ADHD (see Landau & Moore, 1991) are strikingly similar to one another and to social skills programs designed for maladjusted children without these complicating developmental disabilities.

A common treatment program for children with maladjustment across diagnostic categories would be even more attractive if the intervention could remediate both academic and social skills deficits. Because of the link between academic weakness and social maladjustment, Hinshaw (1992a) suggested that both areas should be addressed in treatment programs, particularly in the early grades. It is possible, in fact, that academic gains may themselves enhance children's social adjustment. Coie and Krehbiel (1984) randomly assigned fourth-grade underachievers who were also rejected by peers to either a social skills training condition, a reading tutoring condition, a combination training condition, or a no-treatment control condition. Children who experienced academic training, either in isolation or combined with social skills training, showed improvement in both academic and social domains, whereas children receiving the social skills training alone showed limited gains in peer acceptance only.

## Aggression and Peer Rejection

A strong, but not perfect association exists between aggression and peer rejection in children. About two thirds of children who are aggressive are also rejected by peers (Bierman, 1989; Coie, Underwood, & Lochman, 1991). In one study, instances of arguing in the playground at the beginning of the school year predicted peer rejection for preschoolers later in the year (Ladd, Price, & Hart, 1988). All acts of aggression, however, do not always result in peer rejection. Fighting, for instance, is not necessarily negatively perceived by other children unless it occurs at high rates or is initiated by children with additional unadmired attributes, such as academic difficulties or physical unattractiveness (Bierman, 1989). Nonetheless, between 30% and 40% of rejected children are also aggressive (Coie et al., 1991). This overlap between childhood aggression and peer rejection is depicted in Figure 2.2.

Peer expectations are negatively affected by the reputation of a rejected child (Hymel, Wagner, & Butler, 1990). Dodge and Frame (1982) found that peers both blame rejected children for difficulties in play and exclude them from play. Moreover, peers respond more favorably to group entry attempts of popular children, even when both popular and unpopular groups employ similar techniques (Dodge, Schlundt, Schockern, & Delugach, 1983). Although reputational bias may hamper a child's ability to gain acceptance by a new group of children, it does not explain why particular children

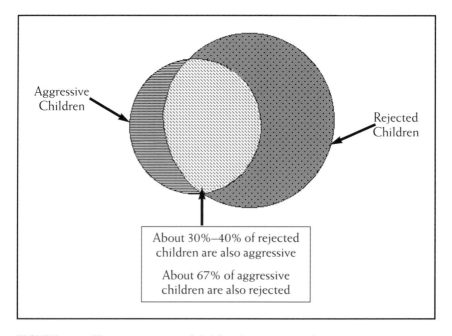

FIGURE 2.2. The co-occurrence of childhood aggression and peer rejection.

become rejected in the first place. In one instance, boys rejected by peers in their initial play group quickly reestablished rejected status in an unfamiliar play group where reputational bias was not a possible factor (Dodge, 1983).

The importance of peer reaction to the maintenance of aggressive behaviors suggests that social skills instruction must be coupled with increased opportunities for children to practice prosocial alternatives (Hawkins & Weis, 1985). To address this issue, Bierman (1986) assigned unpopular children to groups including popular children to work toward a "superordinate" goal of producing a videotape. Providing this opportunity for unpopular children to interact positively with popular peers resulted in increases in both peer-rated social status and self-rated social competence for unpopular children. Moreover, these increases in social status were found to sustain over 6 weeks.

It should be pointed out that much of the evidence linking aggression and peer rejection has not been focused on gender differences. Boys have been found to exhibit higher rates of aggression than girls (Parke & Slaby, 1983). Crick and Dodge (1994) suggested that the higher rate of aggression for boys than girls is a reflection of the restricted way in which aggression has been defined and assessed. If the definition of aggression is broadened from its typical interpretation as overt verbal (e.g., teasing, swearing) and nonverbal (e.g., hitting, kicking) behaviors to also include indirect and covert actions (e.g., excluding others from friendship relationships), then the prevalence of aggression for girls approaches levels shown by boys (Crick & Grotpeter, in press). When attempting to inflict harm on peers, boys and girls may each do it, but in different ways. Boys focus on asserting their dominance by verbal and physical aggression, whereas girls are more likely to focus on affecting the relationships among peers by covert means.

## A Working Model: The Self-Perpetuating Cycle of Aggression

As described in Chapter 1, once maladjustment is initiated, a number of factors seem to contribute to its maintenance. The social reactions of others to difficult children is particularly important in perpetuating maladjustment (Hawkins & Weis, 1985). A working model of a self-perpetuating cycle of aggression is offered to summarize the social development mechanism described by Hawkins and Weis (1985), among others, and to suggest targets for intervention. This model is based on the premises that (a) multiple events contribute to children's aggressive behaviors, and (b) these events interact in a "self-perpetuating cycle" (Bierman, 1986). As shown in

Figure 2.3, the elements included in this model are social skills deficits, antisocial behaviors, immediate reactions of others, and longer term reactions of others. The causal cycle of events can be initiated at any point. For purpose of this discussion, social skills deficits is considered first. Maladjusted children tend to lack social skills to deal effectively with interpersonal conflict and to develop positive relationships. Deficits in social behaviors required to initiate and maintain positive peer interactions combine with deficits in both cognitive and affective domains, impelling children to react to social problem situations with aggression. (See Connection A in the cycle depicted in Figure 2.3.)

Their aggressive behaviors are strengthened by the immediate reactions of others. In some situations, aggression enables the child to either avoid or escape a demand situation. For instance, Patterson (1986a) reported that 70% of aggressive children's counterattacks successfully resulted in the withdrawal of coercion from the "attacking" family member.

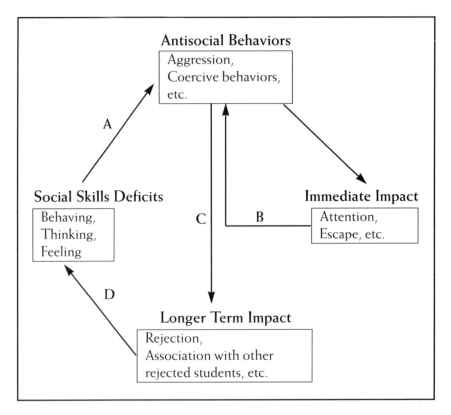

FIGURE 2.3.   A hypothetical self-perpetuating cycle of aggression.

Aggression also recruits social reinforcement through the attention it generates from either peers (Solomon & Wahler, 1973) or teachers (Strain et al., 1983). Thus, aggressive responses to interpersonal situations are strengthened, initially by negative reinforcement from family members (Parke & Slaby, 1983) and later by positive reinforcement from peers (Patterson, 1986b). (See Connection B in the cycle depicted in Figure 2.3.)

Longer term reactions to childhood aggression may bring into play factors that impede learning about alternate coping strategies for problem social situations. Aggressive, inept choices selected by maladjusted children in their interpersonal dealings precipitate rejection from both peers and teachers. (See Connection C in the cycle depicted in Figure 2.3.) Rejection may not only contribute to these children's sense of loneliness, depression, and helplessness, but also diminish the likelihood of teacher praise for the child's prosocial behavior, even if it occurs. In addition, the negative reputation of aggressive children contributes to their rejection by peers. With few ways of gaining acceptance, these children turn to other socially rejected and deviant children for affiliation. The bonding and social learning that comes with this association may further strengthen patterns of social deviance and rejection (Hawkins & Weis, 1985). In this way, longer term reactions to aggression limit opportunities for aggressive children to acquire positive social skills as an alternative to aggression.

The diminished exposure to prosocial behavior coupled with the lack of reinforcement of prosocial behavior when it does occur reduces opportunities for aggressive–rejected children to acquire social skills. So the cycle continues. (See Connection D in the cycle depicted in Figure 2.3.)

This model suggests consideration of three intervention targets to interrupt the self-perpetuating cycle. One target for intervention is the enhancement of social skills that enable children to make friends, get along with others, and cope with life stressors. A second target is the structuring of social environments that provide a high frequency of reinforcement for children's positive behavior, as well as clear and firm consequences for misbehavior. A third target is the encouragement of meaningful opportunities for children to practice the social competencies that are being promoted, in an environment that encourages and reinforces prosocial behaviors.

## The Goals of Social Skills Intervention

Gresham (1986, 1993) has argued that the acquisition of improved social skills is a necessary but not sufficient outcome of intervention programs.

Rather, acquired skills must contribute, with other factors, to overall increased social competence in children. Social competence conveys more than the ability to apply a learned set of social skills.

Although numerous definitions of social competence have been proposed, almost all have included the two concepts of *effectiveness* and *appropriateness* of behaviors. Social competence implies a degree of successful outcome to one's actions, achieved in a manner consistent with norms of conduct (Gresham, 1993). For instance, Guralnick (1990) defined social competence as the "ability of young children to successfully and appropriately select and carry out their interpersonal goals" (p. 4). Likewise, the definition suggested by Rubin and Rose-Krasnor (1992) was "the ability to achieve personal goals in social interaction while simultaneously maintaining positive relationships with others over time and across situations" (p. 285).

An emphasis on equipping children with aptitudes to achieve social goals in addition to eliminating social skills deficits provides a new direction for social skills interventions, one that is consistent with a "wellness" or positive health model of service provision (Seeman, 1989). In a wellness model of health care, the goal of intervention is to assist individuals in attaining states of functioning qualitatively different from the absence of illness. In the area of physical health, physical fitness defines a wellness state. In the area of psychological health, Cowen (1991) suggested that "psychological wellness" of children might be achieved through interpersonal skills, communication skills, anger control skills, and coping strategies that mediate major life stressors.

The capacity to adapt to deleterious life circumstances (e.g., divorce or major illness) without succumbing to prolonged emotional problems has been referred to as a child's "resilience" or "invulnerability" to stress (Garmezy, Masten, & Tellegen, 1984). Resilient children are not likely to develop mental health problems even after prolonged exposure to multiple and significant stressors (Compas, 1987). The identification of precise social factors that either enhance or impede resilience may help to pinpoint competencies that, when acquired, serve to buffer children from the harmful effects of stress. In one study, for instance, the support of an extensive network of both friends and adults was found to enhance childhood resilience in a sample of children (Pryor-Brown & Cowen, 1989). Helping children to build support networks and to acquire personal coping strategies may thus be considered examples of positive health interventions in the area of social adjustment.

In practice, social skills intervention may simultaneously target a number of distinct goals, depending on the different needs of specific groups of children. For children who are already maladjusted, intervention may address issues of social competence in remediation of fully developed adjustment problems. For children at risk for maladjustment but not yet dysfunctional, the goals of intervention may be to promote social competencies that prevent the later development of behavior and emotional problems. For the majority of children, those who will never become maladjusted, intervention may enhance social competence to make friends, gain social acceptance, and increase self-esteem. The question is how to structure social competence–enhancing interventions capable of meeting all of these goals.

# Conclusion

## IMPLICATIONS FOR BEST PRACTICE

- Social skills assessments and interventions typically have included skills in behavior, cognitive, and affect response domains.

- Similar, if not identical, social skills interventions may be appropriately used with some children of differing diagnostic labels (e.g., learning disabilities, mild mental retardation, attention-deficit/hyperactivity disorder).

- Because of the strong association between the two variables, interventions should couple strategies to enhance children's social competence with strategies to enhance academic competence.

- Social skills interventions should not only have students acquire social skills but also provide them with meaningful opportunities to practice their newly acquired skills, in a social environment that encourages the occurrence of prosocial behaviors and discourages negative behaviors.

- Social skills interventions need to meet a range of social competence goals in schools. For the few children with already established maladjustment, the social competence intervention should reduce negative behaviors. For the larger number of children who are at risk for maladjustment, the social competence intervention should prevent later maladjustment. For the majority of children who will never develop maladjustment, an intervention should promote existing social competencies for psychological wellness.

This chapter presented a description of social skills deficits associated with maladjustment in children. These include weaknesses in social behavior, cognitive skills, and affect, weaknesses that interact in complex ways to produce maladjustment. Similar social deficit patterns are found in children with disorders such as learning disability, attention-deficit/hyperactivity disorder, and mental retardation. These deficits may interact with other factors in a self-perpetuating cycle that maintains behavior problems in children. Interrupting this cycle may require multiple targets of intervention: equipping children with additional social skills, structuring environments that both reinforce prosocial behaviors and prohibit negative behaviors, and providing meaningful opportunities for children to apply skills they have learned. Social skills intervention provided in schools may need to take different forms for enhancing the psychological wellness of all children, in preventing the future occurrence of maladjustment in high-risk students, and in remediating existing social skills deficits in poorly adjusted students.

# chapter 3

# Selecting Programming Targets

## ISSUES IN PRACTICE

■ What role does the selection of programming targets play in planning interventions to promote social competence in children?

■ How can practitioners minimize faculty judgments and biases that distort their selection of programming targets?

■ What are methods for selecting appropriate programming targets for promoting social competence?

■ What are the advantages and disadvantages of these methods?

In one of his adventures, Winnie-the-Pooh stalked a "Woozle" by tracking its footprints around a tree (Milne, 1926). As over and over he retread the circular path of the trunk's circumference, Pooh convinced himself that he was on the trail of more and more of the mysteriously elusive beast, which, despite Pooh's best hunting efforts, managed to remain just out of sight. His unwavering persistence notwithstanding, Pooh never got any closer to his quarry, for the tracks he so doggedly followed were, of course, those of his own making. Having selected an inappropriate target of pursuit from the outset, neither the rigor nor the precision of his tracking method made any difference to the success of the hunting expedition.

Likewise, neither the rigor nor the precision of any treatment intervention will result in meaningful benefit unless the program itself targets appropriate changes in children's maladjustment. The issue of appropriate, relevant choice of programming targets becomes particularly challenging not only in light of the myriad of problem areas that typically can be identified in maladjusted children, but also in acknowledgment of limitations in both resources and opportunities to deliver children's mental health interventions.

Clinicians tend to base their selection of programming targets for individual children on a combination of clinical intuition and general impression. Weist, Ollendick, and Finney (1991) reviewed studies targeting social interaction for children from the ages of 3 to 18 in two clinical journals over a 9-year period. Of 25 studies published, only one had used an empirical method of selecting target behaviors.

What factors should be considered in the selection of treatment targets? The following paragraphs discuss alternative strategies for selecting program targets, and point out the merits and deficits of each one. These strategies are summarized in Table 3.1.

## Debiasing Practitioner Judgment

To increase the precision with which they select programming targets, practitioners may need assistance in recognizing factors that contribute to faulty clinical judgments, and increasing their reliance on available assessment information. Weist et al. (1991) encouraged the formulation of practitioner judgment based on information provided by multiple sources of child assessment, including naturalistic observations and child behavior ratings obtained from teachers, parents, and peers.

However, a couple of difficulties are associated with this approach. First, practitioner reliance on general impressions for the selection of pro-

TABLE 3.1. Summary of Methods to Select Social Competence Programming Targets

| METHOD | ACTION |
| --- | --- |
| Debiasing practitioner judgments | Select targets that converge from multiple sources of assessment information. |
| Positive relationship to important social competence outcomes | Select targets that enable a child to access socially important outcomes. |
| Susceptibility to "behavior trapping" | Select targets that can be maintained by "natural communities of reinforcement" in environments. |
| Correspondence to students' social skills deficits | Select targets that correspond to a child's social skills deficits. |
| Social validation | Select targets that are endorsed by program consumers. |
| Comparison to socially competent children | Select targets that match social behaviors of socially competent children. |
| Models of developmental pathways | Select targets that will hinder the developmental pathway toward child maladjustment. |
| Functional equivalence | Select targets that are the functional equivalent of the problem behaviors in the context. |

gramming targets is both strong and resistant to change by the addition of further objective information. Simple awareness of potentially biasing affects on clinical judgment may not provide sufficient impetus for clinicians to alter their decision-making tendencies. In fact, literature on the diagnosis of such childhood disorders as learning disabilities, conduct disorder, and attention-deficit/hyperactivity disorder reveals that clinicians continue to rely on biased judgment for making diagnostic decisions despite the availability of actuarial information (Algozzine, Morsink, & Algozzine, 1988). It appears that, more often than not, the availability of program space and other "system" factors tends to determine placement of children with learning or behavior problems more consistently than assessment information concerning child factors (Friedman & Street, 1985).

Second, the availability of multiple sources of assessment may increase rather than eliminate the need for practitioner judgment, which is required both to interpret information and to reconcile discrepancies across information sources. Moreover, practitioner reliance on the number of measures that identify a specific problem area may not be the most pertinent basis for selection of target intervention. Arguably, depending on the situation, any one particular source of information about any individual instance of maladjustment may carry more weight in defining problem areas than the convergence of all available data.

## Positive Relationship to Important Social Competence Outcomes

Gresham (1986) suggested that the social importance of an intervention depends on whether changes in target behavior impact positively on areas deemed socially significant for children, particularly in such areas as peer acceptance and adult (parents and teachers) positive behavioral assessment. He also reported that of 33 studies using cognitive behavioral techniques to train child social skills, only five included measures relating changes in the target behavior to socially important outcomes.

Which specific social behaviors, when acquired by children, result in increases in socially important outcomes? Some examples of child behavior related to increased peer acceptance include asking questions, teaching, and offering to support others, all of which have been related to positive changes in children's social status (Ladd, 1981). Ironically, the frequency of child–child play interaction does not appear important on its own. Increases in the frequency of play with peers has not been found to increase peer acceptance (La Greca & Stark, 1986). In contrast, the type of behavior used to gain entry into a play group does seem to affect peer acceptance. Dodge (1983) contended that the use of appropriate means to gain entry into a peer group is a prerequisite skill for further social interaction, which differentiates popular from rejected children. Popular children initially judge the (perhaps subtle) prevailing expectations of a play group before joining in, and consequently adjust their behavior, maintaining consistency with the perceived expectations. Unpopular children tend not to regulate their behaviors to fit play group norms; consequently, their attempts to gain entry are likely to be rebuked (Ladd, 1981).

Selecting programming targets connected to socially important outcomes begs the question of what precise social outcomes hold promise for maladjusted children. At present, no consensus on what constitutes socially important outcomes exists. Furman and Robbins (1985) suggested that social skills programs should target behaviors that result in children's increased friendships, in addition to their acceptance by peers. Close personal relationships satisfy personal needs of intimacy, loyalty, and companionship not typically achieved by general peer acceptance. Programs that target peer acceptance may increase the total number of a child's acquaintances, but have no impact on the formation of friendships (Gresham & Nagle, 1980; Odom & Asher, 1977). Interventions to promote the development of friendships may need to include programming elements different from interventions to promote acceptance.

Another important question is whether particular social skills exist that are universally related to particular social outcomes. In other words, are there skills that, when acquired, result in improved social outcomes for all children? These particular skills may depend upon a host of child factors, including:

- *Gender*—Sex-typing may determine which specific behaviors are viewed as socially acceptable for each gender. For example, rough-and-tumble play is frequently associated with positive peer interaction for boys, but rarely for girls (Strain, Odom, & McConnell, 1984).

- *Developmental level*—Skills involved in group entry for young children (e.g., hovering and then entering the play activity) may not be appropriate for more mature children, whose interactions depend more on verbal mediation (Ladd, 1989).

- *Context*—Different programming strategies may be used to achieve the same social outcomes, depending upon the context. Burstein (1986), for example, found that more peer interaction occurred during outdoor play than during "center time" for preschoolers without disabilities.

■ *Cultural and socioeconomic differences*—The types of behaviors that result in improved social outcomes may differ for children of different cultural backgrounds or socioeconomic status. For example, being in trouble with the law is associated with diminished social status for children of middle and upper socioeconomic status, but not for children of lower socioeconomic status (Rolf, Sells, & Golden, 1972).

Figure 3.1 organizes the skills addressed in six commercially available social skills programs into a matrix that categorizes response domains of behaving, thinking, and feeling (as suggested by Ladd, 1985), as well as social domains of self-related, other related, and task related (as described by Stephens, 1992). As the table suggests, several social skills are targeted by a number of the programs. For example, skills of beginning a conversation, complimenting, listening, and responding to teasing—behavior responses in relating to others—were included in four of the programs. In contrast, behaviors in relation to self and feeling in relation to tasks rarely were included in the social skills programs.

The popularity of any particular social skill in terms of its inclusion in commercial programs is not necessarily an indication of the strength of its relationship to socially important outcomes. In fact, of the programs described in Figure 3.1, only the ACCEPTS Program (Walker et al., 1988) provided evidence in the manual that children who have successfully completed some or all of the skills in the program showed greater gains than those who did not receive the program. They reported the results of two studies indicating that groups of elementary school children with handicaps who received the ACCEPTS curriculum showed greater gains on a role-play test, during behavior observation in the classroom, and on the playground. However, the benefits of the program tended neither to persist nor to be perceived by teachers.

## Susceptibility to "Behavior Trapping"

Stokes and Baer (1977) proposed that children may maintain certain social behaviors because they spontaneously elicit desired reactions from others. For instance, a pleasant social greeting is likely to be reinforced by a response in kind. "Natural communities of reinforcement" that exist within

## Social Context Domain

| | Relating to Self | Relating to Others | Relating to Tasks |
|---|---|---|---|
| **Behaving** | • self-care 6<br>• dealing with boredom 4 | • accepting a compliment 3,4<br>• accepting consequences 4<br>• accepting others who are different 2<br>• accepting peer suggestions 2<br>• accepting responsibility 4<br>• apologizing 4<br>• answering to someone talking 5,6<br>• asking a favor 4<br>• asking a question 6<br>• asking do you like 5<br>• asking permission 4,2<br>• avoiding trouble 3,4<br>• basic interaction skills 6<br>• beginning a conversation 2,3,4,6<br>• communication/conversing 4<br>• complimenting 2,3,4,6<br>• continuing a conversation 3,6<br>• contributing to discussions 4<br>• cooperating 2<br>• dealing with accusations 4<br>• ending a conversation 4<br>• eye contact 6<br>• finding out what people like 5<br>• friendship making 6<br>• following rules 6<br>• giving suggestions for improvement 3<br>• greeting 4<br>• helping 6<br>• ignoring distractions 2,4<br>• introducing other people 3<br>• introducing yourself 2,3,4<br>• interrupting a conversation 3<br>• inviting others to join in activities 2<br>• joining in 2,3,4<br>• listening 2,4,5,6<br>• making a complaint 4<br>• making sense of conversations 6<br>• offering help to a classmate 2,3,4<br>• offering help to an adult 4<br>• paying attention to a speaker 2<br>• playing a game 4<br>• questioning rules that may be unfair 2<br>• refusing unreasonable requests 2<br>• reporting accidents 2<br>• responding to aggression 2<br>• responding to criticism 2,3,4<br>• responding to teasing 2,3,4,6<br>• saying no 3,4<br>• saying thank you 2,4<br>• sending an ignoring message 3<br>• sending an "I'm interested message" 3<br>• sharing 3,4,6<br>• showing sportsmanship 4<br>• smiling 6<br>• staying out of fights 4<br>• suggesting an activity 4<br>• taking turns talking 6<br>• telling an adult about unfair treatment 2<br>• touching the right way 6<br>• using polite words 6<br>• using positive consequences 3<br>• using the right voice 6<br>• when someone asks you to do something you can't do 6<br>• when someone says "NO" 4,6<br>• when someone tries to hurt you 6<br>• when things don't go right 6 | • answering the phone 2<br>• asking for help 3,4<br>• asking questions 4<br>• bringing materials to class 4<br>• doing your best work 6<br>• care of the environment<br>• completing assignments 2,4<br>• deciding on something to do 4<br>• following classroom rules 6<br>• following instructions 3,4<br>• keeping desk clean, putting away materials 2<br>• listening to the teacher 6<br>• lunchroom behavior 4<br>• making corrections 4<br>• making transitions 2<br>• on-task 4<br>• performing before others 4<br>• producing correct work 2<br>• quality of work 4<br>• using free time 2<br>• using time appropriately when waiting 2<br>• when a teacher asks you to do something 6 |
| **Thinking** | • auditory sequencing 1<br>• before–after words; now–later words 5<br>• building a matrix 1<br>• compromising 3<br>• deciding what caused a problem 4<br>• developing alternative plans 1<br>• developing flexibility in planning 1<br>• do–don't words 5<br>• expanding solution categories 1<br>• evaluating solutions 1,5<br>• expressing problems by drawing 5 | • find out others' preferences to solve problems 5<br>• flexible categorizing 1<br>• generation of solutions/creative thinking 1,5<br>• goal settings 4<br>• how one's acts affect others 5<br>• if–then words 5<br>• illustrate you can't assume what the problem is 5<br>• impatience and problem solving 5<br>• introducing questions and answers 1<br>• is–not words 5<br>• making a decision 4<br>• negotiating 4<br>• predicting consequences 1,5<br>• problem identification 4<br>• problem solving 3,4,5<br>• remembering 5<br>• role-play problem solving 5<br>• same–different words 5<br>• story comprehension 5<br>• some–all words 5 | • time and problem solving 5<br>• understand connection between act and consequence 5<br>• understand others might not know what happened 5<br>• understand reasoning behind events 5<br>• understand sequential thinking 5<br>• understand what the problem is 5<br>• using self-control 4<br>• using social skills to solve problems 1<br>• verbal planning 5 |
| **Feeling** | • being honest 4<br>• complimenting self 2<br>• dealing with embarrassment 4<br>• dealing with fear 4,5<br>• dealing with feelings 4<br>• dealing with frustration 5<br>• dealing with wanting something that isn't yours 4<br>• dealing with your anger 2,4,6<br>• expression of feelings 4<br>• identification of feelings 1,4<br>• learning about pride 1,5<br>• liking different things at different times 5 | • being aware of other people's angry feelings 5<br>• dealing with others' anger 4<br>• dealing with being left out 4<br>• dealing with group pressure 2,4<br>• dealing with losing 4<br>• expressing affection 4<br>• expressing concern for another 4<br>• expression of feelings 4<br>• feeling sorry for others 2<br>• knowing different people like different things 5<br>• knowing you can't always know how others feel 5<br>• listening for feelings 1<br>• paying attention to feelings 5<br>• recognizing another's feelings 4,5<br>• recognizing causes of emotions 1<br>• recognizing people feel different ways about the same thing 5<br>• renaming emotions 1<br>• responding to persuasion<br>• sensitivity to feelings 5<br>• understanding the feelings of others 4,5 | • reacting to failures 4 |

*Response Domain*

FIGURE 3.1. Social skills matrix. *Key:* 1 = Camp & Bash (1985), 2 = Elliott & Gresham (1991), 3 = Jackson, Jackson, & Moore (1983), 4 = McGinnis, Goldstein, Sprafkin, & Gershaw (1984), 5 = Shure (1992), 6 = Walker et al. (1988).

any environment potentially strengthen a child's positive social behaviors. Tactics to "trap" these behaviors within the natural communities of reinforcement are described by Stokes and Osnes (1986), and listed in Table 3.2 along with other strategies to promote generalization of children's social behaviors.

There would be great advantage to selecting target behaviors for children that, once acquired, become maintained by the naturally occurring reactions of both adults and other children. An early illustration of such behavior trapping was reported by Buell, Stoddard, Harris, and Baer (1968). In this study, a socially isolated 3-year-old girl was first prompted and then reinforced by teachers to play with outdoor equipment. Her playing elicited increases in peer attention, which in turn increased opportunities for future play. Teachers were enabled to withdraw their assistance as the girl's behavior became apparently maintained by natural communities of reinforcement.

To maximize the potential for behavior trapping, one must be able to identify behaviors that are most likely to be trapped by naturally occurring contingencies. This procedure may become a very complex endeavor, dependent upon a multiplicity of factors, including characteristics of the target child, the peer group, and the social context. What social behaviors are most likely to elicit reciprocal responses by peers?

---

TABLE 3.2.   Tactics to Promote Generalization of Children's
Social Behaviors

---

Take Advantage of Natural Communities of Reinforcement
    Teach relevant behaviors
    Modify environments supporting maladaptive behaviors
    Recruit natural communities of reinforcement

Train Diversely
    Use sufficient stimulus exemplars
    Use sufficient response exemplars
    Train loosely
    Use indiscriminable contingencies
    Reinforce unprompted generalization

Incorporate Functional Mediators
    Use common physical stimuli
    Use common social stimuli
    Use self-mediated stimuli

---

Adapted from "Programming the Generalization of Children's Social Behavior" by P. S. Stokes and P. G. Osnes, in *Children's Social Behavior* by P. S. Strain, M. J. Guralnick, and H. M. Walker (Eds.), 1986, New York: Academic Press.

One study investigated whether the demonstration of affection constitutes a behavior that naturally evokes a positive peer response in preschool children (McEvoy et al., 1988). In this investigation, common preschool songs and activities were modified to prescribe such affectionate peer responses as hand shaking or hugging. Findings indicated that receiving affection from a peer does seem to result in a reciprocal response directed toward the initiator. Moreover, teaching preschool children to express affection to others resulted in increased social interaction that was generalized across settings.

## Correspondence to Students' Social Skills Deficits

Another strategy is to select intervention targets that correspond directly to particular social skills deficits of children receiving the intervention. The rationale for this approach is based on the assumption that the presence of problem behaviors is an indication of the absence of social competencies. With intervention, maladjusted children may learn to replace problem behaviors with more socially acceptable activity.

Although this approach offers a logically sound conceptualization, it is extremely difficult to implement in practice. First, it is a considerably more simple task to identify the presence of problem behavior than it is to link this behavior to the nonoccurrence of precisely defined social skills. General social skills deficits may be identified by the administration of rating scales such as the *Social Skills Rating System* (Gresham & Elliott, 1990) that provide information about a child's functioning on global dimensions, but not in relation to specific social skills. Second, assuming specific social deficits are known, a mechanism is required for matching the deficient skills to problem behaviors exhibited. For example, a hypothetical child demonstrating high levels of aggression has been identified with skill deficits in areas of social perspective taking, impatience control, and peer group entry strategies. How does one differentiate among these deficits to determine which one(s), when remediated, will reduce the incidence of aggressive behavior? Answering this question draws upon theoretical and empirical frameworks that may not yet be developed.

## Social Validation

Wolf (1978) argued that, in addition to demonstrating actual changes in behaviors, a social skills program should be socially validated by its consumers. In other words, it is important to determine whether teachers, parents, and children (a) consider the impact of a social skills program to be socially important and (b) deem the techniques employed during implementation to be socially appropriate. In one social validation study, for instance, a group of special education teachers, parents, and support professionals (e.g., school psychologists, social workers) rated highly the relative importance of social skills training as an element of the school curriculum for students with disabilities (Odom, McConnell, & Chandler, 1993). Although this study provided endorsement for the inclusion of social skills in school curriculum of children with disabilities, it addressed neither the relative social validity of any specific social skills nor the perceived importance of social skills for typically developing children.

Social validation of specific skills to be included in a social skills program can be obtained by having teachers who have used the program evaluate the appropriateness of each of the social skills it addresses. For instance, 60 teachers who had previously implemented the *Classwide Social Skills Program* rated its original 22 skills, as well as 5 additional skills that could potentially be added (Hundert & Taylor, 1993). Using a criterion of 75% teacher endorsement, all but two of the program's original social skills were retained, with two new skills substituted in their place. Results of teacher ratings of the *Classwide Social Skills Program* are reported in Table 3.3. Due to its subjective nature, social validation derived from consumer acceptability ratings may not be a sufficient basis on which to select the focus of an intervention, unless considered in conjunction with other, more empirically grounded, selection strategies.

## Comparison to Socially Competent Children

Programming targets for maladjusted children may be selected by examining the actions of competent children to suggest standards of behavior. From observations of socially competent children, teachers may be able to select specific skills that connote social competence as programming targets for less competent students.

Another procedure is to ask peers to identify social behaviors of preferred playmates (Cone & Hoier, 1986). In one example, such peer-generated descriptions were instrumental in the creation of a template that was then used to evaluate specific social behaviors of maladjusted children. Using this strategy, the behavior of two maladjusted 11-year-old boys participating in a standardized role-play situation was compared with the previously analyzed performances of 15 popular boys (Weist, Borden, Finney, & Ollendick, 1991). Based on this comparison, three intervention target

TABLE 3.3. Percentage of Teachers Endorsing Each of the 22 Social Skills in the *Classwide Social Skills Program*

| SKILLS | NUMBER OF RESPONDENTS | PERCENT ENDORSEMENT |
|---|---|---|
| Communication Skills | | |
| 1. Listening to others | 39 | 100.0 |
| 2. Following instructions | 40 | 97.4 |
| 3. Introducing myself | 37 | 75.7 |
| Interpersonal Skills | | |
| 4. Staying out of fights | 29 | 96.5 |
| 5. Handling corrections well | 26 | 92.3 |
| 6. Joining in | 40 | 79.2 |
| 7. Sharing | 40 | 95.0 |
| 8. Complimenting | 39 | 98.7 |
| 9. Helping out | 40 | 90.0 |
| Coping Skills | | |
| 10. Relaxation | 38 | 84.2 |
| 11. Problem solving | 41 | 95.1 |
| 12. Expressing anger | 39 | 94.9 |
| 13. Apologizing | 39 | 100.0 |
| 14. Ignoring distractions | 39 | 100.0 |
| 15. Responding to teasing | 39 | 94.9 |
| 16. Negotiating/compromising | 39 | 92.3 |
| Classroom Skills | | |
| 17. Bringing materials to class | 39 | 79.5 |
| 18. Completing assignments | 39 | 89.7 |
| 19. Asking for help | 36 | 91.7 |
| 20. Making corrections | 34 | 85.3 |
| 21. Ignoring distractions | 34 | 85.3 |
| 22. On-task behavior | 36 | 88.9 |
| *Now removed from the skill list:* | | |
| Starting a conversation | 38 | 57.9 |
| Continuing a conversation | 37 | 51.3 |

From "Classwide Promotion of Social Competence in Young Students" by J. Hundert and L. Taylor, 1993, *Exceptionality Education Canada*, 3, 79–101. Reprinted by permission.

behaviors were selected: body orientation, speech intonation, and statement of consequences. Both boys received 6 weeks of training in the target behaviors, using modeling, rehearsal, and feedback strategies. Results of the intervention indicated partially successful outcomes. Although the training increased the boys' use of the target skills, and they were subsequently rated as less problematic by their parents, their peer status remained unchanged.

A related method of target behavior selection makes use of available normative data that describe how average children handle various situations. Reliance on normative data overcomes the potentially biased picture that emerges from observations of only a few competent students. Norms might indicate the extent to which a child's social behavior deficit compares with the performance of most other children. Areas showing the greatest discrepancies from the norm may suggest intervention targets.

The use of normative data for the selection of programming targets has limitations, however. First, the requirement for standardization of both settings and situation variables precludes the development of norms for direct occurrence of children's behaviors other than in contrived situations. Rather, selection of programming targets would necessarily be based on norms derived from respondent ratings of a child's behaviors. A second problem is the limited availability of normative data, particularly for children with disabilities who may not have been included in representative samples (Salvia & Ysseldyke, 1981). Finally, targets chosen on the basis of deviation from norms may not truly reflect skill areas that, once remediated, result in socially significant outcomes.

## Models of Developmental Pathways

Kazdin (1993b) argued that the selection of social competence–enhancing interventions should be derived from theoretical models of pathways leading to maladjustment in children. Theory may suggest target behaviors based on the identification of prosocial skills that impede the developmental trajectory of children toward maladjustment. The developmental model formulated by Patterson and his colleagues was described in Chapter 2. According to this model, primary intervention targets for children aged 4 to 8 should attempt to reduce rates of antisocial behavior, whereas those for children aged 10 to 12 should focus on reducing the likelihood of bonding with deviant peers.

## Functional Equivalence

Haring (1992) argued that children's social behaviors can be understood only by examining the contexts in which they occur, in order to determine their functional causes, such as gaining attention or escaping demand situations (Carr & Durand, 1985). The investigation of motivating, contextual functions of deviant behavior may help identify alternative prosocial behaviors that may serve similar functions (O'Neil, Horner, Albin, Storey, & Sprague, 1990).

By observing children's reactions to different "demand" situations, Carr and Durand (1985) demonstrated that problem behaviors accommodate two major functions: the attainment of something desirable (e.g., attention) or the avoidance of something undesirable (e.g., change in routine). O'Neil et al. (1990) organized problem behaviors into six classes, as shown in Figure 3.2.

In their analysis of the functional properties of aggressive behaviors for children with disabilities, Carr and Durand (1985) discovered different controlling events for different children. For some children, aggression functioned to gain attention. For others, aggression was a learned response that functioned to provide escape from demand situations. For all of these

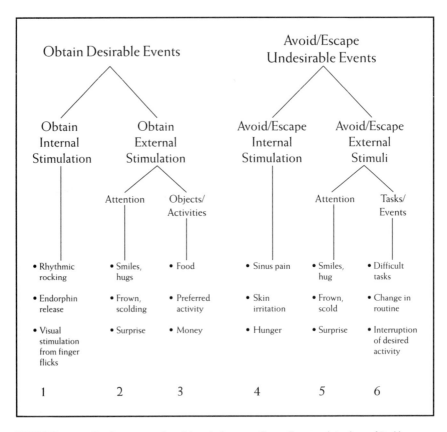

**FIGURE 3.2.** Six functions of problem behaviors. From *Functional Analysis of Problem Behavior: A Practical Assessment Guide* (p. 13) by R. E. O'Neil, R. H. Horner, R. W. Albin, K. Storey, and J. R. Sprague, 1990, Sycamore, IL: Sycamore. Copyright 1990 by Brooks/Cole Publishing Co. Reprinted by permission.

children, high rates of aggression commonly occurred when they were presented with difficult tasks to accomplish. However, aggression was successfully reduced when the children were instructed in "functional equivalents" derived from appropriate communication alternatives. Functional communication training produced behavioral improvements, which were maintained even when naive teachers, unaware of the intervention history, worked with the children. In contrast, a "time-out" procedure also reduced the challenging behaviors of a second group of children, but did not maintain positive effect in the presence of naive teachers.

Interestingly, Taylor and Carr (1993) demonstrated not only that children's challenging behaviors are maintained by the reaction of adults, but also that children's behavior affects both the amount and the type of adult behaviors. For instance, adults tend to respond to attention-seeking children with increased contact and attention, and to the challenging behavior of socially avoidant children with lowered levels of attention. The relation between children's problem behaviors and adult attention is thus both bidirectional and reciprocal.

The selection of target behaviors would be derived from an analysis of the functional properties of the problem behaviors within their specific contexts. Such information could be obtained by questionnaire responses of individuals frequently interacting with the child. On the *Motivation Assessment Scale* (Durand & Crimmins, 1988), respondents predict the likelihood of target behaviors occurring in various situations; a similar format is used in the *Functional Analysis Interview Form* (O'Neil et al., 1990).

Another method of determining the function of a problem behavior is the use of analogue functional assessment. With this technique, possible contextual functions of a behavior are suggested, and then tested by presenting conditions associated with the presumed function of the behavior and measuring changes in its occurrence when those conditions are in place. For example, an increase in aggression when difficult tasks are introduced may suggest that deviant behavior functions as a contextual escape mechanism. To test the function of the behavior, the rate of its occurrence is measured when the difficult tasks are removed (Durand & Carr, 1991). In analogue functional assessment, hypothesized causes of a behavior are directly tested in the field (Repp, Felce, & Barton, 1988).

Once the function of the deviant behavior is identified, appropriate functionally equivalent behaviors to replace the problem behavior are taught. Often this functionally equivalent behavior may be a communication response (Durand, 1990). One of the disadvantages of analogue functional assessment is its complex and time-consuming nature.

# Conclusion

## IMPLICATIONS FOR BEST PRACTICE

■ Assessment of social competence should be based on multiple sources of information.

■ Select social skills programming targets that are known to result in improved child social competence outcomes.

■ Select social skills programming targets that are susceptible to "behavior trapping."

■ Select social skills programming targets that correspond to students' social skills deficits.

■ Select social skills programming targets that are socially validated.

■ Select social skills programming targets that alter children's developmental trajectory toward maladjustment.

■ Select social skills programming targets that are the functional equivalents of the inappropriate behaviors that one is attempting to replace.

■ Because social skills may not be applicable for all children, programming targets should be individually determined.

The selection of appropriate target behaviors provides the necessary foundation for effective intervention. However, the selection of these behaviors is a complex task for which clinical intuition may not provide the optimal decision-making process. This chapter has identified eight methods of selecting target behaviors; they are not mutually exclusive. In fact, given the limitation of any one of the procedures as discussed, a more precise selection of target behaviors may come about by comparing the results of a number of approaches. At present, researchers have not addressed the level of agreement on target behaviors generated by alternative methods.

When considering social skills training delivered to a wide range of children, factors of age, gender, and socioeconomic status may have impacts on the appropriateness of target behaviors selected. Weissberg et al. (1981), for example, devised a social problem-solving program that produced gains for White children in rural schools but not for African American students in urban schools. Other than in general terms, it is unlikely that any specific social skills are universally applicable as intervention targets for all children. A social skills program delivered universally to large groups of children either may not address the social skills deficits of the children with the most difficult adjustment problems, or may dilute them within the broader curriculum to the extent that intervention becomes ineffective. In the end, a program of universal social skills selected for broad exposure may best be combined with social skills programs that focus specifically on high-risk students.

# Conclusion

The development of maladjustment in children is a complex process involving an interaction of factors culminating in deficits in a number of social skills domains. Understanding the developmental pathway both to childhood maladjustment and to social competence would suggest intervention targets to block the harmful effects of risk factors on the one hand, and to plan opportunities to promote social competence on the other. Social skills deficits is a characteristic of a number of developmental disabilities, suggesting that the inclusion of social competence–enhancing interventions may be important components in the remediation of these disabilities. Unfortunately, the selection of intervention targets may be arbitrary or based on clinical intuition, rather than a more systematic process.

# Social Skills Interventions

# chapter 4

# Preschool and Kindergarten Programs

## ISSUES IN PRACTICE

■ What are the advantages of introducing social skills interventions before children reach elementary school age?

■ Do preschoolers with disabilities spontaneously gain in social development by placement in an integrated early childhood setting?

■ What practical strategies can effectively increase children's peer interaction in preschool and kindergarten settings?

■ What factors determine the generalization of social skills interventions to other settings?

There are a number of advantages to promoting children's social competence during their preschool and kindergarten years. First, as discussed in Chapter 1, maladjustment is a stable phenomenon; once developed in preschool years, it tends to persist into the elementary school years and beyond into later life (Fischer, Rolf, Hasazi, & Cummings, 1984; Mize & Ladd, 1990). Interventions initiated in early childhood are likely to have more impact than later attempts to remediate more fully developed behavior and emotional problems. Second, play is a core activity of preschool and kindergarten programs that lends itself well to strategies designed to increase children's social competence. In contrast, as children progress to later grades, an increasing emphasis on academic achievement tends to overshadow the importance of social, play-related outcomes. Finally, encouraging evidence suggests that early intervention in day care settings can produce long-term social benefits for children. For instance, compared with other children, children who attended the High Scope Preschool Program manifested lower rates of juvenile delinquency and other adjustment problems later in their lives (Zigler, Taussig, & Black, 1992). Similarly, a 25-year follow-up study indicated that children of low income families who attended the Perry Preschool Program showed substantially reduced rates of later arrests or receiving welfare than children who did not attend preschool (Barnett, 1993). Providing children with structured, early experiences that promote the acquisition of social competence may increase their resilience to ongoing life stressors.

This chapter describes the lack of spontaneous gains in peer interaction of children with disabilities placed in mainstream preschool or kindergarten classes. Also covered are classroom strategies for promoting social interaction in young students, including teacher mediations, peer mediations, curriculum modifications, curriculum additions, and process-oriented approaches. A discussion of the effects of classroom environment arrangement on children's social behavior is contained in Chapter 9.

## Integration of Young Children with Disabilities

Given the compelling rationale for the early promotion of children's social competence, the issue may become how, and not whether, to include social competency–enhancing strategies in preschool and kindergarten programs. Typically developing children tend to acquire social competence through modeling effects and other learning experiences. In contrast, the development of positive interpersonal relationships in children with disabilities does not occur spontaneously, despite physical proximity with typically developing peers. Compared with their typically developing peers, preschoolers with disabilities interact less frequently (Burstein, 1986; Honig & McCarron, 1988; White, 1980), are more often the recipients of negative peer responses (White, 1980), spend more time interacting with teachers (Novak, Olley, & Kearney, 1980), spend less time engaged with toys (Burstein, 1986), and are generally less well liked by peers (White, 1980). Even when matched for mental age, children with disabilities lag behind peers without disabilities (Guralnick & Weinhouse, 1984). In short, typically developing children prefer to play with other typically developing children. Interactions between children with and without disabilities tend to occur mainly with teacher assistance (Novak et al., 1980).

Studies cited so far in this chapter have compared the social functioning of children with disabilities against standards of typically developing peers in regular preschool programs. A more relevant comparison may be between children with disabilities in integrated and segregated early childhood settings. Evidence exists that children with disabilities who are placed in regular preschool programs fare better than children with disabilities in segregated settings. In one study, Jenkins, Speltz, and Odom (1985) examined the developmental gains of comparable groups of preschoolers with disabilities. One group had been placed in segregated classes; their peers consisted only of other children with disabilities. The second group attended classes in which children with and without disabilities were integrated. Over a 9-month period, both groups achieved significant improvements in cognitive, language, motor, and social development, with no superior gains recorded for children in the integrated setting.

The same authors conducted a second study to correct for some of the methodological weaknesses of the first investigation. In the second study, children were randomly assigned to either segregated or integrated settings, and their interventions came under tighter experimental control (Jenkins, Odom, & Speltz, 1989). One experimental group of children with disabilities received an interactive play condition, in which teachers suggested play ideas, and modeled and prompted appropriate play behavior. Children in the second group received a child-directed play condition, in which they were allowed to select play materials and play freely. Half the children in each of these two experimental conditions were placed in play groups composed of children both with and without disabilities. The other half were assigned to segregated play groups of children with disabilities only. Children with disabilities who experienced the interactive play condition engaged in significantly more interactive play than children who received the child-directed condition, *regardless* of whether the setting included typically developing peers. In other words, gains in children's interactive play did not depend upon the presence of children without disabilities in the play group. Gains did depend, however, on the type of social behavior programming provided.

Placement of children with disabilities into regular classroom settings is a necessary but not sufficient condition for integration success. Additional to placement, a program must be established that specifically targets increased social interaction in order for significant gains to occur. Without effective social competence–building interventions that can be practically implemented in preschool and kindergarten settings, children with disabilities are unlikely to achieve adequate social development. As stated by Guralnick (1990), "Understanding and promoting the social competencies of young handicapped children may well be the most important challenge facing the field of early intervention in the decade of the 1990's" (p. 3).

The need for children to experience activities that increase social skills is recognized by early childhood educators. Results of a survey of 131 early childhood special educators from across the United States suggest that approximately 75% of all preschoolers with disabilities are judged to require remediation in appropriate peer interaction (Odom, Peterson, McConnell, & Ostrosky, 1990). Teacher surveys identifying key competencies for integration of preschool children with disabilities into mainstream kindergarten programs also endorse the need to focus on social competence strategies. In a study by Beckoff and Bender (1989), preschool and kindergarten teachers rated the relative importance of 43 skills for the successful adjustment of children with disabilities in kindergarten. Preschool teachers rated social skills as more important than did kindergarten teachers. This difference may reflect the relative emphasis on play in the two settings. Compared with children in special preschool classrooms, children in regular kindergarten classes spend more time in large instructional groups and less time in play activities (Carta, Atwater, Schwartz, & Miller, 1990).

## Preschool Interventions to Promote Social Competence

Many of the programs to increase the peer interaction of preschool children have been of two types: teacher mediated and peer mediated (McEvoy, Odom, & McConnell, 1992; Odom & Strain, 1986; Strain & Odom, 1986).

### Teacher-Mediated Programs

Some of the earliest strategies to increase preschoolers' peer interaction have consisted of training teachers to deliver prompts and reinforcement to children for using such desired social behaviors as social initiation and sharing. Prompts may be either verbal (e.g., "Why don't you play with Josh?") or physical (e.g., placing the teacher's hand over a child's hand to guide extending a toy to a potential playmate). Prompts may be used to assist children in initiating or responding to a social interaction with a peer (Odom & Brown, 1993; Odom & Strain, 1984). In addition to prompts, teachers have been trained to deliver social or tangible reinforcement when a child exhibits positive social behaviors, but to administer no consequences when the child is not interacting with peers (Strain & Odom, 1986). It is hoped that the delivery of a positive event following a social response will increase the likelihood that the child will engage in the social behavior again.

The use of direct teacher prompting and reinforcement has been criticized on three counts. First, these strategies are often impractical to implement within the time typically available to teachers; second, they encourage children to depend upon the teacher's assistance; and third, gains in children's prosocial behaviors have failed to generalize outside the training situations (Strain & Odom, 1986). Moreover, teachers' regular intervention may disrupt naturally developing child–child interactions (Chandler, 1991; Meyer et al., 1987). For these reasons, both teacher prompts and reinforcement must be faded (Odom & Brown, 1993).

## Peer-Mediated Programs

The need for direct teacher prompts and reinforcement of target students may be avoided by training peers to elicit social responses in these children. Peers have been successfully taught to initiate play with social skill–deficient children, using skills of sharing and play organization (Odom & Strain, 1986). The social initiation of the trained peers is maintained by teacher prompts and reinforcement for successful social bids, and later followed by tangible reinforcement (e.g., happy face stickers exchangeable for a variety of trinkets) (Odom & Brown, 1993).

Studies on the effectiveness of peer-mediated programs have reached the following conclusions:

- The intervention increases peer interactions of socially withdrawn children (Strain & Odom, 1986).

- Introducing a peer-mediated program for some children will increase the peer interaction of other children in the same setting (Strain, Shores, & Timm, 1977).

- Trained preschoolers have been at least as effective as adults in increasing the social interaction of children with disabilities (Odom & Strain, 1984).

- No negative impact is evidenced on the children involved in peer-initiation training (Strain & Odom, 1986).

- Although the peer interaction of children increases in the program setting, improvements in social behavior tend not to generalize to other settings (McEvoy et al., 1992; Odom, Hoyson, Jamieson, & Strain, 1985).

In the Odom et al. (1985) study, three preschoolers with disabilities who received peer-initiation training in a structured play situation demonstrated gains in social interaction in that setting only, and not in other locations or at other times during the day. The same study examined the relative contribution of various components of peer-initiation training to its overall effectiveness. Teacher prompting to the peer trainers was found to be a critical factor. The reward system for peer trainers was removed with no reduction in the levels of children's social behaviors; however, the removal of teacher prompts resulted in the virtual elimination of children's play. Future prompting to encourage peers to interact with target children was critical in maintaining any initial effects that were achieved.

Procedures that rely less on teacher presence and prompting are needed to support children's peer interactions. One potential strategy is to introduce peer-initiation training as described and then to systematically fade teacher prompts. In one case, 10 kindergarten students were trained to initiate play with children with disabilities in a special education preschool class (Odom, Chandler, Ostrosky, McConnell, & Reaney, 1992). After the intervention was well under way, the teacher first reduced the frequency of her prompts to the peer trainers, and then gradually faded out a visual feedback system (number of happy faces stamped on a card). Despite the removal of the prompts and feedback, target children maintained their level of increased peer interaction.

## Curriculum Modifications

The need to find social competence–enhancing interventions that rely on low levels of teacher prompting has spawned interventions that imbed strategies to promote peer interaction into the existing curriculum. Several approaches have been attempted.

**Correspondence training.** One strategy to increase children's social behaviors implemented within the existing curriculum is called correspondence training. Teachers prompt and reinforce children to verbalize their intended behavior during later occurring activities in the school day (e.g., "I am going to play with Jimmy in the dress-up center"). Following the activity, children report on their actual behavior and receive additional reinforcement for say–do correspondence (Risley & Hart, 1968).

Correspondence training was used to increase the toy play of four preschool children (Baer, Williams, Osnes, & Stokes, 1984). Before play, the children were individually prompted by their teacher to verbally select particular materials. By delaying the delivery of reinforcement until after the occurrence of the promised behavior, teachers encouraged generalization of children's say–do behavior both over time and to different situations.

A similar procedure was used to increase the peer-directed talk of two socially withdrawn and language delayed preschool children (Osnes,

Guevremont, & Stokes, 1986). Just before a play period, the children were prompted individually to "talk to the kids a lot." After the play period, they were reinforced for achieving a criterion level of talk with two different peers. For both children, increases in talk to peers maintained after the withdrawal of the correspondence training procedure.

Correspondence training has been combined with peer-initiation training to increase the social interaction of six preschool children with disabilities (Odom & Watts, 1991). Following an initial experimental phase during which peer trainers implemented the peer-initiation procedures, peer-initiation training was combined with correspondence training/visual feedback (CTVF) and implemented during a second daily play session. The peer trainers were prompted to state that they would help "their friend" (i.e. one of several boys with autism) to play. During play sessions, the teacher provided visual feedback to the peer trainers (happy faces drawn on a card) based on the number of times the autistic play partners interacted with them. After the session, the peer trainers received a reward if they had received eight or more happy faces.

The findings of this study indicated that the peer-initiation procedure alone resulted in increases in the social interaction of the boys with autism, but only during the play sessions in which the procedure was implemented. High levels of teacher prompts were needed to maintain the peer trainers' social initiations with these children. During play sessions in which teacher prompts were not provided, the rate of social interaction by peer trainers to targeted children was very low. The CTVF introduced in the second play session produced an increase in both social initiation by peer trainers and social interaction of target children, with almost no teacher prompting.

In a final experimental condition, the peer-initiation procedure was replaced by the CTVF procedure in both daily play sessions. This strategy produced continued heightened levels of social interaction for the targeted children, with few teacher prompts.

**Script training.** Goldstein and his colleagues have used psychodramatic play to increase the peer interaction of preschoolers with disabilities (Goldstein & Cisar, 1992; Goldstein, Wickstrom, Hoyson, Jamieson, & Odom, 1988). They instructed children in aspects of particular common social interactions (e.g., serving a customer at a hamburger stand) through the use of role play and script. An excerpt from a sample script is shown in Table 4.1.

## TABLE 4.1. An Example of a Sociodramatic Script

Setting: carnival-hoop game
Characters: booth attendant (B), assistant (A), customer (C)
A hula hoop and balls representing a ball toss game were used. A money pouch, tickets, and carnival prizes were used to simulate carnival materials.

| | | MINIMAL VERBAL | NONVERBAL | ELABORATED |
|---|---|---|---|---|
| B: | Introduces game. | Ball toss. | Holds ball in front of him. | Come one, come all. Play the ball toss game. |
| C: | Requests price. | How much? | | How much does the game cost? |
| B: | Names price. | One dollar. | Points to sign with the price. | It costs one dollar for three balls. |
| C: | Requests tickets. | Tickets. | Points to roll of tickets. | I'll buy some tickets. |
| A: | Offers assistance. | How many? | | How many tickets would you like? |
| C: | States number of tickets. | Three. | Holds up three fingers. | I'd like three tickets, please. |
| C: | Exchanges money with A. | Here. | Gives money to to A. | I need some change please. |
| A: | Receives money from C. | Thanks. | Extends hand to obtain money. | I'll have to get some change. |
| A: | Gives C three tickets. | Tickets. | Gives tickets to A. | Here are your tickets. |
| C: | Receives tickets from A. | Thanks. | Extends hand to obtain tickets. | I hope I win some-thing. |
| B: | Offers assistance and demonstrates game. | Watch me. | Tosses one ball through hoop. | You have to get each ball through the hoop like this. |
| A: | Tells C the prizes available. | Prizes. | Gestures to all the prizes. | These are all the prizes you can win. |
| C: | Gives A a ticket. | Here. | Hands a ticket to A. | Here, this one's a lucky one. |
| A: | Gives C the first ball. | Good luck. | Gives ball to C. | Just remember to throw it straight. |
| C: | Receives first ball from A. | Thanks. | Extends arm to obtain ball. | I hope I can throw this through the hoop. |
| B: | Directs C to throwing area. | Throw here. | Shakes hoop for attention. | You need to throw the ball through this hoop. |

From "Promoting Interaction During Sociodramatic Play: Teaching Scripts to Typical Preschoolers and Classmates with Disabilities" by H. Goldstein and C. L. Cisar, 1992, *Journal of Applied Behavior Analysis*, 25, p. 268. Copyright 1992 by The Society for the Experimental Analysis of Behavior. Reprinted by permission.

With practice, children were able to enact the psychodramatic play situation, making variations as needed, with little teacher assistance. Children with disabilities were encouraged to apply their role-related behaviors during a free-play period. Of particular interest was the finding that, following script training, children with disabilities increased their peer interactions in situations not specifically targeted in the training sessions (Goldstein & Cisar, 1992). For four children with autism, script training, followed by its fading, produced generalized peer interaction to a different setting, time, teacher, and activity. By the end of the study, the children with autism initiated social interaction with peers as often as did nondisabled children (Krantz & McClannahan, 1993).

Script training may be an important strategy that can easily fit into integrated preschool settings. Not only does it complement existing preschool curricular activities, but it also capitalizes on the developmental mix of children in integrated settings to provide effective language and social modeling.

**Affection training.** Another innovative strategy to elicit social interaction within the existing preschool curriculum is affection training. Using this strategy, the teacher prompts affectionate responses from children during preschool songs or other activities. For example, a typical preschool song such as "If you're happy and you know it, clap your hands" might be modified to instruct children to "hug a friend." Other examples of modifications of preschool songs and games are shown in Table 4.2.

Affection training procedures have been used by teachers to increase social interactions between children with and without disabilities and to generalize those effects to other settings and times after affection training has stopped (McEvoy et al., 1988; McEvoy, Twardosz, & Bishop, 1990). McEvoy, Twardosz, and Bishop (1990), however, suggested two limitations to affection training. First, affection training is most effective in groups where children without disabilities are in the majority. Second, affection training works best for children with disabilities who already exhibit appropriate interaction skills. Because of these limitations, affection training may be applicable only to some children with disabilities and only in some preschool settings.

Like script training, affection training is an intervention that easily fits into the regular preschool program, modifying existing preschool activities to promote increased peer interaction. It also capitalizes on the presence of children without disabilities, whose interactions are the means by which intervention touches target children. Both script training and affection training focus on modifying existing classroom activities, providing

**TABLE 4.2.  Examples of Preschool Activities With and Without an Affection Component**

| PRESCHOOL GAMES/ ACTIVITIES | DIRECTIONS | MODIFIED DIRECTIONS FOR AFFECTION ACTIVITIES | TEACHER PROMPTS/PRAISES |
|---|---|---|---|
| If You're Happy and You Know It | Students sit in a circle with teacher and sing the following verses: If you're happy and you know it clap your hands. If you're happy and you know it clap your hands. If you're happy and you know it, then your face will surely show it. If you're happy and you know it clap your hands. Repeat with . . . stomp your feet, . . . shout hooray, . . . do all three. | If you're happy and you know it hug a friend . . . , tickle your neighbor . . . , give high fives. Continue, using as many affection responses as desired. | Great listening! Doesn't it feel good to be hugged? |
| Simon Says | Students sit or stand in a group facing teacher. Teacher gives verbal directions to students, and if he/she says, "Simon says," the students follow the direction. If he/she does not say "Simon says," the students do not follow the direction. Teacher begins: Simon says, "Jump up and down." "Turn around." Continue, using a variety of simple directions that students can follow. | Simon says, "Pat a friend's back." Simon says, "Hold your neighbor's hand." "Tell _____ that you like her." Continue, using a variety of affectionate responses. | You are doing a good job of becoming better friends! Thank you for paying attention! |
| Role Play | Students sit or stand in a group facing teacher. Teacher presents situations that the students can pretend they are doing. Some examples are: Pretend that you are helping your mother paint a wall in your house. Pretend that you are popcorn popping out of a pan. Pretend that you are a dog running around the yard. | _____ fell and hurt himself. Help make him feel better, _____ (give a hug). _____ is asleep. Help wake her up, _____ (rub her head). _____ is sad. Help make him feel better, _____ (give a compliment). Continue, using situations that allow for affectionate responses. | You are a good helper! That is how friends show each other that they like each other! |
| May I? | Students stand in a straight line facing teacher. Teacher gives directions, and the students must ask, "May I?" If the teacher says, "Yes, you may," then the students follow the directions. If he/she says, "No, you may not," the students stay in place. The students continue following the directions until they reach the teacher. Use a variety of gross motor activities, such as: Take three giant steps. Take five bunny hops. Walk backwards two steps. | Everybody hold hands and jump up and down. Link arms with your neighbor and take eight baby steps. Put your arm around your neighbor and do two frog leaps. Continue. | I like the way you are following directions! Isn't it fun to play with friends? |

From "Affection Activities: Procedures for Encouraging Young Children with Handicaps to Interact with Their Peers" by M. A. McEvoy, S. Twardosz, and N. Bishop, 1990, *Education and Treatment of Children, 13*, p. 162. Copyright 1992 by Pressley Ridge School. Reprinted with permission.

intervention that can be easily implemented by the teacher, without the extensive prompting and praising characteristic of both peer- and teacher-mediated procedures. In both script training and affection training, interactions between children with and without disabilities seem to be maintained by the activities themselves rather than by teacher intervention while the children are interacting.

The report of generalization of children's social behaviors to other situations after script training or affection training is encouraging. Apparently, once patterns of peer interaction are established under the contrived conditions of the intervention, the increased social interaction of children with disabilities is maintained by reciprocal exchanges that continue with children without disabilities.

## Curriculum Additions

The curriculum modification approaches described rely on children's application of positive social behaviors already within their repertoire. Another option is to add curriculum specifically to teach target social skills. Such a strategy may be particularly important when those skills are not in children's repertoire. Through modeling, role playing, practice, and feedback, preschool children may be able to learn components to new social skills and then apply their new knowledge to peer interactions in naturalistic play settings. The value of a curriculum approach to promoting social competence has been discussed previously (McAllister, 1991; Odom & Strain, 1984), but there are few evaluated demonstrations of a social skills curriculum package for preschool children. Odom and his colleagues developed a comprehensive preschool curriculum for promoting social integration of children with disabilities (Odom et al., 1988). The *Integrated Preschool Curriculum* (IPC) provides information about (a) how to group children in preschool settings to promote social integration; (b) how to organize play that encourages social interaction in areas of functional activities, constructive activities, social dramatic play, and games; and (c) how to instruct social skills directly. The package of material includes detailed descriptions for teachers to follow. For instance, the description of how to apply sociodramatic activities of fire fighters is shown in Table 4.3.

Also included in the IPC materials is a description of how to conduct sessions to teach social skills to small, mixed groups of children with and without disabilities. Preschool classes that employed the IPC were found to have higher levels of social integration than comparable classes not using the program (Odom, Jenkins, Speltz, & DeKlyen, 1982).

**TABLE 4.3.** An Example of Material in the *Integrated Preschool Curriculum*

| | |
|---|---|
| *Activity:* | Firelights [Fire fighters] (Level II) |
| *Child Objectives:* | |
| Social: | The child will: |
| | suggest ideas verbally to peers |
| | share materials |
| | assume a role |
| **Materials:** | Fire hats, board or chairs for fire truck, child-sized house, two dolls, hoses (one per two children), phones, space for pretend hospital |
| *Teacher's Role:* | |
| Arrangement: | Table with hats, phones, hoses, fire truck equipment, area for hospital, dolls in house |
| Introduction: | As in Level I, introduce by discussing firelights and their jobs, then demonstrate the play sequence. Arrange roles so that two children are required to do them. Emphasize suggesting play ideas and sharing play materials. Instead of a baby, have one child in the burning house to be rescued. Take the child who was saved to the hospital after the fire is put out. Drive back to the fire station. |

Examples of Prompts:
  Play Organizer:
    "Ask _____ to help save the people."
    "Tell _____ to be the fire fighter now."
    "Say '_____, you drive the truck to the fire.'"
    "Say '_____, quick! Get the hose!'"

  Share/Trade:
    "Ask for help with the hose."
    "Let _____ hold the hose too."

  Role Play:
    "Everyone get onto the truck."
    "Let's put out the fire."
    "The fire's out. Let's go back to the station."

From *The Integrated Preschool Curriculum* (p. 138) by S. L. Odom et al., 1988. Seattle: University of Washington Press. Copyright 1988 by The University of Washington Press. Reprinted with permission.

Another example of a preschool curriculum approach to promoting social competence for four children with behavior disorder in an integrated preschool was described by McConnell, Sisson, Cort, and Strain (1991). For 56 sessions, children received training on 10 social skills grouped into three topic areas: social initiation, social responses, and extending social interaction. Each skill was presented by a verbal description of the rationale and adult modeling of the target behavior, followed by prompting and correction of children's behaviors during role-play practice. Training improved social skills in a controlled role-play situation for three of the four children, but produced only modest effect in a free-play situation.

Hundert and Houghton (1992) found similarly disappointing results for a preschool social skills curriculum targeting skills of initiating play invitations, sharing, persisting at play, compromising, and helping. They introduced social skills training to entire classes of preschool children using teacher modeling, as well as child role-play practice coupled with teacher prompting and praising of children's peer interaction. A description of the lesson format taken from a manual used to train teachers in the classwide social skills program examined in this study is shown in Table 4.4.

Using a five-step format, teachers were trained to instruct the class in the target skills during a series of 20-minute lessons. First, two teachers modeled the target social skills using puppets to depict a play situation. Then, through teacher-led questioning, children were helped to break the skill into about three subskill components (e.g., "What was the first thing Rocky did when he went over to Flower and asked him to play?"). Next, children were invited to use the puppets to role play the same situation with the teacher and receive feedback on their execution of the skill. The next step was for two children to role play the situation with the puppets, and to receive feedback from both the teacher and the class. Children were also asked to state how they would use the skills in the free-play period immediately following the lessons. During that play time, children received teacher prompts, praise, and reinforcement for positive peer interaction. After each free-play period, individual children volunteered to report about an incident when they had used the target social skills.

This social skills program produced a threefold increase in the percentage of positive play shown by children with disabilities in the integrated preschool settings as well as an increase in teacher reinforcement toward them. However, effects neither generalized to outdoor play periods nor maintained during 3- and 6-month follow-up checks. The failure of children to generalize increased levels of positive play was accompanied by comparable failure of teachers to generalize increased levels of reinforcement. The intervention may have required levels of teacher prompting and reinforcement that were not easy to implement under the typical demands of conducting a preschool class.

Another example of a social skills curriculum was used with peer-rejected preschool children (Matson, Fee, Coe, & Smith, 1991). In pairs,

---

**TABLE 4.4.** Content from the Teacher Training Manual for the
*Classwide Social Skills Training*

---

1. Present "Asking to Play" Skill:
   The teacher presents a puppet play to the class that illustrates "asking others to play."

   Teacher: "Class, today the puppets are going to show us another way of showing that you are a good friend. Watch to see what *three* things Flower does when he wants Rocky to play with him."

   *Suggested Puppet Play*

   Flower: "Gee, I don't feel like playing alone today (thinking). . . . Oh look! there's Rocky over there—maybe he'll play with me." (*Walks over* to Rocky and looks right at him.) "Hi Rocky!"
   Rocky: "Hi Flower."
   Flower: "Do you want to play Lego with me?"
   Rocky: "Sure, we could build a garage."
   Flower: "That sounds like fun—let's go."

2. Feedback
   The teacher asks the students questions to *draw out* the skill components.

   Teacher: "What did Flower want Rocky to do?"
   Class: "To play with him."
   Teacher: "That's right! And what did he do first?"
   Class: "He *thought* about whom he wanted to play with."
   Teacher: "Then what?"
   Class: "He *walked over* to him?"
   Teacher: "Right, he *walked over* to where Rocky was, and then where did he look?"
   Class: "He looked right at Rocky's eyes."
   Teacher: "Good!" He walked over, looked at Rocky's eyes and then what did he ask?"
   Class: "He asked Rocky if he wanted to play Lego."
   Teacher: "Right. When Flower wanted to ask Rocky to play, he
   1. *thought* about whom he wanted to play with
   2. *walked* over to him
   3. *asked* him to play
   Who thinks they can use Flower and ask Rocky to play?"

---

Based on "Promoting Social Interaction of Children with Disabilities in Integrated Preschools: A Failure to Generalize" by J. Hundert and A. Houghton, 1992, *Exceptional Children, 58*, pp. 311–320.

the children received eight social skills sessions, 30 minutes long each, in a room outside the classroom. At the end of each session, two nonrejected children joined the two rejected children already in the training session for a brief play period. Four target social skills were taught to the rejected children in a curriculum designed to help them initiate and maintain their positive peer interaction: leading peers, asking questions, commenting, and supporting peers. These skills were taught using a cognitive social learning approach in which puppets were used to model both positive and negative examplars of the target skills. Children were encouraged first to rehearse the social skill verbally and then to enact the skill with puppets. To assist generalization, children were asked to generate ideas about how the skill could be used in other play situations depicted by photographs. With teacher prompts and feedback, children then practiced the skill in a controlled play situation and gradually were introduced to more typical play situations. Finally, adult cues were withdrawn and replaced by self-evaluation.

Findings of the study offer mixed results. On the positive side, rejected preschoolers who received the social skills training interacted with peers at twice the rate of a group of rejected children randomly assigned to a control group. However, the trained children did not make significant gains on sociometric measures of peer acceptance.

There have been few evaluated programs that have introduced social skills as part of the curriculum in preschools or kindergartens. To have sufficient impact, a social skills curriculum would likely need to be implemented over a number of sessions and include strategies to promote social competence within other classroom activities such as games, stories, and psychodramatic play. Such a comprehensive perspective was reflected in the ideas described in *The Integrated Preschool Curriculum* (Odom et al., 1988). The other preschool curriculum programs described in this chapter tended to be brief in duration, did not include ways to incorporate the strategies into other class activities, and were provided only to selected students in the class. Generalized increases in students' social interaction may depend on the introduction of a social skills curriculum that can be easily incorporated into a preschool class, using strategies to promote these skills embedded throughout the school day.

## Process-Oriented Interventions

Most of the programs investigated that promote social competence in preschool and kindergarten students have been implemented by teachers but developed by an experimenter (McEvoy, Shores, Wehby, Johnson, & Fox, 1990). Experimenters train teachers in the program procedures and provide feedback on teacher application in the classroom.

Although an experimenter-designed intervention may ensure that the program is based on sound theoretical and empirical foundations, it may also limit teachers' commitment to the intervention, no matter how effective it might be. As a result, teachers may neither continue with the intervention beyond the life of the study nor tailor the program to be compatible with the ecology of their preschool program.

Some approaches to promoting social competence in preschoolers have focused on training teachers in a process by which they can develop their own intervention strategies. A process-oriented approach is based on the assumption that teachers, with limited assistance, have existing competence to develop effective intervention strategies. Because it does not involve introducing a large amount of programming content, a process-oriented intervention tends to be brief and consist of a framework that guides teachers in generating their own ideas into a program plan.

A two-session nondirective consultation was provided to two preschool teachers by a special education consulting teacher (Peck, Killen, & Baumgart, 1989). The consultant provided information about the instructional needs in language usage of two children with disabilities and helped teachers think of how each identified child's objectives could be achieved within the existing preschool class activities. At a second meeting, teachers were asked to evaluate the success of their plans. After receiving nondirective consultation, teachers increased their individualized instruction both in a training session that was the focus of consultation and in a generalization setting. Children showed an increase in target language behavior in both settings.

A similar process-oriented approach was used to help day care teachers to generate ideas for increasing the social interaction of children with disabilities within integrated day care settings (Hendrickson, Gardner, Kaiser, & Riley, 1993). During 20-minute sessions, a trained coach led a teacher through a series of questions that helped the teacher reflect on the teaching approach used for a target child. As the coach recorded the responses, the teacher was asked to describe positive aspects of the previous lesson implemented and to identify any aspects to be changed. Furthermore, the coach provided feedback on positive aspects of the measures and added suggestions for the teacher's consideration. The teacher was then asked to describe what additional strategies could be used to support the social interaction of the target children.

Coaching was found to increase teachers' cues, instruction, and feedback to support children's social interaction. Increased levels of teacher and child behaviors were maintained after coaching was discontinued. Moreover, teachers rated the coaching procedure as acceptable.

Another example of a low-cost, process-oriented approach to helping teachers develop their own strategies for promoting children's social competence is a collaborative team approach (Hundert & Hopkins, 1992).

Preschool supervisors were trained during one 2-hour session in a three-step procedure for the classroom and resource teachers (early child special educators) together to develop a plan to increase the peer interaction of an entire class of children, including children with disabilities. The initial step was to meet with the resource and classroom teachers, to present a rationale and a written manual for the teachers to develop a classwide plan to promote social interaction. At a second meeting approximately 1 week later, the supervisors asked the teachers to present their plan and provided positive feedback on the content. The third step consisted of the supervisor delivering positive feedback to teachers on the implementation of their program during at least three on-site visits. A teacher's manual contained a description of the three general programming areas in which teachers were asked to develop their class plan, along with examples of each. These three areas were suggested by Odom and Strain (1984) as important in promoting social competence in preschoolers:

- Organizational level (e.g., changes in adult–child ratios, staffing patterns)

- Activity level (e.g., types of play material available, interaction)

- Teacher interaction level (e.g., teacher prompting and praising)

Teachers were asked to consider each of the programming areas described and, on a one-page sheet (shown in Figure 4.1), indicate aspects of their program they planned to retain and describe any changes planned. Training supervisors in a collaborative team approach produced an increase in the interactive play for both children with and without disabilities in integrated preschools. There was also an increase in the amount of time classroom teachers focused on children with disabilities. These increases in child and teacher behaviors generalized from an indoor play period that was the focus of the intervention to an outdoor play period. Moreover, teachers rated the collaborative team approach as practical and effective.

Process-oriented approaches are low cost and show encouraging effects, at least with the few studies that have been reported to date. It is unclear what factors are important to produce the positive effects that have been described. One common ingredient to the reported studies is that they all involved a process by which teachers generated programming ideas. Teachers have been found to be committed to a program in which

---

## Adaptive Class Plan

Class/setting: _____ For period from: _____ to: _____ Today's date: _____

For activity: _____

SIGNATURES: Classroom Teacher: _____ Resource Teacher: _____

  Supervisor: _____ Others: _____ _____ _____

TARGET OF ADAPTATION (in measurable terms, indicate the charges you are targeting):

| Level of intervention | Keep as is? | Adaptations/ Changes/Additions | Who is to do what? |
|---|---|---|---|
| **I. ORGANIZATION LEVEL** | | | |
| • sequence of activities | _____ | | |
| • location of activities | _____ | | |
| • groupings | _____ | | |
| • adult–child ratios | _____ | | |
| **II. STRUCTURAL/ACTIVITIES LEVEL** | | | |
| • accessibility | _____ | | |
| • appropriate equipment | _____ | | |
| • number of choices/spaces | _____ | | |
| • variety, novelty | _____ | | |
| • developmental variability | _____ | | |
| **III. INTERACTIONAL/TEACHING LEVEL** | | | |
| • labeling | _____ | | |
| • questioning | _____ | | |
| • adult modeling | _____ | | |
| • peer modeling | _____ | | |
| • prompting | _____ | | |
| • guiding | _____ | | |
| • reinforcing | _____ | | |

**FIGURE 4.1.**  The classwide planning format used in the Collaborative Team Approach. Described in "Training Supervisors in a Collaborative Team Approach to Promote Peer Interaction of Children with Disabilities in Integrated Preschools" by J. Hundert and B. Hopkins, 1992, *Journal of Applied Behavior Analysis, 25*, pp. 385–400.

they have had input (Idol & West, 1987; York & Vandercook, 1990). Anecdotally, most of the teachers in Hundert and Hopkins's (1992) study reported spending hours of their own time in planning and classroom preparation—a time commitment that would be unusual if teachers were asked to implement a program of someone else's design. They also reported feeling increased recognition of the value of their own ideas.

All of the process-oriented programs described also provided instruction by which teachers were helped to generate their own programming ideas. In the nondirective consultation described by Peck et al. (1989) and in peer coaching (Hendrickson et al., 1993), teachers' programming ideas were facilitated by cues and prompts provided verbally by a second teacher. In the collaborative team approach (Hundert & Hopkins, 1992), the cues consisted of information contained in a written manual and a class program planning format. This information may have been instrumental in teachers' ability to plan effective strategies.

# Conclusion

## IMPLICATIONS FOR BEST PRACTICE

- Social competence–enhancing interventions should be introduced for children at a young age.

- Gains in peer interaction of children with disabilities depend on the availability of programming to that end.

- Teacher prompts and praise may interrupt natural child–child interactions.

- Social interaction of children can be increased by prompting them to make a positive play statement, followed later by reinforcement for say–do correspondence.

- Preschool and kindergarten curricular activities can be modified to encourage the development of positive peer relationships through such techniques as correspondence, affection, or script training.

- To be effective, social competence–enhancing curriculum needs to be implemented over a number of sessions and include strategies to promote the competencies throughout the school day.

- It is important that teachers are involved in the design or adaptation of social skills programs implemented in their classrooms.

- Generalization of interventions to promote social skills depends upon (a) affecting teachers' adoption and implementation of an intervention and (b) ensuring that the intervention produces gains in children's social behaviors.

This chapter discussed a number of interventions to promote social competence in preschool and kindergarten students. Many of these interventions are able to show initial positive effects, but obtaining generalization of these results across settings or over time has been elusive (Odom & McEvoy, 1988). Chandler, Lubeck, and Fowler (1992) reviewed 51 studies from 22 journals published from 1960 through 1990 that addressed peer interaction among preschool-aged children and included assessment of generalized effects. Of that number, only 12 studies reported successful generalization, and another 8 indicated partial generalization.

Any intervention to promote student's social competence in school settings needs to have at least two levels of change to be successful. First, teachers must accept and then implement the intervention in a manner consistent with its design. Moreover, once teachers modify their practices, they need to persist with the new strategies. After teacher adoption of the intervention, the second level of change is that the strategies, once implemented, produce significant improvement in children's behavior.

A number of articles have discussed programming strategies to promote generalization of social behaviors in children (Brown & Odom, 1994; McConnell, 1987; Stokes & Osnes, 1986). By and large, studies that have attempted to promote generalization of social behaviors in children have focused on second-level changes—how to teach social skills to children and engineer environments to promote generalization (e.g., train diversely, recruit natural communities of reinforcement). Generalization-enhancing strategies will have little effect, however, unless they are implemented by teachers. Generalization of programs to promote social competence in children depends upon teachers first adopting and then using a programming strategy. Unfortunately, little is known about which factors affect teacher's implementation of programming ideas. McConnell, McEvoy, and Odom (1992) proposed that the impact of intervention (presumably also generalization of intervention) is the product of the effectiveness of the intervention and the likelihood of implementation. Effectiveness is not a sufficient, nor perhaps necessary, condition for a program to be adopted by teachers. Teachers may opt to implement an intervention with unknown or little effectiveness. Conversely, highly effective programs may be overlooked. Observation of teacher behavior change practices in early childhood special education classrooms indicated that teachers tended not to use interventions with known high effectiveness for promoting social interaction (Odom et al., 1990). Instead, teachers relied on indirect intervention tactics that target large groups of children and require little ongoing teacher intervention (e.g., selecting toys that promote social interaction). The likelihood of teacher adoption of an intervention may depend upon whether the intervention can be implemented with the time and resources typically available to the teacher (McConnell et al., 1992), whether the intervention is consistent with the teacher's beliefs (Stein & Wang, 1988), and whether training and consultation support are available (Myles & Simpson, 1989). Additional discussion of factors influencing teacher program implementation can be found in Chapter 11.

There has been little or no investigation of factors influencing teacher adoption and implementation of interventions that promote social competence. For example, it would be interesting to determine, after exposure to teacher-mediated, peer-mediated, curriculum-based, and process-oriented interventions, which strategies or combination of strategies teachers adopt and the fidelity of their implementation. An associated point is that unless ways are found to translate research findings into practice, empirical work will have little impact on the field (McConnell et al., 1992). For an intervention procedure to have an impact, consumers of that intervention may need to be involved in the development of the product to ensure its compatibility with factors that influence teacher implementation of interventions.

# chapter 5

# School-Based, Individually Focused Interventions

## ISSUES IN PRACTICE

- ■ How important is social skills training as a psychotherapeutic intervention for children?
- ■ How has social skills training been delivered to children?
- ■ How effective is school-based, individually focused social skills training?
- ■ Is social skills training effective for all children?
- ■ Is social skills training effective on all measures?
- ■ Does the length of training make a difference?
- ■ Do training techniques make a difference?

Social skills training holds promise as an intervention that may be effective for childhood maladjustment. Kazdin (1987) included it as one of four therapeutic approaches that can be supported by research literature as reducing antisocial behavior in children; the other three are parent management, functional family therapy, and community-based treatment. This chapter discusses models of social skills training for children and focuses on programs offered in schools that target specific students. A review of the effectiveness of school-based, individually focused social skills interventions is presented.

Social skills training has been implemented in a variety of settings and with children of various ages and differing problems. Despite these differences, many social skills training programs have targeted similar social skills (e.g., social problem solving) for change and similar training techniques (e.g., modeling, role playing, practice, feedback) to bring about that change. Differences among social skills programs may lie primarily in how they are delivered, particularly in terms of (a) training settings, (b) training agents, and (c) training recipients. Using these differentiating dimensions, three models of social skills training, depicted in Table 5.1, are described in the following section.

TABLE 5.1. Social Skills Training Delivery Models

| MODEL | SETTING | RECIPIENTS OF INTERVENTION | CHANGE AGENT |
|---|---|---|---|
| Clinic-based, Individual-focused | Clinic or specialized setting | Individual children | Experimenter or experimental assistant |
| School-based, Individual-focused | School | Individual children | Experimenter or experimental assistant |
| School-based, Class-focused | School | Class | Teacher |

# Three Models of Social Skills Training

## Clinic-Based, Individually Focused Model

Many early attempts at social skills training were delivered to maladjusted children attending either clinics or other specialized settings, including treatment centers (e.g., Kazdin, Bass, Siegel, & Thomas, 1989; Schneider & Byrne, 1987), schools for children with learning disabilities (e.g., Berler, Gross, & Drabman, 1982), or special summer camps (Kettlewell & Kausch, 1983). In these specialized settings, training was provided to maladjusted children either individually or in small groups, by the experimenter or staff provided by the experimenter.

A major shortcoming of this intervention model is that it is accessible only to children who are already identified as maladjusted and can access the service (Cowen & Gesten, 1978). Its inherent unavailability to most children implies that the clinic-based, individually focused model is unlikely to reduce the overall incidence of maladjustment in the general child population, most children of which are neither formally identified as maladjusted nor referred to mental health clinics (Griest, Forehand, Wells, & McMahon, 1980; Lewis, Dlugokinski, Caputo, & Griffin, 1988).

## School-Based, Individually Focused Model

A second way to deliver social skills training is by targeting maladjusted students in schools. Like the clinic-based model, this approach offers a program of social skills exclusively to preselected students with behavior problems and is delivered either individually (e.g., Adelman & Taylor, 1991; Coie, Underwood, & Lochman, 1991), in dyads (e.g., Gresham &

Nagle, 1980; Ladd, 1981), or in small groups (e.g., Bierman, Miller, & Stabb, 1987; Tremblay, Vitaro, et al., 1992), typically outside the regular classroom and under the direction of a nonteacher. (An in-depth discussion of school-based, individually focused social skills training appears later in this chapter.)

## School-Based, Class-Focused Model

In the attempt both to improve the social adjustment of large numbers of children and to prevent the development of later behavior and emotional problems, social skills training has also been administered to entire classes of students. In this model, rather than targeting identified students only, intervention is made universally available to all children in selected classes, or even the entire school. Typically, a class-focused social skills program is delivered by the classroom teacher, sometimes as part of a social skills curriculum that extends over a period of months, if not years. (School-based, class-focused social skills programs are described in detail in Chapter 6.)

# Review of School-Based, Individually Focused Social Skills Training

A number of literature reviews, listed in Table 5.2, have summarized research on the effectiveness of social skills training with children. These articles have analyzed studies conducted across a variety of settings (not only in schools), using a range of social skills programs.

Studies outlined in Table 5.2 suggested a number of general observations about the state of research conducted on social skills training for children, including:

1. Certain methodological shortcomings weaken conclusions that can be drawn about treatment efficacy. These shortcomings include:

   a. The lack of long-term follow-up evaluation (Meador & Ollendick, 1984; Schneider, 1992; Schneider & Byrne, 1985)

   b. The use of nonclinical subjects, limiting the generalizability of results to clinical populations (Pellegrini & Urbain, 1985)

**TABLE 5.2.** A Summary of Articles Reviewing the Effectiveness of Social Skills Training with Children

| AUTHOR(S) | PARAMETERS OF THE REVIEW |
|---|---|
| Hughes & Sullivan (1988) | Reviewed 38 child social skills training studies published between 1976 and 1985, excluding studies dealing with preschool children. |
| Meador & Ollendick (1984) | Provided a general discussion of studies using cognitive behavior therapy procedures with children. |
| Michelson & Mannarino (1986) | Provided a general discussion of social skills training with children. |
| Pellegrini & Urbain (1985) | Discussed studies that evaluated the social impact of interpersonal cognitive problem-solving training with children. |
| Sancilio (1987) | Provided a general discussion of studies using child–child interactions as a therapeutic intervention. |
| Schneider (1992) | Conducted a meta-analytic review of 79 controlled studies of children's social skills training, from 1985 to 1987, updating findings of Schneider and Byrne (1985). |
| Schneider & Byrne (1985) | Conducted a metal-analytic review of 51 controlled studies of child social skills training, through 1983. |
| Zaragoza, Vaughn, & McIntosh (1991) | Reviewed 27 studies evaluating social skills interventions for children with behavior problems. |

c. The failure to demonstrate pretreatment social skills deficits in participants used (Hughes & Sullivan, 1988; Schneider & Byrne, 1985; Zaragoza, Vaughn, & McIntosh, 1991)

d. The lack of either socially valid or sufficiently ranging outcome measures (Hughes & Sullivan, 1988; Pellegrini & Urbain, 1985)

e. The failure to use control-group experimental designs (Pellegrini & Urbain, 1985)

f. The failure to describe the training content (Schneider, 1992)

2. A number of important issues remained unaddressed in the literature, including:

    a. A component analysis of the salient features of social skills training (Michelson & Mannarino, 1986; Pellegrini & Urbain, 1985; Sancilio, 1987)

    b. The cost-efficiency of large-scale implementation (Michelson & Mannarino, 1986)

    c. The identification of developmental factors contributing to outcome effectiveness (Sancilio, 1987)

3. Few studies have evaluated either the maintenance or the generalization of effects (Hughes & Sullivan, 1988; Schneider, 1992).

4. Social skills training of itself, without additional interventions that restructure children's social environments, does not improve children's peer acceptance (Hughes & Sullivan, 1988; Pellegrini & Urbain, 1985).

5. Social skills training is generally effective for a variety of children (Pellegrini & Urbain, 1985; Schneider & Byrne, 1985; Zaragoza et al., 1991).

6. Peer-rating measures generally report less positive outcomes than either teacher- or parent-rating measures (Zaragoza et al., 1991).

Following the meta-analysis completed by Schneider (1992), which examined social skills interventions available until 1987, a number of more recent examinations of school-based, individually focused programs have been published. Table 5.3 summarizes these studies.

As demonstrated in Table 5.3, school-based, individually focused social skills programs have most frequently been provided to students identified as aggressive, rejected, or both. The target of social skills training has varied from specific behavioral skills (e.g., sharing and helping) to more general skills of either cognitive social information processing or self-management. Many studies have used a combination of interventions, with particular emphasis on coaching, modeling, and role playing. Some studies have also incorporated the use of videotapes either to model appropriate social skills or to record student role-playing experiences.

In most instances, training has been both designed and conducted either by the experimenters themselves or by personnel directly affiliated with them, and delivered to small groups of children in settings outside the

TABLE 5.3. Studies Evaluating School-Based, Individually Focused Social Skills Training Since 1987

| ARTICLE | SUBJECTS | SOCIAL SKILLS TARGETED[a] | TRAINING SETTING[b] | TRAINING TECHNIQUE[c] | CHANGE AGENT | NO. SESSIONS | LENGTH OF EACH SESSION (MINUTES) | DURATION (MONTHS) |
|---|---|---|---|---|---|---|---|---|
| Bierman, Miller, & Stabb (1987) | 32 peer-rejected Grade 1–3 boys | cooperating, helping, questioning, SPS | SG, OC | CA, D, RF | Non-teacher | 10 | 30 | ? |
| Coie, Rabiner, & Lochman (1989) | 49 peer-rejected Grade 3 boys | AC, group entry skills, PS, SPS | SG, OC | D, F, P, RP, V | Non-teacher | 36 | 45 | 6 |
| Kern-Dunlap et al. (1992) | 5 Grade 4–6 students with severe behavior challenges | reduced undesirable peer interactions | SE, SG, OC | C, F, RF, SM, V | Non-teacher | 27 | 20 | 4 |
| King & Kirschenbaum (1990) | 36 K–Grade 4 at-risk students | interpersonal behaviors, SPS | SG, OC | F, M, P | Non-teacher | 24 | 45–50 | ? |
| Lochman (1992) | 31 Grade 4–6 aggressive/disruptive boys | AC | SG, OC | D, F, RF, RP, SS, V | Non-teacher | 18 | 45–60 | 4 |
| Matson, Fee, Coe, & Smith (1991) | 14 Grade 4 and 5 students from specialized preschool | AC, PS | SE | C, M, Pro, Pup, RF, RP | Non-teacher | 12 | 60 | 4–5 |
| Pepler, King, & Byrd (1991) | 40 students, ages 8–12, referred by teachers | interpersonal behaviors, SPS | SG, OC | F, M, P, RF, RP | Non-teacher | 24–30 | 75 | 1.5 |
| Prinz, Blechman, & Dumas (1994) | 48 Grade 1–3 aggressive students | peer information exchange | SG, OC | group rules, "reunion," probes, RF | Non-teacher | 22 | 50 | 5 |
| Tremblay, Masse, et al. (1992) | 46 high-risk K boys | SPS | SG, OC | C, RF, RP, fantasy play | Non-teacher | 19 | 60 | 3–4 |

a. AC = anger-coping; PS = play skills; SPS = social problem solving.

b. SE = special education class; SG = small group; OC = out of the class.

c. C = coaching; CA = cooperative activity; D = discussion; F = feedback; M = modeling; P = practice; Pro = prompting; Pup = puppet play; RF = reinforcement; RP = role playing; SM = self-monitoring; SS = self-statements; V = video.

regular class environment. This exclusion of classroom teachers as active intervention participants poses a major threat to long-term maintenance of school-based, individually focused programs. Without involvement in the actual program delivery, teachers may lack incentive to modify either their own behaviors or their classroom structures to foster targeted social competencies once formal researcher intervention is terminated.

Most studies have been limited to a relatively few sessions conducted over a short period of time. Typically, students have received social skills training in once-a-week, 30- to 50-minute sessions, for a total of about 20 sessions, over a 4- to 6-month period. As successful as they may be in producing initial effects, it is perhaps unrealistic to expect such brief interventions to result in lasting improvements in children's emotional adjustment (Weissberg, Caplan, & Harwood, 1991).

## Program Planning Considerations

A number of considerations are involved in planning a school-based, individually focused social skills program. For instance, one of the first considerations is the determination of which specific children warrant intervention. Most programs have relied on teacher rating (e.g., Ollendick, Oswald, & Francis, 1989), peer rating (e.g., Ollendick, Greene, Francis, & Baum, 1991), or self-rating (e.g., Harter, 1982) as the most common participant identification techniques.

A second consideration is the design of the program itself. A rationale for focusing on some social skills rather than others needs to be formulated; specific training methods (e.g., coaching, modeling, role playing) must be selected. Once the overall plan has been developed, delivery strategies have to be addressed. Who will conduct the training sessions? Where? How often? Over what period of time?

Perhaps even more fundamentally, certain basic questions must be considered. Some of these questions are discussed in the following paragraphs.

### Does Social Skills Training Work?

Meta-analyses of social skills training studies report effect sizes close to those obtained from similar investigations of child psychotherapy outcomes (Casey & Berman, 1985; Weisz, Weiss, & Donenberg, 1992). Children who receive psychotherapy achieve outcomes approximately .43 of a standard deviation greater than untreated children. Similarly, the mean effect size of social skills programs, compared with no intervention, has been identified as between .55 (Schneider & Byrne, 1985) and .89 (Schneider, 1992). This magnitude of effect predicts that about two thirds of children who receive social skills training will demonstrate social gains, compared with one third of children in no-treatment control groups.

Although this somewhat modest difference may cast doubt on the universal effectiveness of social skills training, the accuracy of calculated effect sizes may in fact be called into question by a number of limitations in conducting a meta-analysis. For example, the meta-analysis conducted by Schneider (1992) collapsed a variety of social skills service delivery models, and was not conducted specifically to address school-based individually focused interventions. In the overall results achieved, the effect size of school-based individually focused social skills training may have been diluted when combined into the total data set. Furthermore, the inclusion of some studies and exclusion of others in the meta-analysis may have produced an incomplete and biased overview of findings. Moreover, the manner in which interventions were conducted in studies contributing to the meta-analysis may not reflect conditions under which therapeutic interventions are provided in typical clinical practice (Weisz et al., 1992).

Further to this argument, Weisz and his colleagues (1992) contrasted key differences between child psychotherapy conducted in meta-analysis studies and treatment delivery in the field. These differences, listed in Table 5.4, seem applicable to studies of social skills training delivery as well.

One implication of differences between field- and research-conducted treatment is that overall effect sizes calculated in a meta-analysis may not represent the true magnitude of change produced by treatment conducted exclusively in the field. Weisz et al. (1992) have suggested that effect sizes of field-conducted child psychotherapy tend to be overreported in meta-analyses. However, some of the unique features of research-conducted interventions that are perhaps responsible for superior effect sizes may not be feasible to implement in the field. For example, interventions demanding excessive time commitments from change agents may not be practical to adopt in schools, if teachers are to be involved in implementation (Peterson & McConnell, 1993).

It is important to ask not only whether social skills training works, but also whether it produces sufficient effects to raise the functioning of maladapted children into the normal range. After social skills training, children may demonstrate gains that are statistically greater than chance occurrence, but not large enough to produce a noticeable clinical difference in their adjustment. For instance, Prinz, Blechman, and Dumas (1994) conducted peer coping-skills training with aggressive students in

TABLE 5.4.  Comparison Between Child Psychotherapy Conducted in Meta-Analyses and in the Field

| CONDUCTED IN EXPERIMENTAL STUDIES | CONDUCTED IN THE FIELD |
| --- | --- |
| Subjects are recruited for treatment | Children are referred for treatment |
| Subjects have a homogeneous focal problem | Children have heterogeneous problems |
| Therapy addresses the focal problem, almost exclusively | Therapy is directed to a range of problems |
| Therapists were trained in the technique immediately before therapy | Therapists do not receive recent training in the technique that they are using |
| The therapy involved primary or exclusive reliance on those techniques | Therapy is not restricted to a few techniques |
| Therapy was guided by a manual and was monitored for its integrity | Neither manuals nor monitoring is common |

Adapted from "The Lab Versus the Clinic: Effects of Child and Adolescent Psychotherapy" by J. R. Weisz, B. Weiss, and G. R. Donenberg, 1992, *American Psychologist, 47*, pp. 1578–1585.

Grades 1 to 3. They produced significantly greater improvement in these students' social skills and lowered their aggression more than a randomly assigned group of aggressive students who did not receive this training. However, the improvement was not sufficiently large to move the adjustment of the treated students out of the clinical range. In contrast, Lochman (1992) examined the clinical significance of changes in aggressive boys' behavior after completing a school-based, anger-coping program. Following anger-management training, fourth- to sixth-grade boys who had been identified by teachers as both aggressive and disruptive were tracked over a 3-year period. Compared to a no-treatment group, the boys who received training displayed both lower levels of substance use and higher levels of self-esteem and social problem-solving ability. Moreover, levels obtained by the treated boys in these measures were not significantly different from those taken from a sample of nonaggressive boys.

These latter results provide encouraging findings for the impact of social skills training. Similarly, despite modest outcomes reported in other studies, social skills training has been identified as a promising intervention for children with such maladjustment problems as conduct disorder (Lochman, 1992), attention-deficit/hyperactivity disorder (Pelham & Milich, 1984), developmental disability (Wallander & Hubert, 1987), and autism (Koegel, Koegel, Hurley, & Frea, 1992), as well as the focus of pre-vention initiatives (Kazdin, 1993a; Weissberg et al., 1991).

## Are the Effects of Social Skills Training Durable?

Numerous reviews have discussed the paucity of convincing evidence that social skills training produces durable benefits in maladjusted children. The most promising maintenance effects have been obtained over the relatively brief follow-up periods of either 4 weeks (Ladd, 1981; Lochman, Birch, Curry, & Lampron, 1984) or 6 weeks (Bierman & Furman, 1984). Generally speaking, however, the longer the follow-up period examined, the less pos-itive the lasting results (Schneider, 1992). For example, after receiving instructions both to promote social behaviors and to reduce negative behaviors, rejected Grade 3 students were found to maintain appropriate changes in their social actions over 6 weeks, but not over 1 year (Bierman et al., 1987). One exception to this trend of short duration effect was reported by Odom and Asher (1977), whose research described a group of third- and fourth-grade socially isolated students who maintained social status gains 1 year after their experience of a social skills program.

## Is Social Skills Training Effective for All Children?

Asher's (1985) report that about 40% to 50% of children do not respond to social skills training suggests that such intervention does not affect chil-dren in uniform ways. Indeed, participant responsiveness to a particular social skills program may vary with such individual factors as age and socioeconomic status.

**Age.** Schneider (1992) found that social skills training appeared less effective for latency-age children than for either primary-age children or adolescents. Other studies have also supported the significance of chil-dren's age at the time of treatment. Young children have responded well to modeling techniques (Schneider & Byrne, 1989), whereas children older than 11 have displayed greater benefit than younger children from self-statement modification (Dush, Hirt, & Schroeder, 1989).

**Socioeconomic status.** Both socioeconomic status and ethnicity seem related to child responses to social skills training. For instance, pro-grams that produce gains for White students in rural schools may have little effect on the inappropriate behavior of inner-city African American young-sters (Hawkins, Von Cleve, & Catalano, 1991; Weissberg et al., 1981).

## Is Social Skills Training Equally Effective on All Outcome Measures?

Another important question is whether some indexes of intervention effectiveness are more sensitive to treatment effects than others. Stronger effects of social skills training have been found for results based on role-playing measures (Pellegrini & Urbain, 1985; Schneider, 1992) than on either teacher-rating reports (Schneider, 1992) or direct observation (Schneider & Byrne, 1985). Yet, role-playing measures have been criticized for their unclear relation to important social outcomes (Gresham, 1988). In other words, children's performance on role-playing tasks under experimenter-controlled conditions may not reflect children's actual social adjustment in natural situations. The validity of role-playing measures becomes particularly suspect when children are trained specifically in the situations used to assess role-playing effectiveness (Pellegrini & Urbain, 1985).

While positive changes in children's observed classroom behavior, self-ratings, and teacher and parent ratings have all been documented following social skills training, increases in measures of peer acceptance have been particularly elusive (e.g., Bierman et al., 1987; Hughes & Sullivan, 1988; Lochman et al., 1984; McIntosh, Vaughn, & Zaragoza, 1991; Prinz, Blechman, & Dumas, 1994). Two possible reasons for the resistance of peer acceptance to positive change come to mind. First, having learned social skills in the intervention environment, maladjusted children may not apply them in peer interactions outside the confines of the study setting. Second, improvement levels in the social competencies of many maladjusted children may not be sufficient to alter preexisting low peer social status.

## Does Program Duration Make a Difference?

Kazdin (1993a) suggested that program efforts will not produce durable improvement in social competence of maladjusted children unless they are extended over a long period of time. Weissberg et al. (1991) recommended that school-based social skills programs be conducted for at least 40 sessions to have such an effect. Despite these calls for long-term intervention, reviews of the effectiveness of social skills training programs have not concluded that programs of longer duration necessarily produce greater effects than shorter term programs (Schneider, 1992). In their separate reviews, both Schneider and Byrne (1985) and D...¹ found a nonlinear relationship between d· size. Maximum effect sizes were between 5 and 20 sessions, ¹ tions of both shorter and long

Perhaps the curvilinear relationship between duration of intervention and effect size is explained by the moderating variable of adjustment severity, rather than by direct connection to treatment "dosage." That is, studies requiring longer term interventions may have involved participants with more severe behavior and emotional maladjustment than studies that implemented shorter term intervention. Nonetheless, no clear evidence exists that the effects of school-based, individually focused social skills training increase with the duration of its implementation.

## Does Training Technique Make a Difference?

Most social skills programs employ a composite of training techniques (Michelson & Mannarino, 1986). Although the use of a combination of techniques may increase overall program impact, it also obscures the precise identification of specific active ingredients associated with intervention effectiveness (Pellegrini & Urbain, 1985). Although the relative efficacy of individual training techniques has been a subject of investigation, results of meta-analyses have failed to isolate any greater effect size for either modeling, operant procedures, coaching, or social-cognitive techniques (Schneider, 1992; Schneider & Byrne, 1985).

In one study, the technique of coaching was found to produce positive changes in the peer acceptance of socially isolated Grade 3 and 4 students (Odom & Asher, 1977). In this case, children coached by the experimenter on various interactive play skills showed greater gains in peer acceptance than a noncoached control group. Another study of socially isolated Grade 3 and 4 students investigated the relative effectiveness of techniques of coaching and modeling. In the modeling condition, children watched a series of videotapes demonstrating four social interaction skills. Coached children were verbally instructed in the same skills and encouraged to practice them with a peer partner. Meanwhile, a third group received a combination of abbreviated coaching and modeling. Results of the study revealed no significant effect differences across the three treatment procedures.

In a third investigation, involving a group of aggressive–rejected boys, Lochman and Curry (1986) compared the relative effectiveness of anger-coping training alone (AC) with a combination of anger-coping training and self-instruction (AC-SIT). Boys in the AC group attended 18 weekly 45- to 60-minute sessions conducted in their school. The sessions provided training in self-statements to inhibit impulsive behaviors, social perspective–taking, and generating alternative solutions to social problems, as well as role playing and videotape modeling. Boys in the AC-SIT group learned a five-step self-monitoring sequence ("What is the problem?" "What are my choices?" "Focus in!" "What is my answer?" "Did I do a good job?"). While boys in both training groups showed significant reductions in parent ratings of aggression, as well as increases in classroom on-task behavior and measures of self-esteem, anger coping alone was established as more effective than the combination method in reducing disruptive–aggressive behaviors in class.

Overall, however, no overwhelming evidence supports the claim that any one training technique is more effective in promoting social competence in children than any other. It is possible that specific training techniques may effect change on some dependent measures but not on others. It may be that a composite of training techniques produces superior effects over any technique used individually.

# Conclusion

## IMPLICATIONS FOR BEST PRACTICE

■ There exists a need to consider social skills training that can be implemented for a substantial number of sessions by school personnel.

■ Mechanisms that assist the generalization of effects must be built into social skills training programs.

■ Social skills training needs to be tailored to the developmental level and cultural uniqueness of the children receiving the training.

■ The success of social skills training must be evaluated on multiple child-outcome measures.

■ A composite of social skills training techniques may produce greater results than any single technique.

■ The active and willing participation of teachers is critical to the continued implementation of social skills training.

The general effectiveness of school-based, individually focused social skills training is unclear. Outcome evaluations suggest that targeted children show initial improvements, particularly in their knowledge of behavioral expectations in certain social situations. However, empirical measures of teacher-rating, self-rating, direct observation of behavior, and particularly peer-acceptance measures indicate lower levels of actual improvement. Moreover, the benefits of school-based, individually focused social skills training tend to be short lived. The few studies that have conducted follow-up measures beyond 6 weeks generally report that changes in children's social adjustment tend not to persist 1 to 3 years after intervention.

Sufficiently large and sustainable changes in the social adjustment of aggressive–rejected children may require broad-based interventions, focusing not only on improving social skills deficits of individual children, but also on enriching the surrounding social environments, to include peers and teachers as agents to support the changed behaviors. Virtually none of the reported school-based, individually focused studies have used teachers as change agents. In cases when teachers have participated in social skills studies, they were often paid for their involvement (Furman, Giberson, White, Gavin, & Wehner, 1989). Coie et al. (1991) reported that they used paid staff to serve as social skills group leaders in schools because "our experiences in this system led us to conclude that teachers were too overworked to participate, or too resistant to the concepts involved to cooperate with us" (p. 404).

However, without the willing and active involvement of teachers in the promotion of social competence in their students, it is unlikely that:

■ Social skills programs that are introduced will continue beyond the life of the research project.

■ Natural opportunities for students to apply the acquired social skills (in class, in the playground, in the hallways) will be encouraged.

■ Social environments will be structured to either cue or reinforce prosocial behaviors or deliver prohibitions for negative behaviors.

The lack of teacher involvement in processes of either design or implementation may perhaps doom any social skills program to weak and transitory effects on targeted participants.

# chapter 6

# School-Based, Class-Focused Interventions

## ISSUES IN PRACTICE

- Why provide a school-based, class-focused social competence–enhancing intervention?
- What are the characteristics of a school-based, class-focused intervention?
- How can a school-based, class-focused intervention fit into other behavior interventions at a school level?
- Is a school-based, class-focused intervention sufficient to produce lasting gains in children's social competence?

Probably the biggest challenge facing the field of social skills promotion is determining how to produce sufficiently large and durable effects to reduce the incidence of maladjustment and the burden of suffering caused by that maladjustment for the child population. The high cost of social skills intervention delivered to children with identified maladjustment prohibits its application beyond a small proportion of the children in need. Moreover, although initial effects of individually focused programs may be observed, especially using indirect measures of children's social behaviors (e.g., role playing), interventions specifically targeting maladjusted children tend not to generalize, either to children's actions under natural conditions or over time (Kazdin, 1987; Schneider, 1992). To reach greater numbers of children over longer time periods, some schools are using school-based, class-focused interventions, where the target of intervention is to promote social competence for all students in class or a school, often as a prevention strategy. This chapter summarizes these interventions.

## Advantages of School-Based, Class-Focused Social Skills Programs

A school-based, class-focused intervention differs from a school-based, individually focused approach in a number of ways. Most important, in a class-focused program, intervention is delivered to *all* students in a class or school, with teachers, rather than special service providers, as the primary agents of change. This strategy suggests a number of advantages, as discussed in the following paragraphs.

## Prevention and Remediation Focus

Without a proactive strategy to assist students' social development, teachers are forced mainly to react to problems after they occur. Schools may or may not have in place consistent strategies for dealing with behavior incidents. A school-based, class-focused social skills program provides training to all students in a classroom, most of whom are not maladjusted. The intervention is designed not only to reduce the incidence of social problems in children with already developed behavior difficulties, but also to prevent future maladjustment of at-risk children and to strengthen the existing social competencies of all children. Intervention is provided at a point in time prior to the development of problems, and targets all children in either specific classes or the entire school.

## Little or No Stigma

Interventions provided only to high-risk students may contribute to the stigma of these children being isolated because of their social incompetence, thus adding to their problems. For instance, students who are withdrawn from classrooms to receive academic remedial programs rate the experience as embarrassing (Jenkins & Heinen, 1989). The provision of social skills training to all students in classrooms enables those with more pronounced behavior and emotional problems to be exposed to intervention without stigma.

## Use of Natural Groupings of Students

In a social skills program delivered to students withdrawn from various classrooms, there may be little occasion or desire for participants to interact with one another at other times in the school day. Moreover, targeted students may be unlikely to apply acquired social skills with untrained peers who have not been primed to initiate or respond to social invitations of students undergoing social skills training. In fact, untrained peers tend to provide attention to the disruptive behavior of their classmates in ways that strengthen, not diminish, these behaviors (Solomon & Wahler, 1973).

An associated issue is that students in withdrawal programs have limited opportunity to be exposed to appropriate models of targeted social skills. In homogeneous groupings of maladjusted students, socially inept students are likely to be exposed only to behaviors of other equally socially inept students. In contrast, the mix of social competence levels in typical heterogeneous classrooms would enable a classwide approach to provide numerous examples of positive models of social behaviors.

Furthermore, classwide training exposes all students in classes to common social stimuli (e.g., classroom art depicting the social skills being practiced, the presence of classmates who have gone through the same training), which might help students mediate applying their acquired social skills across settings and over time (Stokes & Osnes, 1986).

## Teachers as Prime Change Agents

A quick visit to a few typical classrooms would convince almost everyone of the diversity of developmental levels of students and instructional styles of teachers. To be effective, school-based interventions must allow for sufficient flexibility to accommodate individual differences in schools and classes. Powers (1988) labeled the capacity of an intervention to become compatible with key features of a setting as its "ecological sensitivity." Any intervention that cannot become compatibly adjusted to critical features of individual classrooms may be either rejected by the teacher or, if initially implemented, quickly abandoned.

On the other hand, haphazard alterations to a program would likely weaken the integrity of factors vital to its effectiveness. A balance is needed between fitting a program to the ecology of a particular classroom and ensuring adherence to key features of the intervention. The answer may lie in the distinguishing of those intervention components that *must* be implemented with fidelity in order for the program to work, from components that *may* be altered to the specifications of a class without compromising program integrity.

In practice, school-based, class-focused interventions use teachers as prime change agents. In fact, the actual adjustments required to adapt an intervention to specific classes may not be as important as the process of involving teachers as decision makers in the selection of those adjustments. Teacher involvement in program design not only ensures better compliance with the demands of the classroom, but also increases their commitment to program implementation.

## Access to Other Classroom Changes

Social skills training alone may be insufficient to produce durable improvements in children's social behaviors (Dumas, 1989b; Kazdin, 1987). Bierman, Miller, and Stabb (1987) found that, in order to be effective, social skills training needed to include prohibitions and other behavior-controlling techniques to reduce negative behaviors. In their study, groups of aggressive–rejected first- to third-grade students were randomly assigned to one of three experimental treatments: (a) instruction in positive social behaviors (i.e., questioning others, helping and sharing); (b) prohibitions and a token response–cost for negative behaviors; or (c) a combination of both conditions. Although children who received instruction in positive social behavior sustained increases in their social interaction with peers, and students who received prohibitions decreased their negative behaviors, only the combination of both instructions and prohibitions produced an increase in children's sociometric ratings from nonaggressive peers.

Social skills training may work best when coupled with interventions that optimize the classroom social environment to support students' newly acquired social behaviors. A classwide approach lends itself well to incorporating class discipline strategies to deal with negative student behaviors, strategies to provide learners with meaningful opportunities to practice the social skills being promoted (Bierman, 1989; Hawkins & Weis, 1985; Ladd & Mize, 1983), and strategies to reinforce the defined social skills once they occur. For instance, in preschool and kindergarten classes, social skills instruction can be followed by a play period during which children are encouraged to apply the target social skills and receive teacher feedback (Odom & Asher, 1977). In more senior classes, one needs to capitalize on naturally occurring opportunities during the school day (e.g., physical education activities, classroom transitions, recess), when students can be cued to use their social skills and later receive teacher feedback (or self-evaluation in the case of older students) on their use of those skills.

Similarly, one needs to consider strategies to encourage students' use of social skills outside the classroom, in such settings as hallways, playgrounds, and lunchrooms. Student behavior problems that occur in these "public" locales may be handled differently by different staff, or perhaps not handled at all. Staff consistency in dealing with student problem behaviors outside of classrooms may require consensus from all school staff (including lunchroom supervisors and other support personnel), parents, and others in the community regarding (a) the positive behaviors that will be promoted; (b) the negative behaviors that will not be tolerated; and (c) a plan for consistently handling negative behaviors and promoting positive prosocial alternatives (Cauce, Comer, & Schwartz, 1987).

The mechanism by which to obtain staff consensus on a schoolwide plan to deal with problem behaviors and to promote social competence is unclear. One possibility is the development of a planning committee under the direction of the principal to guide the unfolding of a school plan. Comer (1980) assisted a school in forming a school management and planning team to which "governance" of a schoolwide program was delegated. Whether through such a school-based team or some other mechanism, it is important to ensure broad-based input, planning through consensus, continuity of a plan over a long period of time, and evaluation of the effects of schoolwide efforts.

# Review of Classwide Programs

Relatively few systematic evaluations of school-based, class-focused interventions have been conducted. Examples of programs that have been evaluated, summarized in Table 6.1, are described below.

## Interpersonal Cognitive Problem Solving

In a seminal work that provided impetus for many of the social skills programs that followed, Spivack and Shure (1974) completed one of the earliest studies of a classwide model of promoting social competence in students. A total of 131 inner-city African American nursery school and kindergarten students received a class-based program that taught interpersonal cognitive problem-solving skills (sensitivity to interpersonal problems; alternative thinking; means–end thinking; consequential thinking; and social causal thinking). The program consisted of a 20-minute game format, in which children learned to generate and evaluate alternative solutions to various presented social situations. The 3-month program was repeated the following year for nursery school children entering kindergarten.

The study generated several very positive results. Trained children showed greater gains than untrained children in their ability both to devise alternative solutions and to anticipate social consequences. The greatest gains were shown by children who had received training for 2 years. Improvements in social problem solving and behaviors tended to continue for at least the year following training. These results prompted other researchers to replicate the study, but with little success (Gillespie, Durlak, & Sherman, 1982; Rickel & Burgio, 1982).

**TABLE 6.1.** A Description of Selected School-Based, Class-Focused Programs to Enhance Students' Social Competence

| PROGRAM | ARTICLE | SUBJECTS | COMPONENTS | TEACHER TRAINING AND SUPPORT | PROGRAM EXPOSURE |
|---|---|---|---|---|---|
| Child Development Project | Battistich, Solomon, Watson, Solomon, & Schaps (1989) | 642 K students | Cooperative learning, developmental discipline, class activities promoting social understanding | 1-week summer workshop, monthly staff and individual meetings | Integrated into daily class program over 5 years |
| Improving Social Awareness—Social Problem-Solving Project | Elias et al. (1986) | 158 Grade 5 students | Story or videotape presentation of social skills; class discussion, role play, class activities, and notebooks to teach problem solving; life space intervention | On-site consultant, curriculum material | Twice weekly, 40-minute lessons for 10 weeks for instructional phase, followed by 3/week use of life space interventions |
| | Elias & Allen (1992) | 158 Grade 3–4 students | Videotape presentation of social skills; class discussion, role play of how problem solving can be applied to everyday situations | Weekly 1-hour workshops for 6 weeks; undergraduate or teacher aide to assist in class; curriculum material | Twenty-two 35- to 40-minute lessons over 6 weeks |
| Interpersonal Cognitive Problem Solving | Shure & Spivack (1979) | 131 nursery & K students | Game format for providing instruction in lessons | Scripted lessons | Daily 30-minute lessons for about 3 months |
| Norwegian Victim/Bully Project | Olweus (1991) | 130,000 Grade 4–7 students in Norway | Booklet with teacher suggestions, advice folder, student questionnaire, feedback to staff | A consultant visited school, government project | Ongoing |
| Comer Social Development Program | Cauce, Comer, & Schwartz (1987), Comer (1980) | 24 Grade 7 students in one inner-city middle school | Mental health team, school planning and management team, parent involvement in planning activities to improve school climate | A coordinator to guide the process | Ongoing |
| Yale–New Haven Social Development Project | Weissberg et al. (1981) | 122 Grade 3 students in three schools | Videotape modeling, games, class discussion, role play | Sixteen 1.5-hour training sessions; 2 undergraduate assistants | Fifty-two 20- to 30-minute lessons/week, over 13 weeks |
| | Gesten et al. (1982) | 158 Grade 2–3 students | Videotape modeling, games class discussion, role play; abbreviated program had only videotape and discussions | Nine 2-hour training sessions; 2 undergraduate assistants, 1 senior program staff | Seven 30- to 40-minute lessons over 9 weeks; five 40-minute sessions for the abbreviated program |
| | Caplan et al. (1992) | 61 Grade 4–6 students | Didactic instruction, class discussion, role play, worksheets, homework assignments | Six 2-hour workshops and weekly on-site consultations; community agency staff as co-teachers | Twenty 50-minute lessons/week over 15 weeks |

The interpersonal cognitive problem-solving model has had considerable influence on the content of social skills programs in the field, and was recommended as among the most promising formats for the prevention of mental health problems (President's Commission on Mental Health, 1978). The work of Spivack and Shure (1974) provided one of the earliest suggestions that social behaviors of children can be modified indirectly by teaching social problem-solving skills. More recently, an 82-lesson version of the program has been developed for commercial distribution (Shure, 1992).

## Yale–New Haven Social Development Project

One of the most studied classwide social skills programs is the *Yale–New Haven Social Development Project*, designed by Weissberg and colleagues (1981). Used with six classes of third-grade students, this program consisted of a series of 52 lessons of 20 to 30 minutes duration each, presented over a 4-month period, covering such social problem-solving skills as recognized feelings, generating alternative solutions, and considering consequences. The influence of Spivack and Shure's (1974) interpersonal cognitive problem-solving program can clearly be seen in the approach taken in this project.

The program was implemented by teachers and undergraduate assistants who trained students in social problem-solving skills, using modeling, class discussions, role-playing exercises, and games. Teacher training in the procedure was provided during training sessions held four times a week over a 13-week period. More recently, teacher training has been conducted in 5-day training sessions held during the summer (Weissberg, Stroup Jackson, & Shriver, 1993). It is important to note that, although perhaps necessary, the amount of time required for teacher training in the procedures may not be available in many schools.

Children who received the program showed greater improvement and use of social problem-solving skills than a control group of no-treatment children in other classes in the same schools (Weissberg et al., 1981). However, these positive effects occurred only for students attending suburban schools, not those in urban schools. A second study, which used a shortened 17-session version of the program, provided similar unequivocal results (Gesten et al., 1982).

More recently, a further revised program for young adolescents was developed, consisting of 20 sessions focusing on stress management, self-esteem, problem solving, substances and health, assertiveness, and social network building (Caplan et al., 1992). During 50-minute sessions conducted twice weekly for 15 weeks, skills were co-taught by teachers and program staff using didactic instruction, class discussion, diaries, small-group role plays, work sheets, and homework assignments. Students were encouraged to apply the skills to hypothetical dilemmas involving drug and alcohol problems. Gains obtained by 282 students from Grades 6 and 7 were compared with those of students attending randomly assigned, no-intervention classes in the same schools. Program students showed superior gains in (a) skills of handling interpersonal problems and coping with anxiety, (b) teacher rating of student social-emotional adjustment and popularity, and (c) self-report of problem-solving efficacy and decreased use of alcohol. In contrast to the results of Weissberg et al. (1981), these positive outcomes applied equally as well to African American students in inner-city schools as to White students in suburban schools.

## Improving Social Awareness—Social Problem-Solving Project

The Improving Social Awareness—Social Problem-Solving Project (ISA-SPS) was a collaborative effort of a community mental health center, a university, and a local school district, with the goal of improving the ability of fourth- and fifth-grade students to cope with school stressors (Elias & Weissberg, 1990). Students were taught social problem-solving skills organized into curriculum units of (a) interpersonal sensitivity (attending to one's own and others' feelings); (b) means–end thinking (consideration of alternative ways to reach one's goal and the consequences for alternative strategies); and (c) planning and anticipation (developing ideas to implement one's chosen solution).

This content was introduced to students in a series of lessons divided into three phases. During the *Readiness* phase, students were taught such self-control and social awareness skills as listening, following directions, self-calming, and appropriate ways to show caring. This phase was followed by the *Instructional* phase, during which students were exposed to a strategy for problem solving in social situations. Finally, in the *Application* phase, students were taught to use their acquired skills on real-life social and academic problems.

The ISA-SPS has been used to help fifth-grade students cope with the stress of entering middle school. The project was implemented over a 1½-year period, to 158 fifth-grade students in four elementary schools. Teachers applied the Instructional phase of the program during twenty 40-minute lessons, followed by once weekly sessions for the Application phase over the course of a school year. Teachers were trained to mediate conflicts between students and to fit a problem-solving approach into the regular classroom routine. An on-site consultant (predoctoral psychology student) worked with teachers on the implementation of the program. Although the amount of teacher training was not described in this study, another account of the implementation of the ISA-SPS indicated that teacher training usually consists of a 2-day workshop (Elias & Clabby, 1992).

Elias et al. (1986) compared the gains of students who received the full program (Instructional and Application phases from October to May), students who received only the Instructional phase (from January to May), and students who received no training. Results indicated that students who received the full program reported better coping with school stressors than students who received partial training. Students who received either full or partial programs, in turn, showed superior results to students receiving no training. Neither direct observation nor teacher ratings of student behaviors were included, thus limiting the generality of the conclusions that could be drawn from this study.

In a more recent study, Elias and Allen (1992) compared three methods for teaching social decision making and social problem solving to elementary school children. One method was a condensed version of the ISA-SPS. A second method consisted of discovery learning, in which students observed a series of thirty 15-minute videotapes to train children in interpersonal problem resolution. The third method was a direct learning approach. In this condition, students observed the same videotapes used in the discovery condition, but additionally were taught a cognitive-mediational strategy similar to that developed by Meichenbaum (1977). Interventions were applied by teachers during twenty-two 30- to 40-minute lessons conducted during the social studies class, for a period of 6 weeks.

Students in all three treatment conditions showed gains in social problem-solving abilities immediately after the intervention, as well as 3 months later. The results suggested an interaction between severity of children's maladjustment and treatment method. The direct learning approach was the most effective intervention for socially competent children, but the least effective for at-risk children. The author surmised that the differential effects of treatment condition by children's level of social adjustment may have been due to limitations in the cognitive ability of at-risk children, limitations that restricted their ability to generate problem-solving strategies.

## The Child Development Project

School-based, class-focused interventions have been extended to incorporate all students within a school. One example of a schoolwide intervention was the *Child Development Project*, introduced in three suburban elementary schools in northern California (Battistich, Solomon, Watson, Solomon, & Schaps, 1989; Solomon, Watson, Delucchi, Schaps, & Battistich, 1988). The purpose of this project was to prepare students to be responsible and caring citizens through the development of moral character and social values. Over a 7-year span, the program was introduced successively to an additional grade a year, from kindergarten to Grade 6. Teachers were trained to create a caring classroom environment that promoted prosocial student behaviors through the use of co-operative learning, developmental discipline, and activities promoting social understanding, prosocial values, and helping. Teachers participated in a week-long workshop during the summer, monthly staff meetings, and weekly individual teacher meetings with "coaches" who provided feedback on teacher implementation of the program.

Sequential cohorts of kindergarten children were followed over a 5-year period and compared with children in three randomly assigned comparison schools. Students in the intervention schools showed greater gains in social problem-solving skills, as measured by the responses to hypothetical scenarios. In addition, observations conducted in classrooms indicated that program students displayed higher levels of prosocial behaviors (Solomon et al., 1988).

## Comer School Development Program

A systems-oriented approach to student adjustment problems was developed to improve the social environment and to develop supportive social networks in a middle school (Anson et al., 1991; Comer, 1980). The major elements of the project consisted of:

■ Paid parent aides to help in classrooms.

■ The formation of a multidisciplinary team of mental health professionals to (a) consult with staff on the management of student behaviors, (b) recommend policy changes to prevent behavior problems in the school, and (c) assist in staff development.

■ A parent program that conceived and planned a social calendar to improve school climate and involve parents.

■ The creation of a school planning and management team composed of teachers (elected and nominated); parents (elected by other parents); members of the school's professional support staff (e.g., school psychologist); a representative of the nonprofessional support staff (e.g., secretary or custodian); and the principal, who served as team leader. The team's primary purposes were to plan and guide a school strategy for improving school climate and to develop a community and public relations program.

This project is interesting on a number of counts. Its target was to affect the climate of the school by both adding and altering planning structures at a school level. There was no specific program that schools were expected to implement other than the described structural changes. A school would be free to develop specific plans that met a goal of improved interpersonal relationships as long as the plan involved a cross-section of individuals representing groups that should have a stake in the functioning of the school. The programs that were the focus of each planning group targeted not only student–student relationships but also staff–staff and staff–parent relationships. In contrast to other school-based interventions discussed to this point, the *School Development Program* (a) focused on an improved process for deriving solutions rather than implementation of already developed solutions; (b) targeted interpersonal relationships among staff, students, and parents, rather than only among students; and (c) enlisted a broad base of teacher support rather than participation of selected teachers only.

Unfortunately, there has been little evaluation of the impact of the *School Development Program*. Cauce et al. (1987) identified a sample of 24 seventh-grade African American students who had participated in this program from Grades 1 to 4 and, as a control group, matched samples of students from the same middle schools who had previously attended other primary schools. In comparison to control students, students who had received the program 3 years earlier attained higher academic test scores, higher grade point averages, and higher perceived school and self-competence. These results, although encouraging, are difficult to interpret because of limitations in the experimental methodology used in the study.

## Norwegian Victim/Bully Project

Concerns about the aggression and intimidation occurring in school yards prompted a nationwide campaign in Norway against bully/victim problems, with all schools in the nation invited to participate (Olweus, 1991). The major components of the intervention consisted of:

- A 32-page booklet for school personnel providing suggestions for dealing with and preventing the bully/victim problems

- A 4-page folder of information and advice to parents

- A 25-minute videotape depicting the impact of bullying on students

- An inventory completed by students on the level of problems at their school

- Feedback, at some schools, comparing results for their schools to nationwide findings

The program was introduced in about 830 schools with approximately 130,000 students participating. Effects were evaluated after 8 and 12 months of intervention using consecutive cohorts of approximately 600 to 700 students in Grades 4 to 7. Results indicated that the program was associated with a 50% reduction in student reports of being bullied or bullying others, a reduction in student self-report of antisocial behaviors, and an increase in student satisfaction with school life.

# Conclusion

### IMPLICATIONS FOR BEST PRACTICE

- Schools need in place not only strategies to deal with behavior-related incidents when they occur, but also to prevent the emergence of behavior problems by promoting social competence development.

- School-based, class-focused interventions have advantages of providing little or no stigma, using natural groupings of children, using the teacher as key change agent, and accessing other classroom changes.

- School-based, class-focused interventions should draw on multiple components, implemented by multiple socializing agents, in multiple settings over multiple years.

What interventions or set of interventions will have sufficient impact to reduce the burden of suffering for children with maladjustment, as well as reduce the likelihood that other children will develop maladjustment? The school-based, class-focused programs described in this chapter all contained multiple components, and in the Comer School Development Project multiple socializing agents (i.e., school personnel, parents, community agent). These programs all treat children through their broader social environment rather than through isolated interventions (Zigler, Taussig, & Black, 1992). The interventions target not only children but also teachers to effect changes at class and school levels. To produce large effects, class-wide interventions may require multicomponents, involving multiple socializing agents who implement consistent strategies over multiple years (Weissberg, Caplan, & Harwood, 1991).

Multicomponent intervention is not without its disadvantages. First, the complexities of multifaceted programs make them difficult to implement correctly and consistently (Schneider, 1992). Second, with so many treatment variables being implemented at the same time, it is difficult to discern the relative contribution of any single variable to obtained effects (Meador & Ollendick, 1984). Improvements in the packaged intervention would require a component analysis to isolate the active ingredients in the comprehensive program.

School-based, class-focused interventions draw on an ecological or system perspective, which assumes that a child's behavior is maintained if not caused by the arrangement of factors in the child's surrounding social environments (Bronfenbrenner, 1979; Zigler et al., 1992). It would be important to identify the critical ecosystems to target in a school and the process by which change in school ecosystems can come about. For instance, can durable reductions in students' aggression in the playground be obtained through class-based interventions? If not, how many additional settings and how many other people must an intervention incorporate to have sufficient impact to produce generalized increases in children's social competence? Pentz et al. (1989) argued that, to promote successfully social competence, one needs to involve multiple socializing agents, including parents, community leaders, government, and mass media in an integrated approach with schools.

No matter how well designed, a social skills program delivered to all students in classes may not have sufficient strength to improve the behaviors of the most troubled. A tiered system of progressively more focused and intensive social skills interventions may be needed to reduce maladjustment in the child population. Such a model is depicted in Figure 6.1. At the first tier are interventions that are universally delivered to all children, interventions that, if successful, can strengthen students' existing competencies and help to avert future maladjustment for a broad range of

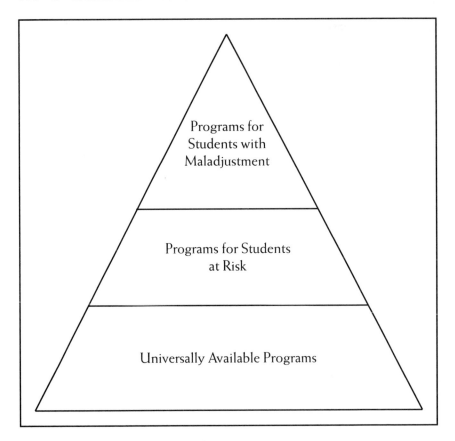

**FIGURE 6.1.**   A three-tiered model of social skills interventions.

children, most of whom will never develop maladjustment. Many of the school-based class-focused interventions discussed in this chapter are examples of interventions that can be universally delivered to students.

A second tier of interventions may be to provide programs not universally, but targeted at particular students at risk for later development of maladjustment. One form of at-risk intervention is to provide a program at a developmental milestone associated with increased risk of behavioral and emotional problems. For example, a school-based program can be delivered to children of divorce. The *Children of Divorce Intervention Program* (CODP) (Pedro-Carroll, Cowen, Hightower, & Guare, 1986) is a 10-week school-based program that provides experiences to help fourth- to sixth-grade students cope with the stress of divorce. Compared with children from intact families, children of divorce were found to be less well adjusted before they began the CODP. Their adjustment improved after the intervention, approaching levels similar to children from intact families.

Another example of a milestone program is the provision of interventions to students who are experiencing school transition, such as from middle to secondary school. In making transitions, students are simultaneously faced with adjusting to a new physical setting, unfamiliar peers and teachers, and a new learning format. The effectiveness of a program to help students with this transition was evaluated by Felner, Ginter, and Primavera (1982). Fifty-nine students entering high school were placed in homerooms with teachers who assumed responsibilities more typically performed by guidance personnel (aided students in choosing classes, counseled students regarding personal difficulties, contacted parents when students were absent, etc.). Students in the program were also scheduled into primary academic classes (e.g., English and mathematics) with other program students, in order to maintain peer-group consistency from class to class. Compared with students in a matched control group, program students had significantly higher grade point averages, attendance records, and positive self-concept, and also rated the school climate more positively.

Even with universal and at-risk programs, there will always remain a need to respond to those students who have already developed maladjustment. Interventions targeted specifically to children with maladjustment, as described in Chapter 5, can be added as a third tier of interventions to a backdrop of universal and at-risk programs.

It is likely easier to provide a specialized intervention to identified maladjusted students individually or in groups if school staff have already arranged classrooms, school hallways, and playgrounds to promote and reinforce social competence in all students. Movement toward a multiple-level or tiered approach will require a balance in determining the resources that should be allocated to each of the various tiers that need to be put into place. Currently, most resources are spent responding to children with already developed behavior and emotional problems, often at a point of crisis (Weissberg et al., 1991). In moving to a multitiered approach, more resources would need to be set aside for programs delivered to children before maladjustment develops and to promote social competence in all children. Specialized programs to provide children at high risk for maladjustment would work best when incorporated into this multilevel system of service delivery.

# chapter 7

# The *Classwide Social Skills Program*: An Example of a School-Based, Class-Focused Intervention

### ISSUES IN PRACTICE

■ What are the features of the *Classwide Social Skills Program*?

■ What factors affect schools' implementation and continuation of the intervention?

Chapter 6 discussed school-based, class-focused interventions to promote social competence in children. This chapter describes one such intervention in detail. The *Classwide Social Skills Program* (CSSP), currently implemented across the Province of Ontario, Canada, is one of the interventions being examined in a 5-year longitudinal study[1] comparing the effectiveness of various school-based interventions for children at risk for maladjustment, as a follow-up to the *Ontario Child Health Study* (Offord, Boyle, & Racine, 1991). At the point of this writing, the project is in its third year.

The purpose of this chapter is to illustrate some of the issues that pertain to implementation of a school-based, class-focused social skills program. A brief overview of methodology used in the longitudinal research study is presented, followed by a program description and brief discussion of implementation issues.

## Longitudinal Study

The purpose of this large study is to assess the benefits of alternative school-based interventions by measuring changes in the social adjustment

---

1. Principal investigators for the study are Dr. Dan Offord and Dr. Michael Boyle, McMaster University, Hamilton, Ontario, Canada. Coinvestigators are Dr. Chuck Cunningham, Dr. Joel Hundert, and Ms. Yvonne Racine, McMaster University. The *Classwide Social Skills Program* was developed by Joel Hundert and Penny Burlak and is being implemented in schools and preschools in the Hamilton area.

of five successive cohorts of elementary students identified at either high or low risk for maladjustment. Subjects were selected from students in kindergarten through third grade, from a total of over 50 schools in 10 Ontario school boards.

As illustrated in Table 7.1, a yearly random selection of about 4,000 of these students receive initial screening to determine proportions at high and low risk of maladjustment. Screening consists of teacher and parent ratings of student behavioral adjustment on items adopted from and added to the *Child Behavior Checklist* (Achenbach & Edelbrock, 1983). Ten percent of students (about 400) receiving the highest and lowest scores derived from these measures were selected for inclusion in the high-risk and low-risk groups, respectively. One school from each of the 10 school boards was selected at random to receive one of three interventions, with the particular intervention itself determined at random. The remaining nonintervention schools serve as controls for that year. The subsequent year, another set of 10 intervention schools is selected at random from the remaining control schools. This research design is illustrated in Table 7.2.

## Interventions

Interventions were initiated in January of one school year and continued until December of the next school year, with opportunity for further continuation at the discretion of each school. The late intervention start allowed for pretest data to be collected in the fall, prior to program implementation. The three interventions were the *Classwide Social Skills Program* (Hundert & Taylor, 1993), "buddied" reading (Topping, 1989), or a combination of both

TABLE 7.1. Yearly Selection of Student Cohort Samples in Longitudinal Study

| | TOTAL NUMBER OF STUDENTS (*N* = 12,400) | NUMBER SCREENED (*N* = 4,000) | NUMBER OF STUDENTS SELECTED FOR DETAILED FOLLOW-UP | |
|---|---|---|---|---|
| | | | HIGH RISK (*N* = 200) | LOW RISK (*N* = 200) |
| Intervention schools | | | | |
| Social skills | 800 | 600 | 60 | 60 |
| Reading program | 800 | 600 | 60 | 60 |
| Combined | 800 | 600 | 60 | 60 |
| No-intervention schools | 10,000 | 1,200 | 120 | 120 |

**Table 7.2.** Assignment of Schools to Intervention and Follow-Up for Longitudinal STUDY

| | NUMBER OF SCHOOLS | | | | |
|---|---|---|---|---|---|
| | YEAR 1 | YEAR 2 | YEAR 3 | YEAR 4 | YEAR 5 |
| Intervention schools | 10 | Follow-up | Follow-up | Follow-up | Follow-up |
| No-intervention schools | 40 | | | | |
| Intervention schools | | 10 | Follow-up | Follow-up | Follow-up |
| No-intervention schools | | 30 | | | |
| Intervention schools | | | 10 | Follow-up | Follow-up |
| No-intervention schools | | | 20 | | |
| Intervention schools | | | | 10 | Follow-up |
| No-intervention schools | | | | 10 | |
| Intervention schools | | | | | 10 |
| No-intervention schools | | | | | 0 |

programs. The reading program was selected as an intervention for two reasons. First, evidence suggested that maladjusted children can improve their peer relationships as a result of tutoring in academic areas (Coie & Krehbiel, 1984). Second, academic failure has been well articulated as an important ingredient in the developmental pathway toward maladjustment (Patterson, Capaldi, & Bank, 1991; Tremblay, Masse, et al., 1992).

A fourth intervention, consisting of school-based parent training, was originally included in the study. This intervention was discontinued because of the low attendance rate, despite rigorous recruitment activities of parents whose children were at high risk for maladjustment. Projections indicated that even if parent training produced significant improvements for every student whose parent attended, the small numbers of parents involved would not have resulted in sufficient effect to show a significant difference from high-risk students in nonintervention schools.

## Measures

Details of the measures used to evaluate changes in high-risk, low-risk, and nonintervention students, as well as other in-depth aspects of the methodology used in the study, exceed the scope of this chapter. In brief, measures assessing children's social adjustment drew upon multiple dimensions of children's social functioning, taken from different settings and sources, including:

- Child self-rating of perceived social competence (Harter, 1982)

- Test of reading achievement (Jastak & Wilkinson, 1984)

- Teacher rating of student social adjustment (Gresham & Elliott, 1990)

- Parent rating of student social adjustment (Boyle et al., 1987)

- Naturalistic observations of student classroom behavior (Stanley & Greenwood, 1981)

- Naturalistic observations of student playground behavior (Ollendick, Greene, Francis, & Baum, 1991)

Measures were collected during the fall, before the start of interventions, and subsequently at the beginning of each school year of the study.

# Components of the Classwide Social Skills Program

The *Classwide Social Skills Program*, implemented to all children in primary division classes, targeted a number of elements that structure classroom and school environments in order to foster heightened social competence in students. Specific components included:

1. Classroom presentation of targeted social skills

2. Teachers' use of naturally occurring opportunities throughout the school day to prompt and reinforce targeted social skills

3. On-site coaching and consultation to teachers

4. Regular monthly meetings with teachers to review the program progress and refine class discipline strategies

5. Involvement of all school staff in developing a schoolwide plan to prevent and react to aggression in school hallways, playgrounds, and so forth

## Social Skills Selection

The CSSP contained 22 social skills (shown in Table 7.3) clustered into four domains: communication skills, interpersonal skills, coping skills, and classroom skills. These skills were organized to represent response domains of behaving, thinking, and feeling, applied to social situations relating to tasks, to others, and to self. Skill selection was based on a review of the literature, content analysis of other social skills programs (see Figure 3.1), and teacher feedback on the perceived suitability of various social skills. Teachers who implemented the social skills program during the first year of the project were asked to rate (yes or no) whether each of the 22 social skills and five alternative skills was applicable to their class. A cutoff of 75% teacher endorsement was used to retain a social skill in the program. Based on this evaluation, two of the original social skills (starting a conversation, continuing a conversation) were substituted by two other skills shown in Table 7.3.

## Pace of Social Skills Presentations

The pace of introducing new social skills was left to the classroom teacher's discretion, with a recommendation to initiate a new social skill once a week

TABLE 7.3. Percentage of Teachers Endorsing Each of the 22 Social Skills in the *Classwide Social Skills Program*

| SKILLS | N | PERCENT ENDORSEMENT |
|---|---|---|
| Communication Skills | | |
| 1. Listening to others | 39 | 100.0 |
| 2. Following instructions | 40 | 97.4 |
| 3. Introducing myself | 37 | 75.7 |
| Interpersonal Skills | | |
| 4. Staying out of fights | 29 | 96.5 |
| 5. Handling corrections well | 26 | 92.3 |
| 6. Joining in | 40 | 79.2 |
| 7. Sharing | 40 | 95.0 |
| 8. Complimenting | 39 | 98.7 |
| 9. Helping out | 40 | 90.0 |
| Coping Skills | | |
| 10. Relaxation | 38 | 84.2 |
| 11. Problem solving | 41 | 95.1 |
| 12. Expressing anger | 39 | 94.9 |
| 13. Apologizing | 39 | 100.0 |
| 14. Ignoring distractions | 39 | 100.0 |
| 15. Responding to teasing | 39 | 94.9 |
| 16. Negotiating/compromising | 39 | 92.3 |
| Classroom Skills | | |
| 17. Bringing materials to class | 39 | 79.5 |
| 18. Completing assignments | 39 | 89.7 |
| 19. Asking for help | 36 | 91.7 |
| 20. Making corrections | 34 | 85.3 |
| 21. Ignoring distractions | 34 | 85.3 |
| 22. On-task behavior | 36 | 88.9 |
| *Now removed from the skill list:* | | |
| Starting a conversation | 38 | 57.9 |
| Continuing a conversation | 37 | 51.3 |

for students in Grades 1 to 3 and once a month for students in junior and senior kindergarten. (Students in kindergarten were exposed to only 5 of the 22 skills: listening to others, joining in, sharing, helping others, and problem solving.) Exposure to new social skills was interspersed with a review of previously presented skills. Emphasis was placed on applying the social skills acquired rather than on "covering" a specific number of skills. In monthly teacher meetings to discuss CSSP implementation, attention was placed on the synchronization of social skills across classes in order to achieve a schoolwide focus on the "skill of the week."

## Social Skill Presentation

Each social skill was introduced to a class in a training procedure lasting 20 minutes. The purpose of this initial presentation was to orient students to the target skill and its subskill components. Designed to be fun, its aim was to help students focus on their social behaviors in and outside of the classroom. Components of the introductory session are outlined below.

**Adult–Adult Modeling of the Social Skills.** Each social skill was first modeled by two adults (the classroom teacher and an on-site facilitator) who role-played a scene depicting the social skill in use. The CSSP manual provided an example of a role-play situation for each social skill, but teachers were free to substitute other examples. For kindergarten classes, the adults used puppets in the role-play scenarios. Once the program became more familiar to the class, the teacher employed the assistance of a student rather than the second adult to model new skills.

Following brief modeling of each social skill, the teacher asked the class to identify the skill's more specific components (e.g., by asking, "What was the first thing Ms. Gomez did when she shared her toy with Ms. Edgar?"). To help the class identify and recall subskill components, the teacher displayed pictorial cue cards for each one. Cue cards identifying components of the skill labeled "ignoring distractions" are depicted in Figure 7.1.

**Adult–Adult Inappropriate Demonstration.** Following the discussion of subskill components, the two adults role-played the social skill a second time, intentionally omitting a skill component, which students were then invited to identify. This step provided students with additional practice in discriminating skill components, a teaching strategy important for concept formation (Becker, 1971) that has been previously used to introduce social skills to preschool children (Mize & Ladd, 1990).

**Child–Adult Role Play.** Presentation of the social skill to this point took approximately 10 minutes. In the next step, a child was invited to practice the target social skill with the teacher in front of the class. The remaining students became "good detectives" for the purpose of providing feedback on skill execution. At the completion of the child–adult role

STOP &
CALM DOWN

DON'T LOOK

DON'T TALK

KEEP WORKING

**FIGURE 7.1.** Pictorial cue cards for the social skill of ignoring distractions.

play, the teacher referred to each of the cue cards, prompting the class to decide whether or not each skill component had been demonstrated (e.g., by asking, "Did Frank stop what he was doing?").

**Child–Child Role Play.** Finally, pairs of students were invited to practice the target social skills, either spontaneously in front of the class or following a practice session, during which the teacher encouraged children to use the cue cards for recalling skill components.

## Daily Program Activities

The main thrust of the *Classwide Social Skills Program* relied on teacher use of naturally occurring opportunities to promote target social skills. After the initial lesson introducing a social skill, no further direct instruction was conducted unless the teacher perceived the need for the class to practice identifying skill components. However, teachers were encouraged to conduct periodic reviews of previously presented social skills on a regular basis.

**Reinforcement System.** Amid the bustle of activities typically occurring within classrooms, teachers often find it difficult to praise students' prosocial behaviors at sufficiently high rates to maintain student behavior change (White, 1975). To assist teachers in praising student use of targeted social skills, as well as to provide additional cues to students for using those skills, a reinforcement system was suggested in the CSSP. Following the presentation of any new social skill, and at the beginning of each subsequent school day, the teacher led a class discussion on typical school situations where students might apply the target social skills (e.g., at recess, during music period, in the gym). Five students were selected at random to wear a stick-on "sunshine badge" (see Figure 7.2) for the day. Upon observing these students practicing the social skills, the teacher gave positive feedback and "a ray of sunshine" (a yellow marker line) on the sunshine badge. To reinforce the prosocial behaviors of children not wearing badges, and also to fade the badge system, the teacher increasingly relied on "invisible rays of sunshine" (an imaginary line from a finger) and praise alone. In addition, students were encouraged to praise one another and grant each other imaginary rays of sunshine for social skills demonstrations.

Teachers were granted the option to change this reinforcement system by substituting another. The only stipulation was that any acceptable reinforcement system must have prompted high levels of teacher praise, cued students to practice social skills, and provided feedback that was sufficiently motivating to students.

**Daily Review.** At the end of each school day, the teacher asked the students wearing sunshine badges to explain how they received their rays of sunshine. This review allowed the teacher to provide additional praise to badge-wearers, and also to recognize other students observed practicing the target social skill.

**Parent Involvement.** Communication with parents was an essential component of the CSSP, both before and during its implementation. At

**FIGURE 7.2.** "Sunshine badge" used in the *Classwide Social Skills Program.*

the beginning of the school year, a CSSP brochure was sent home with each student in participating classes; teachers described the program to parents during fall report card meetings; and a special "open house" for parents was conducted just before implementation began.

Parents were also encouraged to participate in a home note system, enabling them to provide encouragement and praise to their child for the use of targeted social skills. Whenever a new social skill was introduced, parents received a home note describing the skill and inviting them to describe a situation when their child displayed the skill at home. Completed home notes were used by the teacher at the beginning of the school day to discuss students' application of social skills at home and also to remind students of the skills being promoted. Like the badge system, the home note system was faded over time. After a while, parents received home notes approximately once a month. An example of a home note for the social skill of sharing is shown in Figure 7.3.

## Supports to the Classroom Teacher

**In-Class Facilitators.** Workshops may not be feasible as the main vehicle for introducing school-based interventions to teachers. Moreover, teacher learning in workshops tends not to be applied in classrooms

# Classwide Social Skills Program Home Sheet
## Skill #7: Sharing

Dear Parents:

Our class is learning some new ways to be good friends and to work well in the classroom. Each week we will be learning a new skill and the students will try to practice that skill both at school and at home.

This week, the class will be learning about sharing with others. The students know that to share, they must:

| **THINK** | **ASK** | **SHARE FAIRLY** |
| about whether you want to share | if they want to share | |

If you observe your child trying to share at home, please fill out the form below and we shall discuss it in class.

------------------------------------------------------------

☺ **HAPPY NEWS!** ☺

_____ did a good job of sharing when _____
(Name of student)

_____

_____
(Parent's signature)

FIGURE 7.3. An example of a home note for the social skill of sharing.
©1994 by PRO-ED, Inc.

(Joyce & Showers, 1982). A suggested alternative is the use of on-site coaches who support teachers in both the learning and the implementation of a new intervention (Weissberg, Caplan, & Sivo, 1989).

For school boards in the Hamilton, Ontario, vicinity, on-site coaching was performed by clinic staff who worked within the schools approximately 6 hours a week over a 2-month period. In the longitudinal research project, delivery of the CSSP was accomplished through the in-class involvement of trained social skills facilitators, who initially co-taught the program with the classroom teacher, and gradually transferred control of the entire program to that teacher.

Identified by the school boards, these social skills facilitators were predominantly consultants (e.g., special education consultants, psychologists) already experienced in working with teachers. Prior to implementation of the CSSP project, facilitators underwent a 3-day training period that included a written manual, participation in simulation exercises, and demonstration of their mastery of the program content and consultation skills both on a paper-and-pencil quiz and in a role-play task. After the formal training period, facilitators observed a class already implementing the program. Next, they practiced providing consultation to a teacher in a class not participating in the CSSP project, and received feedback on their skill implementation. During all phases of the training period, facilitators completed a "self-monitoring log," which guided them through the progressive implementation steps and monitored the integrity of their involvement. (A copy of a self-monitoring form used by social skills facilitators is shown in Table 7.4.)

During implementation, facilitators were present in each primary class an average of 2 hours per week for the first month, and gradually less often during the remainder of the project. Each facilitator provided consultation for approximately three to five classrooms; most often, a number of facilitators worked within each school, with one of them providing overall site-specific coordination.

**Monthly Teacher Meetings.** Sharing reactions about classroom techniques has been described as an important learning experience for teachers (Weissberg et al., 1989). During implementation of the CSSP, monthly meetings of primary-division teachers and facilitators were held both to discuss experiences arising from the project and to provide additional information to teachers about the promotion of social competence in students. Issues raised include coordination of the program across classrooms and suggestions for alternative implementation strategies.

**TABLE 7.4.** Self-Monitoring Sheet Completed by Facilitators of the *Classwide Social Skills Program*

*Before Presentation of a Social Skill*

| | | | |
|---|---|---|---|
| 1. | Did you inform the teacher about what will be covered in the presentation? | yes | no |
| 2. | Did you clarify roles and responsibilities? | yes | no |
| 3. | Did you discuss how to accommodate individual children? | yes | no |
| 4. | Did you have all the material you needed ready? | yes | no |

*During Presentation*

| | | | |
|---|---|---|---|
| 5. | Did you read at least two home notes? | yes | no |
| 6. | Did you review the previous day's lesson (skill and skill components) and solicit at least one example of a student's application of the skill at home or school? | yes | no |
| 7. | Did you introduce a new social skill using adult–adult role-playing? | yes | no |
| 8. | Did you solicit the skills components using cue cards? | yes | no |
| 9. | Did you have children practice identifying the skill components by an adult–adult inappropriate presentation of skill? | yes | no |
| 10. | Did you have one or two child–adult role plays to practice the skill? | yes | no |
| 11. | Did you have one or two child–child role plays to practice the skill? | yes | no |
| 12. | Did you select about five children to wear badges? | yes | no |

*After Presentation*

| | | | |
|---|---|---|---|
| 13. | Did you solicit the teacher's feelings and comfort level? | yes | no |
| 14. | Did you add your own evaluation and feedback? | yes | no |
| 15. | Did you discuss how to promote skill at other times of the day? | yes | no |
| 16. | Did you review the teacher's lesson plan for the rest of the week? | yes | no |

*Throughout the School Day*

| | | | |
|---|---|---|---|
| 17. | Did you prompt individual children to practice the desired social skills? | yes | no |
| 18. | Did you provide instruction to practice the skill during opportunities that arise in the day (e.g., physical education, recess)? | yes | no |
| 19. | Did you award rays of sunshine throughout the day, and explain to children why they earned the rays? | yes | no |
| 20. | When you praised, did you describe the behavior that was praise-worthy? | yes | no |
| 21. | For mild behavior problems, did you use planned ignoring? | yes | no |
| 22. | For mild behavior problems, did you praise another child who was behaving appropriately (suggestive praise)? | yes | no |
| 23. | Between two and four times a day, did you choose a child to self-evaluate his or her demonstration of the social skill and to add to the activity poster? | yes | no |

*End of the Day*

| | | | |
|---|---|---|---|
| 24. | Did you distribute home notes to students? | yes | no |

**Teacher Manuals.** Along with a brief written description about the program and its expectations, teachers received a manual containing skill-by-skill implementation procedures for the CSSP. A separate manual was available for first- to third-grade students (approximately 250 pages) and for kindergarten students (approximately 75 pages). Both contained cue cards depicting each social skill as well as sample scripts that could be used during introductory presentations.

## Other Components of the Classwide Social Skills Program

**Self-Management.** An additional self-management component was introduced for students in second to third grades in September of the second year of the social skills program. Its purpose was to encourage student self-awareness in implementing acquired skills. One important self-management strategy involved "self-talk" instructional statements (Meichenbaum, 1977) that mediate student social skills implementation. Self-talk techniques were first modeled by teachers and then practiced by students in instructional sessions similar to those already described for introducing new social skills.

A second self-management skill involved student goal setting and reflection about the use of target social skills. In workbooks, students described plans for their use of target social skills in naturally occurring situations. During daily reviews, students recalled in their workbooks the number of times they had practiced the target social skills, and then evaluated their own degree of success. Figure 7.4 provides a sample page from the student workbook for the skill of helping others.

**Class Behavior Plan.** Bierman (1986) suggested that social skills instruction is not sufficient in itself to reduce the occurrence of negative behaviors in classrooms, and recommended the use of prohibitions and other consequences for negative behaviors. For this reason, classroom teachers were provided with additional information about effective classroom behavior management strategies. In an eight-page handout, teachers read about important components of effective classroom behavior planning, and were asked to review their own plan. They were encouraged to consider classroom structures that facilitate positive social interaction (e.g., heterogeneous student groupings, cooperative learning formats, planned seating arrangements); antecedent conditions (e.g., preparatory statements, rules, visual cues and instructions); feedback and reinforcement (e.g., effective use of praise, use of activities as rein-

Classwide Social Skills Program

How I Used the Social Skill
(Draw or Write Examples)

Social Skill #9
Helping Others

THINK about ASK if help HELP if
whether help is needed needed
is needed

MY GOALS

I can use this social skill:

In the classroom: _____

_____

On the playground: _____

_____

Other places at school: _____

_____

At home: _____

_____

Each day, I will try to use this social skill
_____ times.

MONDAY
Number of times

How I did ☹ 😐 ☺

TUESDAY
Number of times

How I did ☹ 😐 ☺

WEDNESDAY
Number of times

How I did ☹ 😐 ☺

THURSDAY
Number of times

How I did ☹ 😐 ☺

FRIDAY
Number of times

How I did ☹ 😐 ☺

FIGURE 7.4. An example of a page from the student workbook.

forcers); and consequences for behavior (e.g., planned ignoring, turnouts, sitouts). During a meeting of teachers and facilitators, teachers read the brief document and subsequently reviewed aspects of their classroom plans. A one-page planning sheet (shown in Figure 7.5) was provided to teachers for this purpose. At the next meeting, teachers reported on planned classroom changes and received additional consultation from facilitators.

## Teacher Planning Sheet for Class Discipline Plan

| COMPONENTS | ASPECTS TO: | |
| --- | --- | --- |
| | KEEP (enter ✓) | MODIFY (describe) |
| 1. Promotion | | |
| 1.1 Mixed students groups | | |
| 1.2 Cooperative tasks assigned | | |
| 1.3 Use of "learning centers" | | |
| 1.4 Conducive seating arrangements | | |
| 2. Structuring Antecedent | | |
| 2.1 Clear rules | | |
| 2.2 Visual cues | | |
| 2.3 Removal of events that elicit inappropriate behavior | | |
| 3. Feedback/Reinforcement | | |
| 3.1 Way of reminding teachers to recognize students' social skills | | |
| 3.2 Feedback system | | |
| 3.3 Review of feedback received | | |
| 3.4 Descriptive praise (frequent, immediate) | | |
| 3.5 Suggestive praise | | |
| 3.6 Cues for feedback system will be faded | | |
| 4. Handling Discipline | | |
| 4.1 Planned ignoring | | |
| 4.2 Reprimands (brief, clear, firm) | | |
| 4.3 Clear instructions (e.g. "options") | | |
| 4.4 Consequences (turn-out, sit-out, privilege removal) | | |
| 5. Other | | |

FIGURE 7.5. Teacher planning sheet for class discipline plan.

**School Plan to Promote Social Competence.** Although the bulk of the *Classwide Social Skills Program* was implemented in the primary division, it was important to formulate a schoolwide focus for dealing with problems in playgrounds, lunchrooms, and hallways. Schools typically have developed written policies and codes of conduct, but rarely have considered ways of either translating existing policies into practice or ensuring consistency of procedures dealing with behaviors. To encourage staff consensus about school disciplinary issues, the principal was asked to arrange a half-day workshop, during which staff developed a framework for a schoolwide plan to deal with behavior problems and promote social competence alternatives. In the workshop, staff were led through a number of exercises in which they:

1. Identified the positive qualities of the school

2. Identified disciplinary problems of concern

3. Developed consensus on how to deal with these problem areas

4. Formulated decisions for preventing these problems

A staff committee was then charged with developing a school plan from the framework derived from the session. The plan was further revised by staff before being drafted in final form.

# Conclusion

## IMPLICATIONS FOR BEST PRACTICE

■ The *Classwide Social Skills Program* is a multiple-component intervention, universally delivered to all students in the primary grades. Components include (a) modeling, practice, and feedback of social skills; (b) prompts to students to use acquired social skills during naturally occurring opportunities during the school day; (c) supports to classroom teachers to implement the intervention; (d) assistance in teacher review of the class discipline plan; and (e) assistance with all school staff in the development of a schoolwide plan to promote social competence and to deal with behavior problems.

■ Initial implementation and continued involvement of staff in the intervention require the active support of the school principal and the stewardship at the school and school system levels, along with supporting policies and procedures adopted by the school board.

At the point of this writing, the research data are not yet available to determine the impact of the *Classwide Social Skills Program*. As a general indicator, teachers implementing the program each year were asked to complete a satisfaction questionnaire. Results of feedback from over 100 teachers are summarized in Figure 7.6. As indicated by the figure, the majority of teachers considered the program to be practical and effective; however, less endorsement was provided for either the primary teacher meetings or the schoolwide meetings. Moreover, although teachers perceived the program as helpful for most students in their classes, they found it less beneficial for the more behaviorally challenged students. Despite these provisos, 93% of teachers indicated that they would choose to continue with the program.

A number of implementation issues have arisen in conducting the longitudinal project and implementing CSSP. One recurring factor is the commitment of educators to an intervention targeting student social competence, given the competition for teacher time and priorities. The extent

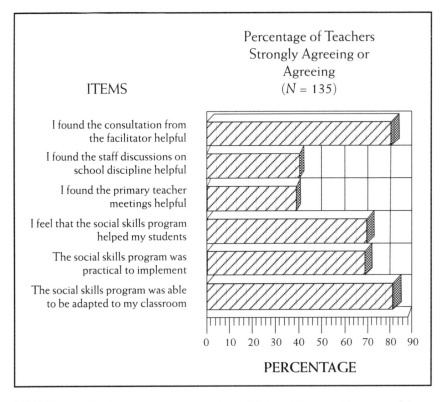

FIGURE 7.6. Teacher agreement to questions of their satisfaction with aspects of the *Classwide Social Skills Program*.

to which educators view a social skills focus as a legitimate activity of educators is an issue for debate. Perceptions about the relative priority of promoting student social competence are of paramount importance at an administrative level. Schools in which principals are committed to such a focus seem to be able to implement this intervention with less difficulty than schools in which principals are not as actively involved or committed. At a local level, CSSP is being implemented only in schools where principals initiate a request for the program and not in schools selected by central administration only.

A second issue involves longer term implementation and continuation of the intervention. Sustained program maintenance is dependent on ways of imbedding the project into the organizational structure of school systems. Given the mobility of school staff, program stewardship within schools needs to be addressed. It may be vital to nominate a key individual in the school system to assume responsibility for ensuring the continued support necessary for schools to implement a social skills program. Policies and procedures identifying expectations around the use of a social skills intervention may also need to be clarified and codified. Without the scaffolding of such systemic infrastructures, any interventions falling outside the traditional scope of education are destined to create transitory impact at best. Structures that enable schools to implement social skills intervention over a number of years, with sustained commitment to essential resources and supports, are necessary components of successful long-term implementation.

Part of the answer may lie in building supports at the school level. A school management team may need to develop collaborative plans for dealing with maladjustment and promoting social competence. At the school level, it seems important to incorporate structures that provide support to teachers. In the *Classwide Social Skills Program*, for instance, facilitators are located within schools, become familiar with the school culture, and provide assistance to both individual teachers and the school as a whole.

Neither the desirability of promoting social competence in students nor the soundness of program strategies used for these outcomes may spark issues of intense debate. The greatest challenge in delivering these strategies may lie in operationalizing the necessary support structures within school organizations to introduce and sustain a sufficiently powerful intervention.

# chapter 8

# Using Peers and Parents to Promote Social Competence

## ISSUES IN PRACTICE

- How can peers and parents contribute to school-based, social competence–building interventions?

- What are the advantages of using peer mediation of conflicts at school?

- How have peer mediation, conflict resolution programs been implemented in schools?

- In what ways can parents be involved in enhancing their child's social competence?

- What are the barriers to parent involvement with school programs?

- How should a school–home note system be designed?

- How has training in child management procedures been delivered to parents?

An understanding of the development, prevention, and treatment of student maladjustment needs to draw upon an appreciation of the impact of the broader contexts in which students' behaviors occur. For example, family environment and parent–child relationships may play central but not exclusive (Emery, Fincham, & Cummings, 1992) roles in the development of childhood maladjustment (Fauber & Long 1991; Reid & Patterson, 1991). Over the years, there have been substantial changes in the composition and functioning of families, affecting children's adjustment. For example, it is now estimated that only about 40% of U.S. children will reside with both biological parents throughout their entire childhood (Office of Technological Assessment, 1986). Even in two-parent families, the increased need for households to generate two incomes diminishes the time available for careful rearing and supervision of children (Johnson & Abramovitch, 1988).

Peers form a second important context for the development of children's social behaviors. Peer rejection in childhood (Dodge, 1983) and subsequent "bonding" with deviant peers during early adolescence (Hawkins & Weis, 1985) contribute to the consolidation of formative anti-social behaviors (Kazdin, 1993a; Patterson, Capaldi, & Bank, 1991).

School-based programs designed to strengthen students' social competence may be enhanced by the involvement of parents, peers, or both. Enlisting multiple change agents in multiple settings as part of a social-building program may provide more pervasive and durable impact than a single-component intervention. In a multidimensional program, each component may potentially interact with others to exceed the impact of any one component in isolation (Kazdin, Siegel, & Bass, 1992).

This chapter identifies and describes examples of peer-mediated and parent-mediated initiatives to promote social competence in conjunction with school-based social skills programs. In particular, peer mediation of school conflicts and parent involvement in school-based programs are discussed.

## Peer-Mediated Conflict Resolution

In recent years, a number of programs have been developed to teach students to mediate conflicts with fellow students (Krenz, 1991). These peer-mediated conflict resolutions have been implemented in elementary, middle, and secondary school settings (Davis & Porter, 1985; Deutsch, 1993). Conceptually based on advocacy for peaceful solutions to violence, peer-mediation programs draw heavily from dispute training techniques (Roderick, 1988). According to Lane and McWhirter (1992), one of the earliest examples of peer-mediation programs in schools was the *San Francisco Community Board Program*, which served as a prototype for many subsequent programs.

Despite the proliferation of peer-mediated conflict resolution programs, there exist few (if any) empirical or controlled evaluations of the impact of such interventions (Deutsch, 1993). There are, however, positive anecdotal reports. McCormick (1988), for example, reported a 47% reduction in aggression at one school following the introduction of a peer-mediation program, and Schrumpf, Crawford, and Usadel (1991) claimed that 95% of peer disputes at one middle school were successfully resolved using a similar intervention. However, without empirically based substantiation of these endorsements, it is difficult to gauge the actual benefits of a peer-mediation approach to conflict resolution.

A few potential advantages to a peer-mediation program have been suggested. First, peer leaders may provide credible models of prosocial behaviors (Jason & Rhodes, 1989). Second, peers may be more likely than teachers to witness and intervene in playground disputes. Based on their observation of bullying in school playgrounds, Pepler and Craig (1993) reported that peers interceded three times as often as teachers to halt peer-bullying episodes.

Although the efficacy of peer-mediated conflict resolution is to date empirically untested, there is reason to believe that student mediators may themselves profit from their involvement in such programs. A "helper effect" may be obtained when students assist peers (Fowler, Dougherty, Kirby, & Kohler, 1986). Through their experiences, peer mediators, some of whom may display adjustment problems of their own (Krenz, 1991), may be made more aware of their own interpersonal actions and adopt positive resolution strategies (Lane & McWhirter, 1992; Maxwell, 1989; Roderick, 1988). All in all, peer-mediated conflict resolution holds promise when considered as one element within the arsenal of strategies available to schools to promote social competence in students.

A number of delivery issues demand attention in the introduction of a peer-mediated conflict resolution program. How does one initially present the concept to school administration and staff? By what criteria and means should student mediators be selected and trained? How should peer mediators be deployed in schools? What ongoing supports does the program need? Table 8.1 summarizes the ways in which selected programs have addressed these planning and implementation issues. Generally, before initiating a peer-mediation program, the idea has been presented to staff and received staff commitment. In some cases, a committee composed of staff and a parent is formed to guide program implementation. Recruitment of student mediators is based on a number of factors, but is primarily determined by the student's high acceptance by peers. Peer mediators are initially trained in mediation techniques; during program implementation, regular weekly meetings are held to provide additional support and training.

Peer mediation has been deployed in schools in a variety of ways, but most often is used to help students generate solutions for interpersonal problems they face at school. Resolution is not attempted at the time of the conflict, nor do mediators intercede in fights or tell other students what to do. Typically, the mediator makes an appointment to meet with the students in conflict, often in a designated "mediation room" at the school. At this meeting, the mediator leads the students through a predetermined series of conflict resolution steps, such as those included in Table 8.1.

Peer mediation offers promise in enhancing school climate for the promotion of alternatives to violence. Unfortunately, little or no controlled

TABLE 8.1. Summary of Components of Selected Peer-Mediated, Conflict Resolution Programs

| | SCHRUMPF, CRAWFORD & USADEL (1991) | LANE & McWHIRTER (1992) | KRENZ (1991) | CAHOON (1988) | DAVIS & PORTER (1985) |
|---|---|---|---|---|---|
| How the intervention was introduced | An advisory committee was formed to develop the proposal | An orientation was provided to staff, followed by staff completion of an interest questionnaire; a total of 8 hours of teacher training in the use of mediation techniques was provided | A committee of two staff, a parent, the school secretary, and the project coordinator planned the implementation | Not specified | Introduced by an organization outside of school |
| Mediator recruitment and selection | Based on communication and thinking skills; representative of a cross-section of students | Nominated by students and then put to a vote | Selected from upper two grades in school; selected by students and representatives of minority groups | Teachers selected two students from each class, every 2 weeks | 4th- and 5th-grade students selected by peers, based on leadership ability and representation of ethnic identity of the school |
| Mediator training | 10, 90-minute sessions | 5 half-day sessions | Two half-day sessions, 2 weeks apart | Orientation by principal during one recess period | 15 hours |
| Supports to mediator | Informal meetings with a coordinator | Twice weekly meetings with coordinator | Not specified | Not specified | Teachers trained by outside experts |
| How deployed | Students who wish to resolve conflicts come to a "mediation" center | Pairs of mediators deployed in playground | Paired to resolve conflict at recess with follow-up at a separate location in school | Deployed in playground and lunchroom to mediate conflicts for students in their class | Pairs of mediators used during lunch and recess periods |
| Mediation procedure | 6 steps, from how to open and gather information to how to write the agreement and close | 4-step procedure of introduction, listening, wants, and solutions | Not specified | Help students to state what they want from the other, get agreement, ask students to apologize, check on resolution, take it to adult if needed | 14-step resolution process to help others solve problems for themselves |

program evaluation is available to substantiate its potential benefits. If peer mediation works, how does it operate? Does it positively alter the behaviors of the mediators themselves? If this were found to be the case, it would suggest that a strategy of rotating students in the mediation role may increase the impact of the approach. In one Las Vegas school, for example, new peer mediators were selected from each class every second week (Cahoon, 1988).

Peer mediation may not benefit all students equally. Because it is used only with students who identify that they are in conflict and wish to find a resolution, it may not be accessed by students with strongly entrenched antisocial behaviors. Bullies, in particular, may not voluntarily seek resolution for their conflicts. Moreover, students entering into conflict resolution must have the requisite skills to negotiate a resolution and follow through on their plan. Students who are either impulsive or weak in transferring verbal plans into action may have difficulty following the conflict resolution steps, and may not apply these steps in other conflict situations following the mediation session. For these reasons, peer mediation would probably work best if it was included as one element of a more global school strategy to curtail violence and promote social competence. All students may need to learn how to resolve conflicts, as well as how to prevent conflicts from arising in the first place. In addition, the mediation steps taught to students would also need to be employed by teachers and school administration in their handling of discipline problems (Schmidt, Friedman, & Marvel, 1992).

## Parent Involvement in School-Based Programs

As socializing agents, parents play an important role in the social development of their children and may lend added effectiveness to school-based programs that promote social competence in children. The potential linkage between home and school should not be taken to suggest that school-based programs cannot work on their own. Moreover, children who display maladjustment at school do not necessarily experience adjustment problems at home, and vice versa (Bernal, Delfini, North, & Kreutzer, 1976; Offord et al., 1987). Furthermore, even when parents are successfully trained to reduce the disruptive behavior of their child at home, there is no automatic transfer of effects to the school, unless teachers implement similar behavior change strategies in their classrooms (Breiner & Forehand, 1981). With some exceptions (e.g., Bodiford McNeil, Eyberg, Hembree Eisenstadt, Newcomb, & Funderburk, 1991; Peed, Roberts, & Forehand, 1977), efforts to change children's behaviors are restricted to the specific setting (i.e., school, home, or clinic) in which the intervention is delivered (Chandler, Lubeck, & Fowler, 1992).

Nevertheless, teachers tend to assume that parent involvement has the potential to either enhance or diminish the impact of school-based programs. This view has extended to school administrators as well, who appear to perceive lack of parental involvement as a major factor contributing to increases in school violence (Boothe, Bradley, Flick, Keough, & Kirk, 1993). Unfortunately, the level of parents' participation in school planning and programming for their children tends to be low (Winton, 1986). For example, one study found that only about 43% of parents of children at risk attended one or more sessions of a child management course offered at the school (Hawkins, Von Cleve, & Catalano, 1991). Parents who do become involved at school tend to either discontinue their involvement (Winton, 1986) or assume passive roles (Turnbull & Winton, 1984).

## Barriers to Parent Involvement

A number of obstacles undermine parental participation in school-based behavior programs. One is the fact that intercommunication between home and school is often unclear (Turnbull & Turnbull, 1986). Similarly, barriers caused by cultural and first-language differences may prevent parents from developing a clear understanding of how schools function and recognizing ways in which they can become meaningfully involved in their child's school program.

Another barrier to home-school relations is the intimidation and blame some parents feel when dealing with schools about their child's problems (Turnbull & Winton, 1984). Results of a national survey suggest that teachers tend to attribute student behaviors and learning problems to factors external to their control, such as poor home environment (National Education Association, 1979). Parents as well as their children may be perceived as "sick" and in need of treatment (Seligman & Benjamin Darling, 1989). Rather than treated as equal partners in planning, parents may become the recipients of pedantic instructions for managing their child at home, alienating them further from school personnel.

Parent availability to attend school meetings constitutes another obstacle to home–school partnerships. Career responsibilities may make it impossible for parents to attend meetings held during school hours; responsibilities of child care may make it difficult to attend meetings held at night (Turnbull & Turnbull, 1986). Additional meetings also make further demands on teacher time (Witt, Miller, McIntyre, & Smith, 1984).

Considered together, these barriers suggest that parent involvement in school-based programs should be approached with both care and sensitivity. Communication to the home must be composed in clear and simple language, free of jargon and technical terms. It may be desirable to field test written information intended for parents before full-scale distribution.

A cooperative, co-equal relationship between home and school will flourish only in an atmosphere of mutual respect and support. Teachers may need to ask for advice as much as they offer it. Common home and school goals for a child may need to be negotiated, rather than declared. Finally, parent involvement should be seen as desirable (and therefore invited) rather than essential (and therefore insisted upon) in helping schools proceed with their efforts to promote social competence in students.

## Levels of Parent Involvement

As illustrated in Figure 8.1, parent involvement in school-based social programs can differ in terms of both quantity and quality. The minimum level of involvement is achieved when parents merely receive communications about activities occurring at school. Typical formats are newsletters, or even more technologically sophisticated communications. Bauch (1989), for example, described a school-to-home communication system that involved a computer-driven telephone on which teachers transmitted messages about homework assignments. Such one-way communication methods help to keep parents informed about programs at the school, but typically fail to solicit parent support activities. This level of parental involvement may be appropriate when the bulk of a student's program is occurring at school, with no specific action expected of parents. In such cases, extracurricular parental involvement would be both self-determined and incidental. Guidelines for setting up a school newsletter to inform parents how to promote social problem solving in their child have been described by Hett and Krikorian (1993).

## School–Home Notes

An increased level of parental involvement is achieved by the use of school–home notes inviting parents to reinforce aspects of a school-based behavior program at home. School–home notes have been used to address such student social behaviors as staying on task (Coleman, 1973), inappropriate talking out in class (Dougherty & Dougherty, 1977), and completion of assignments (Blechman, Taylor, & Schrader, 1981). The teacher reports

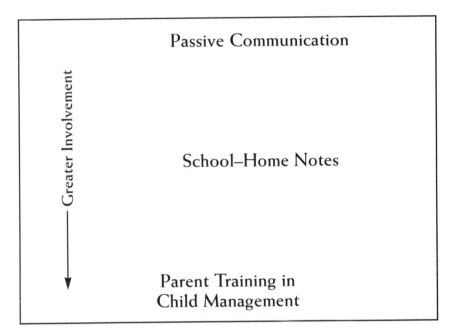

FIGURE 8.1. Levels of parent involvement in school-based programs to promote social competence.

specific student behavior on a note sent home to parents (Kelley, 1990). Parents are asked to provide feedback, praise, and more tangible forms of reward (e.g., privileges) based on the information contained in the school–home note. Kelley (1990) suggested a number of components essential to an effective school–home note program, reproduced in Table 8.2.

Evaluation of school–home notes has generally been favorable. Home-based rewards have been found to be more effective than school rewards in changing student classroom behaviors (Budd, Leibowitz, Riner, Mindell, & Goldfarb, 1981; Kelley, 1990; Schumaker, Hovell, & Sherman, 1977).

Blechman et al. (1981) compared a school–home note system with family problem solving as interventions for aiding students' math work completion in 17 elementary school classrooms. Classrooms were randomly assigned to one of the two interventions. Parents in the school–home note condition were expected to reward their child on days when they received a "good news" note. Good news notes were sent home whenever the child achieved 80% or better in math work completion. Parents in the family problem-solving condition received the same school–home note system, but in addition attended a 1-hour session on contracting desirable math performance with their child. Teachers in the family problem-solving classes

## TABLE 8.2. School–Home Note Program Checklist

*Target Behaviors*

1. _____ Target behaviors are defined in a specific manner.

2. _____ Target behaviors occur frequently and are potentially sensitive to change.

3. _____ The behaviors are judged as important by the teacher, parents, and student.

4. _____ Target behavior definitions are understood by the parents and student.

5. _____ Target behaviors are easy for the teacher to monitor.

6. _____ Target behaviors are worded positively.

7. _____ Target behaviors are evaluated by the teacher in all relevant situations.

*Evaluation Criteria and Performance Goals*

1. _____ The evaluation anchors (e.g., happy vs. sad face) are well defined.

2. _____ The parent, teacher, and student understand what behaviors warrant positive versus negative evaluations.

3. _____ The child clearly understands what must be done to earn rewards.

4. _____ The parent, teacher, and student agree that the required level of performance is fair and within the student's current ability to achieve.

5. _____ Improvements in the student's performance result in improved global evaluations by parents and teacher.

*The Note*

1. _____ The actual school–home note is uncluttered, organized, and easy to complete.

2. _____ The note is pleasing to the child and developmentally appropriate with regard to wording and performance criteria.

3. _____ Data derived from the note are easy to summarize.

*Administration*

1. _____ Parent, teacher, and student responsibilities are clear to all involved (e.g., it is understood who provides the blank note daily).

2. _____ Each teacher completes the note daily and provides meaningful comments to the student and parent.

3. _____ The note is minimally intrusive for the student and teacher.

4. _____ The child is not ridiculed or excessively questioned by other students about the note.

5. _____ Each teacher completes the note in a friendly, facilitative manner and avoids making hostile, embarrassing, or excessively critical statements to the child.

6. _____ Parents provide feedback to the teacher about home consequences and ask questions when they arise.

7. _____ Both the parents and teacher use the note as a communication tool rather than a weapon, and take time to acknowledge improvement and each other's problem-solving efforts.

8. _____ The note is used for at least a few weeks after behavior is quite acceptable and then faded systematically (or reintroduced if performance diminishes).

*(continues)*

TABLE 8.2. (Continued)

*Feedback and Consequences*

1. _____ The target behavior goals and consequences for goal achievement are clear and written in a contract.

2. _____ The child earns both daily and weekly rewards.

3. _____ The child participates in generating the rewards for goal achievement.

4. _____ Rewards are important and *truly* rewarding to the child.

5. _____ Teacher provides feedback about performance and goal achievement at regular intervals throughout the day.

6. _____ Parents review the teacher's comments daily and promote improved performance through problem solving with the child.

7. _____ Parents and teacher praise the child for goal achievement.

From *School–Home Notes: Promoting Children's Classroom Success* (pp. 105–106) by M. L. Kelley, 1990, New York: Guilford. Copyright 1990 by The Guilford Press. Reprinted by permission.

telephoned parents each week to monitor contract compliance. While students in both groups improved in their math performance, those in the family problem-solving condition not only produced higher rates of accuracy in their math work, but also maintained these rates when home rewards were withdrawn. It is unclear, however, how much of the effectiveness of family problem solving was due to such features as increased parent–teacher contact rather than to the family contracting procedures per se.

Modifications to a school–home note system would probably be needed to adapt its use for young students (e.g., K–Grade 2). A young student may be able to focus on only one or two simple goals. Moreover, feedback on the student's performance against this goal would need to be simple to understand (e.g., use of absolute rather than percentage scores; visual representation of the results). Another modification may be to review the goal with a young student before each session.

A school–home note system may be particularly useful when developing behavior change programs for individual students where access to more powerful home rewards is seen as important. There seem to be at least a couple of situations where the use of school–home notes may be counterindicated. When the target behavior is not already within the child's skill repertoire (e.g., knowledge of math operations), one would need to provide skill-building interventions prior to establishing a home-based reward system. School–home notes may also be inappropriate in home settings where parents are apt to punish their child for not achieving behavioral goals, despite instructions that the program is based on rewarding positive behaviors. Because of this possibility, one may need to meet with and train parents before introducing a school–home note system.

## Parent Training in Child Management

A more involved level of parent participation entails training parents in specific skills to be applied with their children at home. Reviews of interventions for children's antisocial behaviors have concluded that parent training is among the most effective strategies to help children adjust (Dumas, 1989b; Kazdin, 1987). Parent training has been delivered in a variety of ways, including:

- Clinic sessions for individual families (e.g., McMahon & Forehand, 1984)

- Clinic sessions for groups of families (e.g., Hall, 1984)

- Direct coaching of parents at home (e.g., Dangle & Polster, 1984)

- Self-instructional material (e.g., Webster-Stratton, 1989)

Regardless of the method of delivery, most parent training programs share similar basic elements and concepts, as summarized in Table 8.3.

Early parent training approaches were based on the premise that poor child rearing was caused by the lack of parent knowledge how to deal effectively with their child's misbehavior (Blechman, 1984; Wahler & Dumas, 1989). As a result, early parent training programs focused almost exclusively on equipping parents with new behavior management skills.

---

TABLE 8.3.  Basic Elements of Social Learning Approaches to
Parent Training

---

Pinpointing and accurate labeling of child behavior
Emphasis on prosocial goals
Daily tracking of specific child behavior
Tangible and social reinforcement
Use of alternatives to physical punishment
Clear communication
Anticipating and solving new problems

---

Based on "Enhancement of Social Learning Family Interventions for Childhood Conduct Disorder" by G. E. Miller and R. J. Prinz, 1990, *Psychological Bulletin, 108*(2), pp. 291–307.

For the most part, parent training has produced generally favorable outcomes (e.g., Patterson, Chamberlain, & Reid, 1982; Peed et al., 1977; Zangwill, 1984) and has often resulted in generalization of effects from home to school (e.g., Bodiford McNeil et al., 1991; Breiner & Forehand, 1981), from clinic to home (e.g., Peed et al., 1977), and over time (e.g., Cunningham, Bremner, & Secord-Gilbert, 1993; Pisterman et al., 1989).

## Dissemination of Parent Training

One remaining challenge of parent training efforts is how to disseminate interventions to the high number of families who have children with maladjustment, the vast majority of whom are not referred to a clinic (Kazdin, Mazurick, & Bass, 1993). Low-cost, high-efficiency strategies for disseminating advice to parents need to be considered (Forgatch & Toobert, 1979; Risley, Clark, & Cataldo, 1976). For example, Webster-Stratton, Hollinsworth, and Kolpacoff (1989) developed a series of parenting skills videotapes to be used by parents on their own. In one study, parents from a diversity of social backgrounds were randomly assigned to conditions of videotape modeling alone, discussion group alone, or a combination of both (Webster-Stratton et al., 1989). Results indicated that all groups both improved significantly more than a no-treatment control group and maintained their improvements for a 1-year period (Webster-Stratton et al., 1989).

Another efficient model of parent training consists of large-group programs offered in neighborhood schools and childcare centers. Cunningham et al. (1993) described their model of large-group, school-based training for parents of children with attention-deficit/hyperactivity disorder. A series of eight weekly parenting sessions was offered in local schools, in conjunction with social skills training for children. This arrangement proved beneficial for a number of reasons. Parents were provided with the opportunity to observe adult models with their children, children were exposed to a social skills curriculum, and the problem of child care during parent training sessions was eliminated. Following the program, monthly parent booster sessions were held to help maintain effects over time.

## Serving Multiply-Stressed Families

A major challenge to parent training is the fact that less favorable outcomes have been associated with families experiencing multiple sources of stress (e.g., low income, marital discord, personal adjustment), many of whom are coerced into treatment by public agencies (Miller & Prinz,

1990). Patterson (1976) reported that, of the parents entering the *Oregon Social Learning Center* parent training program, approximately one third dropped out, one third completed the program but showed negligible effects, and the remaining one third demonstrated substantial improvements in their parenting skills (Patterson, 1976). Several other studies have reported similar estimates of parent response to parent training programs (e.g., Kazdin et al., 1992; Pekarik & Stephenson, 1988).

Families that drop out of parent training tend to be characterized by financial problems, social isolation, depression, and single-parent status (Dadds & McHugh, 1992; Kazdin et al., 1993; McMahon, Forehand, Griest, & Wells, 1981; Miller & Prinz, 1990). A similar profile emerges from examination of families that finish parent training programs but do not change their style of interacting at home. Dumas (1984) found that economic disadvantage and socialized isolation accounted for 43% of the variance of parent training outcomes. Dumas concluded, "Thus, although the child is typically identified as a source of 'problems' at the time of referral, his/her chances of benefiting from treatment appears to depend upon the extent to which his/her family has additional 'problems' than upon the child's background characteristics" (p. 358). Similar characteristics of poor responders to parent training have been described by others (Clark & Baker, 1983; Griest & Forehand, 1982).

More detailed examination of the day-to-day experiences of insular and economically disadvantaged parents suggests a direct link between the quality of interaction with their children and social contacts outside of the home (Wahler, 1980). On days when these parents have few exchanges with individuals outside the family, they tend to resort to high levels of aversive behaviors with their children.

Wahler and Dumas (1989) suggested that multi-stress families have difficulties attending to their child's cues in the midst of trying to handle other stressors. As a result, they tend to be unresponsive and inconsistent in their parenting style. These results suggest that the parenting difficulties of insular families may have more to do with factors that influence their parenting *performance* than their lack of parenting *knowledge*.

A model to understand how families respond to stress was proposed by Hill (1958) and later refined by McCubbin and Patterson (1983). Hill (1958) suggested that a family's capacity to adapt to crisis depends not only on resources available to the family, but also on their perception of the crisis. Bailey and Simeonsson (1988b) proposed three categories of support available to families: personal resources (values and beliefs that serve as a foundation for social conduct), internal resources (instrumental and socioemotional supports from family members), and external resources (support from individuals outside of the family). The availability of these social supports appears pivotal to parental well-being, and indirectly affects interactions with their children (Dunst, Trivette, & Deal, 1988). Strong social networks have been associated with both resilience to stress (Pryor-Brown & Cowen, 1989) and utilization of mental health services (Mitchell, 1989).

The above considerations suggest that parent training programs need to address issues of social support. Dunst et al. (1988) proposed a social system perspective for working with families of developmentally at-risk preschoolers. They indicated that family interventions should be broadly conceptualized to include the identification and utilization of family social networks to help deal with family needs and goals. Similarly, Wahler and Dumas (1989) suggested that socially isolated parents need help in differentiating between the stress caused by their general life situation (e.g., conflict with social services) and their frustration in rearing their child. In a like-minded approach, Blechman (1987) taught parents to apply communication and problem-solving skills to social factors that interfere with successful parenting.

**Multisystems Approach.** The parent training programs proposed by Wahler and Dumas (1989) and Blechman (1987) both targeted broader ecological factors that hamper parenting skills. Miller and Prinz (1990) described a multisystem approach that extends the consideration of these ecological factors further by including the environments maintaining children's antisocial behaviors (school, home, and community settings). An example of a multisystem approach is the coordination of social skills programs in schools with parent training programs. Greater gains, and generalizations of those gains, may be realized by concurrently focusing on children's social skills and parents' child management skills. Because child and parent behaviors continuously affect one another (Tronick, Ricks, & Cohn, 1982), changes in one are likely to elicit changes in the other.

Social skills training in schools has been combined with parent training in an attempt to prevent the development of antisocial behaviors in young students (Hawkins et al., 1991). First-grade classes in eight Seattle schools were randomly assigned to receive a combined intervention or no intervention. The combined intervention consisted of (a) *The Interpersonal Cognitive Problem-Solving Curriculum* (Spivack & Shure, 1982), (b) teacher training in proactive classroom management procedures, (c) teacher training in interactive teaching methods, and (d) a 7-week parent training course. Results indicated that although superior gains in teacher-rated student adjustment were found for White students, no significant effects were observed for African American students.

Tremblay, Vitaro, et al. (1992) also combined social skills training and parent training in a 6-year longitudinal study for high-risk boys. First-grade disruptive students were randomly assigned to treatment or control groups. Children in the treatment group received a combined intervention over a 2-week period. One component was a small-group social skills program held at school. A second intervention was individual parent training using the *Oregon Social Learning Center Model* (Patterson et al., 1982). Students receiving the intervention showed greater reductions in fighting, as well as greater teacher and peer ratings of adjustment over the 6-year period than students who did not receive the intervention. However, no significant differences in mothers' perceptions of their sons' adjustment were found.

Although these results are encouraging, the study was unable to address whether the combination of parent training and social skills instruction was superior to either intervention alone. Such a study was completed by Kazdin et al. (1992) with children aged 7 to 13 years referred for severe antisocial behavior to a psychiatric facility. One group of children received about 25 individual sessions of problem-solving training, derived from the work of Spivack, Platt, and Shure (1976) and Kendall and Braswell (1985). Parents were assisted in prompting and reinforcing their children's application of social skills at home. The second group of children and families received 16 individual parent management training sessions based on the *Oregon Social Learning Center Model* (Patterson, Reid, Jones, & Conger, 1975). Finally, a third group of children and their families received a combination of both parent management training and problem-solving skill training.

Results indicated that children in all three intervention groups showed significant improvements in adjustment at home, at school, and in the community. Moreover, gains were maintained for a 1-year follow-up period. The combination of parent management training and problem-solving skills training produced more marked gains in children's and parents' adjustment than either intervention alone. These results suggest that simultaneous programming for children's social behavior at home and school is better than programming for either setting on its own.

**Multisystemic therapy.** A similar rationale for effecting change in the multiple ecologies that maintain a child's problem behaviors has been used with families typically recalcitrant to treatment. Multisystemic therapy

(Henggeler & Borduin, 1990) consists of first working with the family to identify and understand the multiple social systems (e.g., peer group, neighborhood, family) that cause and maintain a child's antisocial behaviors. A systems perspective (circular causation model) is assumed; that is, each causal factor to children's behavior affects all other causal factors. The therapist develops a plan with the family, attempting to change the identified "system" of causal elements contributing to the child's behavior. For instance, the therapy for a single-parent family may consist of teaching the parent more effective disciplinary practices, finding a neighbor to monitor the child after school until the parent returns home from work, teaching the child self-control strategies as an alternative to aggression, finding ways for the child to maintain peer status without resorting to aggression (e.g., participation in sports), and encouraging the teacher to strengthen the child's prosocial behaviors and the parent's newly developed disciplinary strategies (Henggeler & Borduin, 1990).

Henggeler et al. (1986) examined whether multiproblem families who received multisystemic therapy showed more improvement than comparable families who received equivalent exposure to other types of community treatment. Families receiving multisystemic therapy showed a significant reduction in adolescent conduct problems and an increase in family functioning; in contrast, families receiving other forms of treatment realized little or no improvement. Similarly positive outcomes have been found when multisystemic therapy has been used for abusive or neglectful families in comparison with parent training programs (Brunk, Henggeler, & Whelan, 1987) and individual counseling for adolescent sex offenders (Borduin, Henggeler, Blaske, & Stein, 1990).

# Conclusion

## IMPLICATIONS FOR BEST PRACTICE

■ School programs to promote students' social skills can be strengthened by the active involvement of peers and parents.

■ Peer-mediated conflict resolution programs need to consider the introduction of the program to the school; the process for the selection, training, and ongoing support of peer mediators; and the integration of the approach with other behavior change strategies at the school.

■ Parent involvement in social competence enhancement should be encouraged, with sensitivity to the barriers that hamper their participation.

- Parent training needs to be designed to be delivered to large numbers of parents, using components that help multistress families in recruiting social support and differentiating other sources of stress from their child.

- Parent training is more effective when combined with social skills training and when targeting the "systems" contributing to the families' problems.

There may be promise in drawing from a broader systemic or ecological perspective to consider multiple change agents in promoting children's social competence. This perspective assumes that understanding and changing children's behavior can occur only by affecting the contexts of that behavior, some of which may be distal but still functionally connected to the behavior. For instance, weak social supports of "insular" parents affect the quality of their interaction with their children (Wahler & Dumas, 1989).

Interdependence among elements composing the broad systems affecting children's adjustment seems to contribute to the high stability of their ongoing problems. It also suggests that a single-component intervention is unlikely to have sufficient impact on the contextual systems that maintain childhood maladjustment. Prevention and treatment strategies for childhood maladjustment must involve multiple socializing agents, in multiple settings, over multiple years (Kazdin, 1992). Yet the move to broader, multielement, longer term interventions carries with it increased demands on participants. Obtaining and maintaining either parent (e.g., Hawkins et al., 1991) or teacher (Kupersmidt, Coie, & Dodge, 1990) involvement are challenging enough, without increasing the demands for participation. The increased participation demands engendered by multi-components may be minimized by integrating or combining interventions. A "blended" package entails the formulation of a new intervention from distilled critical ingredients of each separate one.

It may be safe to assume that most programs to promote social competence in children are conceptually defensible and promoted by well-intentioned individuals. Lacking may be substantive evaluation of program effectiveness (Kazdin, 1992). For instance, despite their promise and widespread use, peer-mediation programs have not been well evaluated (Deutsch, 1993). Moreover, the active ingredients of effective interventions may be either unknown or subject to change when combined with other ingredients. These issues and others affecting the concurrent targeting of multiple socializing agents must be addressed in research studies.

■ *section 2*

# Conclusion

This section described a number of interventions that focused on promoting social competence in young students. They share an attempt to teach social skills to children and encourage them to use those skills in natural social contexts, which also may have been the target of intervention. Intervention strategies differed in who delivered the program, who received the program, where (in what setting) the program was implemented, and what other components (e.g., peer involvement, parent involvement) were also included. The needs of the children involved, the nature of the setting, and the resources available would determine which combination of social competence–enhancing interventions would be applicable in what situations.

# Assessment and Implementation Issues

# chapter 9

# Ecobehavioral Analysis of Classroom Behaviors

## ISSUES IN PRACTICE

■ What classroom ecological variables affect students' social behaviors?

■ How do classroom organizational variables, such as spatial variables, spatial density, student groupings, staffing ratios, and staff deployment, affect student behaviors?

■ How do classroom activity variables, such as the type and sequence of activities, affect student behaviors?

■ How do teacher variables affect student behaviors?

■ What information is provided by an ecobehavioral analysis of classrooms?

■ How does one conduct an ecobehavioral analysis?

As described in Chapters 5 and 6, strategies to enhance children's social competence have often involved direct teaching of social skills in specialized settings. However, transfer of acquired skills to natural settings is unlikely to occur unless the environments in those settings support the use of social skills. Without question, the arrangement of physical and social events in classrooms can affect student behaviors (Rogers-Warren, 1982; Willems, 1974). Yet, the optimal arrangement of classroom ecological variables to enhance children's social competence is unclear. Knowing more precisely what ecological classroom variables, in what arrangements, contribute to children's enhanced social competence may suggest ways to engineer classroom environments to prevent future behavior problems by enhancing students' social development. This chapter discusses ecological classroom events that affect children's social behaviors and describes how to conduct an ecobehavioral analysis of environment–behavior relationships.

Classroom ecological variables have been categorized in a number of ways (e.g., Bailey, Harms, & Clifford, 1983; Carta, Sainato, & Greenwood, 1988; McEvoy, Fox, & Rosenberg, 1991; Sainato & Carta, 1992). One classification approach is to group classroom ecological variables according to the level of planning involved in modifying the variable. This method results in a three-level conceptualization of classroom variables. One level (organizational level) consists of variables pertaining to the global organization of the classroom, including the physical structure of the classroom, the number and characteristics of students, and the number of staff present. Classroom organizational variables tend to be set and altered only periodically. Once set, they are difficult to rearrange. A second level (activities level) includes variables pertaining to the type and sequence of daily student activities. Classroom activity variables are more readily under the influence of classroom teachers than are classroom organizational variables. The third level (teacher behavior level) focuses specifically on teacher variables regarding the planning, frequency, and manner of interactions with students to bring about desired behavioral changes. These three levels of classroom ecological variables (organizational, activity, and teacher variables) are shown in Table 9.1 and are described in more detail in the following sections.

## Classroom Organizational Variables

### Spatial Variables

It has been suggested that classrooms for young students should be spatially organized into distinct areas, each corresponding to a curriculum theme, with associated materials and equipment (e.g., sand play, dress-up, vehicle play) (Bailey & Wolery, 1984; Rogers-Warren, 1982; Whaley &

---

TABLE 9.1.  Examples of Classroom Ecological Variables

---

Organizational Variables (the global arrangement of the class)
- Spatial variables
- Student groupings
- Staff–student ratios
- Staff deployment

Activity Variables (the arrangement of curriculum and instructional activities available to students)
- Types of instructional activities
- Sequence of instructional activities

Teacher Behavior Variables (teacher presence and actions toward students)
- Rules, prompts, reinforcement
- Spatial proximity

---

Bennett, 1991). In this arrangement, each area can be defined by clearly designated boundaries, perhaps using low furniture barriers (e.g., shelves) or carpets as demarcation (Whaley & Bennett, 1991). Location of play materials can also affect children's behaviors. Placing toys on shelves rather than in boxes encourages children to choose materials and play independently (Montes & Risley, 1975).

## Spatial Density

Another classroom organizational variable concerns the number of students located within a defined physical space. Increases in child aggression have been noted when density falls below one child per 20 square feet (Smith & Connolly, 1976). The effects of manipulating spatial density on the behavior of young children with disabilities was examined by Brown, Fox, and Brady (1987). They contrasted the social interaction of a group of 3- and 4-year-olds in a large play area consisting of the entire classroom, compared with their social behaviors in a play area one third that size. Other variables, such as the number of toys available, were held constant. More socially directed behaviors, as well as no increase in aggressive behaviors, were associated with the smaller play areas. Well-defined play areas led to smaller groupings of children, with less noisy interactions and more task involvement than larger play areas (Fitt, 1974; Sheehan & Day, 1975).

## Student Groupings

Based on such factors as age, disabilities, and number of children, the composition of children in play groups affects peer interaction. A number of studies suggest that more sharing and peer interaction, together with less aggression, occur if children are arranged in mixed-age groupings (Bailey & McWilliam, 1990; Bailey & Wolery, 1984). Group size is also important, particularly for younger children (Lougee, Grueneich, & Hartup, 1977), socially withdrawn preschoolers (Furman, Rahe, & Hartup, 1979), and children with disabilities in integrated preschools (Rogers-Warren, Ruggles, Peterson, & Cooper, 1981; Speigel-McGill, Bambara, Shores, & Fox, 1984). Similarly, there has been investigation of the effect of grouping children with developmental delay with nondelayed preschoolers. Although preferred by children with disabilities (Guralnick & Groom, 1987), being placed with typically developing children in itself does not seem to affect their rate of peer interaction (Guralnick & Groom, 1988; Jenkins, Odom, & Speltz, 1989).

## Staffing Ratios

A logical assumption would be that more advantageous staff–student ratios would be associated with increased student social interaction. However, studies on the effect of staff–student ratios in preschools suggest the opposite result. O'Connor (1975) compared the behaviors of children in nursery schools with staff–student ratios of 1 to 3.5 and 1 to 7. Children not only interacted significantly less often with peers, but were also more dependent on adults in the enriched staff–student ratio. Similarly, Stodolsky (1974) found that in preschools with higher adult–child ratios, students engaged in both shorter periods of activity and more transitional tasks.

## Staff Deployment

The number of staff present may not be as important as how staff are deployed. LeLaurin and Risley (1972) compared a "zone" to a "man-to-man" staff assignment on children's participation in a preschool setting. In the zone procedure, teachers assigned to an area supervised any children who came into that space. In man-to-man coverage, teachers responsible for a group of 6 to 12 children followed the group from one activity to another. The zone staff assignment produced two advantages over the man-to-man assignment. First, it was associated with higher child involvement in activities, and second, coverage was easier for staff to implement.

# Classroom Activity Variables

## Types of Activities

The variety and types of classroom activities in which children are engaged affect how they interact with one another. Unfortunately, students tend to spend a low percentage of class time actively engaged in tasks. In one study, for instance, fourth-grade students were found to engage in academic tasks only 25% to 30% of their school day (Stanley & Greenwood, 1983). The highest rate of student task engagement occurred when teachers assigned work from either readers or paper-and-pencil worksheets. Lowest rates of task engagement occurred when teachers used audiovisual media or conducted teacher–student discussions (Greenwood & Carta, 1987).

Similarly low levels of task engagement have been found for a group of preschool students. During typical preschool days, the students were found to be engaged on-task about one third of the time (Greenwood, Carta, Kamps, & Arreaga-Mayer, 1990). While task engagement almost doubled during self-care or fine motor activities, the lowest levels of task engagement were associated with periods of story-telling, transition, and gross motor activities.

Classroom activities also affect children's social interaction. In one study, the highest rate of verbal social interaction among preschool children with and without disabilities occurred during either free play or clean-up activities (Odom, Peterson, McConnell, & Ostrosky, 1990). Not only is the type of activity important in facilitating peer interaction, but also the amount of structure in activities seems to be an important environmental variable. DeKlyen and Odom (1989) rated 25 different play activities according to the amount of structure introduced by the teacher to facilitate successful peer interactions. An example of a highly structured activity was bowling. An example of a low structured activity was water-table play. Children both with and without disabilities were more likely to interact with peers, but not with teachers, during highly structured play activities. Teacher actions in setting rules, establishing themes, and assigning play roles before play began facilitated students' interactions.

The type of play material available also affects the way students interact with one another. Some play materials have been found to facilitate social interaction, others to encourage isolated play (Hendrickson, Strain, Tremblay, & Shores, 1981; Quilitch & Risley, 1973). A list of "social" and "isolate" toys for preschool children, composed by Martin, Brady, and Williams (1991), is shown in Table 9.2.

These results suggest that student academic and social performance is affected by the types of activities in which they engage. A greater frequency of targeted student behavior may be facilitated by increasing the amount of classroom time devoted to activities that promote the targeted student behavior.

## Sequence of Activities

Another area for consideration is the sequencing of activities planned for a school day. Bailey and Wolery (1984) suggested that preschool classroom environments need to be predictable so that there is a clearly designated sequence of activities, specifying which students will be involved with which activities, approximate time periods, and responsibilities of each adult in the classroom. Particular sequences of classroom activities may be more conducive than others in promoting certain types of student behaviors. For

TABLE 9.2. Categories of "Social" and "Isolate" Toys

| SOCIAL TOYS | ISOLATE TOYS |
| --- | --- |
| Balls | Puzzles |
| Dress-up clothes | Peg board and pegs |
| Wagon | Art material (e.g., paper, crayons, paints) |
| Toy housekeeping materials (e.g., kitchen set, dishes, dolls, phone) | Play-Doh |
| Puppets | Parquetry |
| Toy vehicles (e.g., cars/track, dump truck, fire engines) | Library material (e.g., assorted picture books, story books) |

From "Effects of Toys on the Social Behavior of Preschool Children in Integrated and Nonintegrated Groups: Investigation of a Setting Event" by S. S. Martin, M. P. Brady, and R. E. Williams, 1991, *Journal of Early Intervention, 15,* p. 156. Copyright 1991 by The Council for Exceptional Children. Reprinted by permission.

instance, a sequence beginning with active children participation and progressing gradually to more sedentary activities limits disruptive behaviors and increases student attention to task (Krantz & Risley, 1977).

Another scheduling issue is the extent to which children are allowed to move from one activity to another, either in a group or individually. Doke and Risley (1972) found that children's participation in preschool activities remained high as long as they could start the next activity individually rather than waiting for others. This result suggests advantages to the availability of concurrent activities, each perhaps associated with different areas of the room.

## Teacher Behavior Variables

Probably the most studied classroom ecological variable is teacher behavior toward students. For example, teacher-delivered rules (Rosenberg & Baker, 1985), prompts (Wolery & Gast, 1984), and reinforcement (Odom & Strain, 1984) have all been found to increase targeted student behaviors.

The spatial proximity of teachers to children during play has also been identified as an important ecological variable that affects students' play, at least in preschool settings (Chandler, 1991; Fagot, 1973; Hamilton & Gordon, 1978). However, spatial proximity itself may not be as important as the nature of teacher interaction with students, especially those with disabilities. Meyer et al. (1987) investigated two levels of teacher intrusion upon elementary school–aged autistic and nondisabled children. Under a high-intrusive condition, teachers were instructed to become involved in children's play once a minute regardless of what the children were doing. Under the low-intrusive condition, teachers were instructed to redirect children's play on no more than three occasions and only if children were not interacting. In both conditions, teachers were located beside the children as they played with one another. Higher levels of appropriate play and toy contact were associated with the low-intrusive condition.

These results suggest that teacher intrusion is best used sparingly, contingent on the absence of peer interactions. More intensive intrusion may both interfere with child–child interactions and increase the likelihood of child orientation toward the teacher.

## Summary of Classroom Ecological Variables

As depicted in Figure 9.1, the three categories of classroom ecological variables may be viewed in a hierarchical relationship with teacher variables dependent on classroom activity variables, which in turn are dependent on classroom organizational variables. The impact of a teacher's use of instruction, prompts, or praise, no matter how well delivered, is thus limited by the extent to which activities in which children are engaged

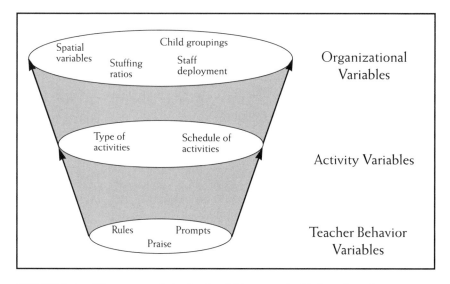

**FIGURE 9.1.** Classroom ecobehavioral variables are embedded one into the next.

also facilitate targeted behaviors. Classroom activities in turn are embedded within the structure of classroom organizational variables, including staff–student ratios and spatial density, which moderate the effects of the other two categories of classroom ecological variables.

It may be unlikely that attending to only one level of classroom ecological variables will be sufficient to produce lasting changes in children's classroom behaviors. The planning of optimal classroom conditions to promote social competence in children may need to occur at all ecological levels. An example of a multilevel change in the ecology of a class for children with autism was described by Nordquist, Twardosz, and McEvoy (1991). First, they arranged the classroom so that a different spatial area of the room was associated with each play activity. They also increased the number and variety of play materials in each area. Second, they assigned staff according to zones rather than specific children. Third, they allowed children, following instruction periods, to move individually to play areas. Not only did these changes have positive impact on children's compliance with adult instruction and time engaged in play, but also teachers' smiling and use of affectionate statements increased as well.

Another example of a program that manipulates ecological variables at all three levels is cooperative learning (Johnson & Johnson, 1986), a strategy that has been applied to a variety of classroom situations, including mainstreaming of elementary school children with disabilities (Johnson & Johnson, 1986; Self, Benning, Marston, & Magnusson, 1991; Slavin, Stevens, & Madden, 1988), regular elementary classrooms (Ross, 1988; Zahn, Kagan, & Widaman, 1986), and early childhood mainstreaming (Miller, 1989). Literature reviews generally have indicated that cooperative learning is more effective than a competitive or individualistic learning format (Hymel, Zinck, & Ditner, 1993; Johnson, Johnson, & Maruyama, 1983; Slavin, 1990), with less clear effects for children with disabilities (Tateyama-Sniezek, 1990). Components of this intervention are divided into four basic elements, depicted in Table 9.3.

Introducing cooperative learning in a classroom entails maneuvering of all three levels of classroom ecology discussed in this chapter. At the organizational level, students of mixed abilities are arranged into small groups, positioned to facilitate direct interaction with one another (Johnson & Johnson, 1986). At the activity level, students work on tasks with interdependent goals, roles, and rewards. Finally, the teacher is expected to monitor the functioning of each group, praising cooperative behaviors and collaborative skills. It is important to note, however, that students who received instruction in collaborative skills have demonstrated higher

TABLE 9.3. Necessary Elements of a Cooperative Learning Classroom

| | |
|---|---|
| Positive interdependence | Groups of 4 to 6 students of differing abilities work toward interdependent goals, tasks, resources, and/or rewards |
| Face-to-face interaction | Direct verbal exchanges are encouraged among students |
| Individual accountability | Each group member contributes fairly to the efforts of the group and evaluated on his or her own learning |
| Interpersonal and small-group skills | Teachers monitor student performance in small groups, praise appropriate interpersonal skills and teacher collaborative skills |

Based on "Mainstreaming and Cooperative Learning Strategies" by D. W. Johnson and R. T. Johnson, 1986, *Exceptional Children, 52,* pp. 553–561.

levels of cooperation with students with disabilities in their group than did their uninstructed peers (Putnam, Rynders, Johnson, & Johnson, 1989).

## Ecobehavioral Space Analysis

Information about the ecobehavioral characteristics of classrooms and their effect on student behaviors may help program developers to identify variables most likely to help students. Carta et al. (1988) suggested that ecobehavioral analysis can be used to influence programming decisions at two levels. At a *molar* level, results of an ecobehavioral analysis provide a description of current ecological events in existing classrooms. From this information may emerge particularly useful comparisons of differing expectations in a variety of classroom settings. For instance, planning the transition of students with disabilities from special preschool classes to regular kindergartens may be facilitated by comparing the two environments on a number of important classroom ecobehavioral variables. An ecobehavioral analysis conducted by Carta, Atwater, Schwartz, and Miller (1990) established two basic differences in instructional procedures between these two settings. First, children in regular kindergartens received most of their instruction in large groups of more than five students, whereas children in special preschool classes were usually taught in small groups. Second, students with special needs received more of their instruction at tables, whereas children in regular kindergartens were seated on the floor for a large proportion of their instruction time.

Such a comparison of environment characteristics assists in determining areas to be targeted for specific programming as children make transitions by suggesting factors that need to be addressed to prepare children for the impact of environmental changes. Results from the Carta et al. (1990) study implied that, to assist their transition into regular kindergartens, children from special preschool classes may need training in receiving instruction with less direct teacher supervision than they are accustomed to experiencing.

Ecobehavioral analysis can also provide information about environment–behavior relationships at a *molecular* level, in revealing the incidence of co-occurrence of a particular behavior category and selected classroom environmental events. In this case, one looks for either heightened or reduced occurrences of the behavior whenever the environment event is present. The temporal relationship between a behavior (B) and a classroom ecobehavioral event (C) is reflected by the conditional probability of B, given C. This formula is:

$$P(B \backslash C) = P(B \cap C) / P(B).$$

The co-occurrence of the behavior with an ecobehavioral event is compared with the base level occurrence of the behavior. Ecobehavioral variables associated with a reduced probability of student behavior in their presence have been referred to as *decelerator* variables (Greenwood, Delquadri, Stanley, Terry, & Hall, 1985); those associated with increased occurrence of student behavior are termed *accelerator* variables. For instance, it is possible to examine such phenomena as the increased probability of student attention whenever a teacher delivers approval, thus determining whether teacher approval constitutes an accelerator variable of the student's behavior. The number of times these two events co-occur within a 30-second cycle would be counted, divided by the total number of times the child was observed to attend, and converted into a percentage.

An ecobehavioral analysis was used to study ecobehavioral events associated with the task engagement of 24 preschool children (Greenwood et al., 1990). At a base level, it was established that children spent about 38% of their time engaged on-task during the preschool day. Significantly higher than base level probability of children's task engagement was associated with fine motor, self-care, play, and clean-up activities. For both fine motor and play activities, the probability of task engagement was almost double the base levels.

Odom, Peterson, McConnell, and Ostrosky (1990) extended the use of an ecobehavioral analysis in preschools to a study of peer interaction.

The behavior of 127 preschool children enrolled in 28 preschool classes was measured on the *Ecobehavioral System for the Complex Assessment of Preschool Environments* (ESCAPE) (Carta, Greenwood, & Atwater, 1985). Results indicated that children were more apt to interact with one another during play than when engaged in any other activity. This finding suggests that social skills instruction may be optimized either during or just prior to play periods, when students typically interact with one another.

## Case Example

An ecobehavioral analysis can be a helpful assessment tool to examine classroom variables affecting the behavior of individual students within classroom environments. A case example is used to illustrate how an ecobehavioral analysis can be conducted in a classroom and the results used to develop a program.

Susan was a 10-year-old with profound mental retardation attending a special education class with a total of five children with disabilities located in a regular school. Susan was referred because of her aggression toward others and self-injurious hand-biting. Over 5 consecutive days, a total of 216 minutes of observation was collected in a variety of classroom situations. The intent was to record environmental events that were simultaneously occurring whenever Susan was aggressive. Of interest were the instructional activities in which Susan was engaged, the behavior of the teacher, and the behavior of the teacher assistant assigned to Susan. As shown in Figure 9.2, the horizontal line represents the base level of Susan's aggression (0.34). Higher than base level probabilities of aggression occurred under each of the following conditions: when Susan was in transition from one activity to another, when the teacher's attention was focused on another adult in the room, when the assistant was interacting with another child individually, when the assistant was out of the room, and when the assistant was expressing disapproval to Susan. Lower than base levels of aggression were noted either during instructional tasks that entailed active components (including music, gross motor exercises, and play) or upon receipt of teacher approval.

Results of this ecobehavioral analysis indicated that Susan's aggressive behavior tended to occur during times of low activity, and suggested that developmentally appropriate, active tasks should be arranged for her. Susan's aggression may also have represented attempts to solicit teacher and/or teacher assistant attention, because it was more than twice as likely to occur either when the teacher was interacting with another adult in the

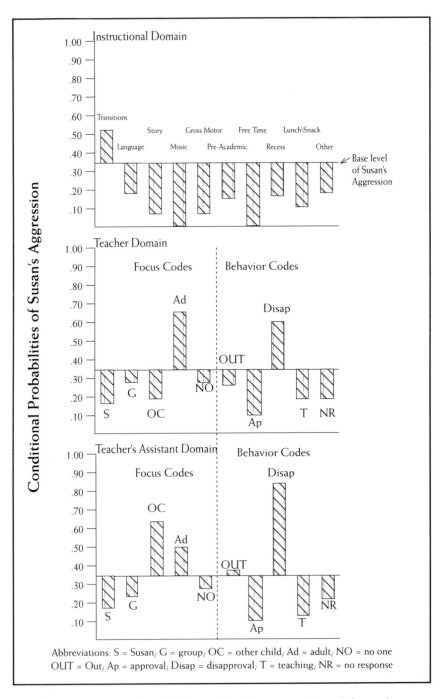

**FIGURE 9.2.** Conditional probabilities of Susan's aggression for ecobehavioral codes in instructional, teacher, and teacher's assistant domains.

room or when the assistant was focused on another child. Hypotheses provided by these data resulted in a program of increased time in developmentally appropriate activities, increased levels of staff praise for appropriate behavior, and increased structures to redirect aggressive behavior. Implementation of this program not only reduced Susan's aggressive behaviors but also increased her time engaged in functional activities.

## Methodological Issues

A traditional behavior assessment examines functional environment–behavior relationships by experimentally manipulating an independent variable (e.g., teacher approval) and measuring the impact on student behavior. In contrast, an ecobehavioral analysis examines moment-to-moment co-occurrences of specified student behaviors and environmental events (Greenwood, Carta, & Atwater, 1991; Greenwood et al., 1990). Greenwood and his colleagues developed a number of ecobehavioral protocols for use in classroom situations. Derived from an original system entitled the *Code for Instructional Structure and Student Academic Response* (CISSAR) (Stanley & Greenwood, 1981), these classroom ecobehavioral coding methods are summarized in Table 9.4.

TABLE 9.4.   Summary Table of Ecobehavioral Analysis Systems for Classrooms

| CODING SYSTEM | APPLICATION |
| --- | --- |
| *Assessment Code/Checklist for the Evaluation of Survival Skills* (ACCESS) (Atwater, Carta, & Schwartz, 1989) | Measurement transition from special preschool to regular kindergartens |
| *Code for Instructional Structure and Student Academic Response* (CISSAR) (Stanley & Greenwood, 1981) | Measurement in regular classroom settings |
| *Code for Instructional Structure and Student Academic Response in Special Educational Settings* (CISSAR-SPED) (Rotholz, Kamps, & Greenwood, 1989) | Measurement in special education settings |
| *Ecobehavioral System for the Complex Assessment of Preschool Environments* (ESCAPE) (Carta, Greenwood, & Atwater, 1985) | Measurement in preschool settings |

To illustrate a method of collecting ecobehavioral information in classrooms, the *Code for Instructional Structure and Student Academic Response in Special Education Settings* (CISSAR-SPEC) (Rotholz, Kamps, & Greenwood, 1989) is described in more detail. This measurement system consists of 73 codes clustered into three general domains: (a) *instructional context codes* (used to record the type of instruction occurring in the classroom), (b) *teacher codes* (used to record the location and behavior of each adult in the room), and (c) *student codes* (used to record student behaviors). Each code is defined in measurable terms; coders are trained in both code definitions and a system of recording observations. A list of general response domains and their subcategories is shown in Table 9.5.

A coder observes and then records appropriate codes for one of the three domains every 10 seconds, starting with the instructional context category, next with the teacher category, and finally with the student category. Following this procedure, codes are entered for each code domain within 30-second cycles that are repeated continuously for a set period of time.

To facilitate this process, coders are instructed to record their observations by marking letter codes provided on a prepared data sheet, an example of which for the CISSAR-SPEC (Rotholz et al., 1989) is shown in Figure 9.3. In addition, 10-second audiotaped sound cues are commonly provided via earphones. Alternatively, computer software is available to enter, store, and analyze codes on portable microprocessors (Barton & Johnson, 1990).

# Conclusion

## IMPLICATIONS FOR BEST PRACTICE

- Optimal arrangement of classroom environments to promote student social competence should involve planning classroom organizational variables, classroom activity variables, and teacher behavior variables.
- Classroom organizational variables that can be modified include spatial variables, spatial density, student groupings, staffing ratios, and staff deployment.
- Classroom activity variables that can be modified include types of activities and sequence of activities.
- Teacher behavior variables that can be modified include rule setting, reinforcement, and spatial proximity.
- Teachers should intervene sparingly when children are interacting with one another.

(list continues on p. 169)

TABLE 9.5.  Code Domains and Subcategories in the *Code for Instructional Structure and Student Academic Response in Special Education Settings*

### INSTRUCTIONAL CONTEXT CODES

| ACTIVITIES | | TASKS | STRUCTURES PHYSICAL | INSTRUCTIONAL |
|---|---|---|---|---|
| Reading | Self-care | Readers | Entire group | Instruction to entire group |
| Mathematics | Arts/crafts | Workbook | Small group | Instruction to small group |
| Spelling | Free time | Worksheet | Individual | One-to-one |
| Handwriting | Class business | Paper/pencil | | Independent activity |
| Language | management | Listen/lecture | | No assigned activity |
| Science | Transition | Other media | | |
| Social studies | Can't tell | Teacher– | | |
| Prevocational/ | | student | | |
| vocational | | discussion | | |
| Motor skills | | Fetch/put | | |
| Daily living | | away | | |
| and | | Time out | | |
| community | | None | | |
| skills | | | | |

### TEACHER CODES

| TEACHER DESCRIPTION | TEACHER POSITION | TEACHER BEHAVIOR |
|---|---|---|
| Head teacher | In front | No response |
| Aide 1 | At desk | Teaching |
| Aide 2 | Side | General teaching |
| Peer tutor | Back | Other talk |
| Other | Out of room | Approval |
| | | Disapproval |

### STUDENT CODES

| ACADEMIC RESPONSES | TASK MANAGEMENT | COMPETING BEHAVIORS |
|---|---|---|
| Writing | Waiting appropriately | Disrupt |
| Academic game play | Raising hand/ | Play inappropriate |
| Reading aloud | signaling for help | Inappropriate task |
| Reading silently | Looking for material | Talking inappropriately |
| Talking academic | Moves to new station | Inappropriate locale |
| Answers academic question | Playing appropriately | Look around |
| Task participation | None | Self-stimulation |
| None | | Self-abuse |
| | | None |

______

Start R M S H L Sc Ss Ac Ft Rr Wb Ws Pp Ll Eg Sg Ie Is 1:1 La Nn
Bm Tn Ct Pv Ms Dl Sf Om Tsd Fp To N

1 If AD O S B NR Gn T OT A D ______ ____________
1 2 3 4 5 If AD O S B NR T OT A D Stop Stop Code

W G RA RS TA ANQ ASK TP NS WA RH LM M PA NT DI PI IT TNA IL LA SST SA NI

Start R M S H L Sc Ss Ac Ft Rr Wb Ws Pp Ll Eg Sg Ie Is 1:1 La Nn
Bm Tn Ct Pv Ms Dl Sf Om Tsd Fp To N

1 If AD O S B NR Gn T OT A D ______ ____________
1 2 3 4 5 If AD O S B NR T OT A D Stop Stop Code

W G RA RS TA ANQ ASK TP NS WA RH LM M PA NT DI PI IT TNA IL LA SST SA NI

Start R M S H L Sc Ss Ac Ft Rr Wb Ws Pp Ll Eg Sg Ie Is 1:1 La Nn
Bm Tn Ct Pv Ms Dl Sf Om Tsd Fp To N

1 If AD O S B NR Gn T OT A D ______ ____________
1 2 3 4 5 If AD O S B NR T OT A D Stop Stop Code

W G RA RS TA ANQ ASK TP NS WA RH LM M PA NT DI PI IT TNA IL LA SST SA NI

Start R M S H L Sc Ss Ac Ft Rr Wb Ws Pp Ll Eg Sg Ie Is 1:1 La Nn
Bm Tn Ct Pv Ms Dl Sf Om Tsd Fp To N

1 If AD O S B NR Gn T OT A D ______ ____________
1 2 3 4 5 If AD O S B NR T OT A D Stop Stop Code

W G RA RS TA ANQ ASK TP NS WA RH LM M PA NT DI PI IT TNA IL LA SST SA NI

Start R M S H L Sc Ss Ac Ft Rr Wb Ws Pp Ll Eg Sg Ie Is 1:1 La Nn
Bm Tn Ct Pv Ms Dl Sf Om Tsd Fp To N

1 If AD O S B NR Gn T OT A D ______ ____________
1 2 3 4 5 If AD O S B NR T OT A D Stop Stop Code

W G RA RS TA ANQ ASK TP NS WA RH LM M PA NT DI PI IT TNA IL LA SST SA NI

Start R M S H L Sc Ss Ac Ft Rr Wb Ws Pp Ll Eg Sg Ie Is 1:1 La Nn
Bm Tn Ct Pv Ms Dl Sf Om Tsd Fp To N

1 If AD O S B NR Gn T OT A D ______ ____________
1 2 3 4 5 If AD O S B NR T OT A D Stop Stop Code

W G RA RS TA ANQ ASK TP NS WA RH LM M PA NT DI PI IT TNA IL LA SST SA NI

**FIGURE 9.3.** A sample data sheet of the CISSAR-SPEC.
From "Ecobehavioral Assessment and Analysis in Special Education Settings for Students with Autism" by D. A. Rotholz, D. M. Kamps, and C. R. Greenwood, 1989, *The Journal of Special Education,* 23, p. 69. Copyright 1989 by PRO-ED, Inc. Reprinted with permission.

- Cooperative learning consists of manipulation of variables at all three levels of classroom ecology.

- An ecobehavioral analysis should be conducted to identify classroom ecological events affecting student behavior.

- An ecobehavioral analysis can influence programming at molar and molecular levels.

- Hypotheses generated by an ecobehavioral analysis should be confirmed by demonstrating the functional relationship between the ecological event and the student behavior.

Ecobehavioral analysis is a useful addition to methodologies currently available for analyzing student behavior. Given the complex nature of classroom environments, access to a methodology for examining fine moment-to-moment relationships between student behavior and ecobehavioral events provides information about possible mechanisms that may contribute to student behaviors. Once identified, these relationships would be confirmed a functional analysis, in which environmental events are manipulated as independent variables and demonstrated to affect student behaviors.

Another use of ecobehavioral analysis is the evaluation of environment–behavior relationships that accompany changes noted after an intervention. Hundert (1994) conducted an ecobehavioral analysis based on the results of a previously published study on preschool supervisor training. Supervisors of preschool settings were trained to introduce a collaborative teaming approach whereby resource teachers (early childhood special educators) and classroom teachers jointly developed a plan to promote peer interaction for all students in their classes, including children with disabilities. This collaborative approach contrasted with a more typical arrangement, in which the resource teacher developed an individualized program for children with disabilities and presented it to the classroom teacher for implementation. The previously published study indicated that supervisor training resulted in increased interactive play of children with disabilities. A subsequent ecobehavioral analysis was undertaken to reveal changes in environment–behavior concurrences that would help to explain these changes in children's behaviors.

Before supervisor training, the interactive play of children with disabilities occurred 16.3% of the time. A higher than base level probability of peer interaction was associated with the presence of resource teachers, but not with any classroom teacher behavior. After supervisor training, both a three-fold increase in the interactive play of children with disabilities and a change in the pattern of ecobehavioral relationships associated with occurrences of interactive play were noted. Higher than base rate levels of interactive play occurred when classroom teachers focused on any group of children that included a child with disabilities, while in contrast resource teacher presence was associated with lower than base rate levels of interactive play.

Inferences may be derived from these results to suggest how supervisor training may have affected children's interactive play. It would appear that, after supervisor training in a collaborative team approach, classroom teachers did not increase the frequency of their focus on inclusive groups of children; when they did provide such focus, however, these occurrences were associated with higher than base rate levels of children's interactive play. This finding suggests that interventions targeting the increased frequency of teacher focus on inclusive children's groupings may help increase interactive play rates of children with disabilities.

One issue facing the field of ecobehavioral analysis is the determination of a framework to guide the selection of variables to be included in a coding system. Given the infinite number of ecological variables in any classroom, what selection process can best identify those that will yield the most meaningful information in an ecobehavioral analysis? Carta, Greenwood, and Robinson (1987) described the process by which the codes for the ESCAPE were developed. First, they reviewed literature on both the effectiveness of special preschool programs and ecological variables that have been linked to instructional gains in preschool classrooms. Second, they observed a variety of existing preschool programs to identify a broad range of features in typical preschool classroom environments. From this information a tentative list of codes was established and then piloted in a variety of settings. The draft instrument was also submitted to experts in the field, from whose feedback revisions were made. A final draft of the observation system then was developed. Such a systematic approach to establishing a coding instrument helped to ensure that measures were consistent with knowledge in the field.

A conceptual framework may help guide the initial selection of ecobehavioral variables that later can be empirically validated significant factors in classroom settings. Without such a framework, ecobehavioral variables would be selected either arbitrarily or by ill-established convention. In either case, the most important areas for consideration in classrooms may not be measured. A number of researchers have conceptualized methods of grouping setting variables (e.g., Bailey & McWilliam, 1990; Carta et al., 1988; McEvoy et al., 1991) that could be used as a starting point for the development of such a framework.

Another limitation of an ecobehavioral analysis is that it assesses environmental events that are both concurrent with and proximal to the target behavior of interest. There may be important environmental events, however, either spatially or temporally distanced from a student's behavior, that exert considerable impact (Dumas, 1989a). For instance, a teacher may arrange a classroom by restricting the number of children who can access a play area, the types of toys that are available, and the freedom of movement between play areas. These actions may be implemented before the play time begins, and hence not identified by an ecobehavioral analysis, yet profoundly affect many observable variables in children's play. In fact, preschool teachers' attempts at increasing children's social interaction tend to consist of either structuring play situations (e.g., determining the type and number of play materials available) or initiating similar manipulative strategies that are executed before the children begin to play (McConnell, McEvoy, & Odom, 1992).

Gewirtz (1972) differentiated between *current* (occurring at the same time as the behavior) and *preceding* (occurring prior to the behavior) setting events. Kennedy and Itkonen (1993) found that preceding setting events were associated with higher frequencies of problem behavior for students with severe disabilities. In one case, a school bus city route that involved numerous stops on the way to school was associated with higher frequencies of problem behaviors later in the school day. When the school bus route was changed to the highway, the frequency of problem behaviors diminished.

Similarly, an ecobehavioral analysis entails the quantitative measurement of consistency between frequently occurring children's behavior and specific environmental events. Thus, low-frequency but powerful teacher behaviors may not be identified by an ecobehavioral analysis unless measures are taken over prolonged periods of time.

It is also important to recognize that an ecobehavioral analysis reflects a correlational but not necessarily a causal link between setting events and target behaviors. It might suggest which specific environmental events *may* be causally linked to target behaviors, for later confirmation by functional analysis.

An ecobehavioral analysis may help to form and support hypotheses about environment–behavior relationships in classrooms. By measuring the concurrency of teacher behavior, classroom environment, and student performance, it allows for a better understanding of how classrooms work and what interventions may be most promising to facilitate gains for children.

■ *chapter 10*

# Assessment of Students' Social Competence

## ISSUES IN PRACTICE

■ What assessment questions are important to the success of social competence–enhancing interventions?

■ What are the characteristics, advantages, and disadvantages of parent or teacher ratings of student social behaviors?

■ What are the characteristics, advantages, and disadvantages of naturalistic observation of student social behaviors?

■ What are the characteristics, advantages, and disadvantages of peer ratings of student social behaviors?

■ What are the characteristics, advantages, and disadvantages of student self-rating of social behaviors?

■ How well do different measures of student social competence agree with one another?

■ How can changes in student and class social adjustment be measured?

The need to consider social competence–enhancing interventions in schools to address adjustment needs of students is compelling. However, the success of programs to promote social competence in students will hinge on at least two assessment questions. One question is whether appropriate students and suitable intervention targets for those students are being selected for intervention. A second question is whether a provided intervention is effective in improving students' adjustment. Answering either question requires inferences to be drawn from information about student adjustment that can be collected practically in schools.

This chapter describes, illustrates, and compares the following measurement approaches for assessing student social competence and discusses associated assessment issues:

■ Teacher or parent rating measures

■ Naturalistic observation

- Peer rating measures
- Self-rating measures

# Assessment Procedures

## Teacher or Parent Rating

One method of measuring social competence is to quantify adults' judgments of students' social behaviors. Typically, a teacher or parent rates on a scale the degree to which a series of written statements of social conduct apply to a student. Results are compared with child norms on which the measure was developed and may be further analyzed into subscales.

Specific teacher or parent rating measures differ from one another in their purpose, the child population being assessed, the types of social behaviors measured, the psychometric soundness of the instrument, and their ease of administration, scoring, and interpretation. For instance, the *Child Behavior Checklist* (CBC) (Achenbach & Edelbrock, 1983) was normed on an initial clinical sample of 2,300 children, aged 4 to 16 years, referred to a mental health clinic in the Eastern United States. To identify items that differentiated clinic referred from non–clinic referred children, a normative sample of 1,300 children was obtained by measuring children in randomly selected homes in three eastern U.S. states. In contrast, the *Social Skills Rating System* (SSRS) (Gresham & Elliott, 1990) was not developed with a clinical sample of children. This measure was normed on a sample of over 4,000 students representative of the U.S. child population, whose social skills were rated by their teachers and parents. Use of the two rating scales discussed would provide divergent sets of information. The results from the CBC would indicate the similarity of a student's rated behaviors to clinic referred and non–clinic referred children, whereas results on the SSRS would reflect a student's social skills in relation to the U.S. child population.

Adult rating scales typically evaluate student behavior problems only, and exclude students' positive social behaviors (e.g., Eyberg & Robinson, 1983; Quay & Peterson, 1983). Assessing negative behavioral functioning provides a limited picture of a child's social competence (Dunst, 1993). The discussion in this section focuses on selected instruments, listed in Table 10.1, in which adults rate students against indicators of positive social functioning.

**California Preschool Social Competence Scale (Levine, Elzey, & Lewis, 1969).** This rating scale, developed for children aged 2.5 years to

TABLE 10.1. Summary Table of Selected Adult-Rating Scales of Student Social Competence

| INSTRUMENT | SUBSCALES | NORMS | AGE RANGE | EASE OF ADMINISTRATION[a] | RELIABILITY[b] | VALIDITY[b] |
|---|---|---|---|---|---|---|
| *California Preschool Social Competence Scale* (Levine, Elzey, & Lewis, 1969) | None | 800 children whose representativeness is unclear | 2.5–5.5 | 1 | 1 | 0 |
| *Child Behavior Checklist* (Achenbach & Edelbrock, 1983) | Activities, Social, School | 1300 boys and girls in three mid-Eastern states | 4–16 | 2 | 1 | 2 |
| *School Social Behavior Scales* (Merrell, 1993) | Interpersonal, Self-Management, Academic, Hostile-Irritable, Antisocial-Aggressive, Demanding-Disruptive | 1800 boys and girls whose representativeness is unclear | K–Grade 12 | 2 | 2 | 1 |
| *Social Behavior Assessment Inventory* (Stephens & Arnold, 1992) | Self-Related, Task-Related, Interpersonal, Environmental | Not applicable | K–Grade 9 | 0 | 2 | 1 |
| *Social Skills Rating System* (Gresham & Elliott, 1990) | Cooperation, Assertion, Responsibility, Self-Control | 4170 boys and girls representative of the U.S. child population | 3 years–Grade 12 | 2 | 2 | 2 |
| *Walker–McConnell Scale of Social Competence and School Adjustment* (Walker & McConnell, 1988) | Teacher preferred social behavior, Peer preferred social behaviors, School adjustment | 1800 boys and girls representative of the U.S. child population | K–Grade 6, Grade 7–9 version | 2 | 2 | 2 |

a.  0 = difficult, 1 = moderate, 2 = easy.

b.  0 = none or minimal, 1 = moderate, 2 = good.

5.5 years, consists of 30 items, each containing four alternative descriptive statements about such social behaviors as following instruction and sharing. A child's raw scores are compared with norms of gender, age, and family occupational level. The scale was normed on 800 children, using 50 children for each of the 16 cells produced by matrix categories of gender (boy or girl), age (2, 3, 4, or 5), and occupational level (high or low). No explanation was provided about the process used to select the 800 children, although it is known that their geographic distribution was proportionate to the U.S. Census Bureau results of the U.S. child population. Moderate interrater and internal consistency reliabilities were reported. No validity data were presented.

**Child Behavior Checklist (CBC) (Achenbach & Edelbrock, 1983).** This scale was developed to identify children with clinically significant behavior and emotional problems. Separate versions of the instrument are available for teachers of students aged 5 to 18 years and parents of children aged 2 to 3, 4 to 11, and 12 to 18; a self-report form for youths of 11 to 18 years old is also included. Only the parent form for children aged 4 to 11 years and the youth self-report form contain items that measure children's social competence in addition to items for rating a child's negative behaviors. Parents are asked to report on both the quantity and the quality of their child's involvement in sports and nonsports activities (Activity Scale); with clubs, friends, and others (Social Scale); and in scholastic tasks (School Scale).

The reliability of the CBC is quite strong, with a median test–retest reliability coefficient over 1 week of .89. [A perfect reliability coefficient is 1.0, but coefficients of $r = .80$ to .90 are considered reasonable (Hauser-Cram & Wyngaarden Krauss, 1991).] Interrater agreement between mothers and fathers on their child's social competence total score was modest ($r = .59$).

**School Social Behavior Scales (SSBS) (Merrell, 1993).** The SSBS was developed specifically for teacher assessment of both the social competencies and the antisocial behaviors of students. Teachers are asked to rate a student on each of 65 statements of social behavior on a 5-point scale ranging from *never* to *frequently*. Results are compared with norms and expressed in two scales (Social Competence and Antisocial Behavior), from which a further six subscales are derived.

This instrument was normed on teacher ratings of more than 1,800 students (including those with disabilities) in Grades K to 12, representing an urban–rural mix and a distribution of socioeconomic status reasonably similar to the U.S. general population (Merrell, 1993). However, the ethnic composition of the sample underrepresents non-White groups.

Internal consistency coefficients of the measure are high ($r$ ranging from .91 to .98). Test–retest reliability, conducted over a 3-week period, is moderate to adequate ($r$ ranging from .60 to .98). Measures of SSBS validity are based on content-, construct-, and criteria-referenced standards. The instrument is highly correlated with similar rating scales, and also discriminates between children with and without disabilities. No predictive validity data were reported.

**Social Behavior Assessment Inventory (SBAI) (Stephens & Arnold, 1992).** This test, produced for students from kindergarten to ninth grade, asks teachers to rate students on a 4-point scale (with categories of *not observed or not applicable, acceptable level, lower-than-acceptable level,* or *never exhibited*) for each of 406 social skills. The SBAI is intended for use in conjunction with an associated social skills curriculum developed by the senior author (Stephens, 1992). Results are presented in 30 subcategories under four domains (Self-Related Behaviors, Task-Related Behaviors, Interpersonal Behaviors, and Environmental Behaviors). The authors reported that the inventory takes approximately 30 to 45 minutes to complete for each student.

The SBAI is a curriculum-based, rather than norm-referenced, measure, which provides a profile of a child's social skills in the curriculum areas composing the test. Both test–retest and internal consistency reliability coefficients are high. The instrument has acceptable content and convergent validity, and it accurately discriminates between students identified with and without either behavior or learning problems. The usefulness of this assessment instrument, as well as the associated *Social Skills in the Classroom* curriculum (Stephens, 1992), relies on the face validity of the social skills included as content in both products. The selection of social skills for both the instrument and the curriculum was based on a content analysis of other behavior rating instruments, a review of relevant professional literature, and teacher feedback on item suitability.

**Social Skills Rating System (SSRS) (Gresham & Elliott, 1990).** This rating scale consists of separate teacher and parent forms for preschool, elementary, and secondary school levels, plus student self-report forms for both elementary and secondary levels. Respondents are presented with between 30 and 40 written descriptions of social behaviors, and asked to rate (a) how often each occurs (*never, sometimes, very often*), and

(b) how important the behavior is to the student's adjustment (*not important, important, critical*).

Depending upon the specific form used, the SSRS is analyzed into a number of subscales (e.g., Cooperation, Assertion, Responsibility, Empathy, Self-control). Parent and teacher forms also contain an additional rating scale for 10 to 18 behavior problems. Academic Competence is another subscale, included only on the teacher form.

Internal consistency, test–retest reliability, and interrater reliability are all quite strong. The SSRS also discriminates between students with and students without disabilities, and the teacher social skills scores indicate a strong relationship with other similar measures.

**Walker–McConnell Scale of Social Competence and School Adjustment (Walker & McConnell, 1988).**   This scale is designed to help teachers determine the social competence of elementary school students. Teachers rate on a 5-point Likert scale (with categories from *never* to *frequently*) the extent to which each of 43 statements applies to a student. The test was normed on 1,800 students representative of the U.S. child population. The manual contains impressive results of the reliability and validity of the scale. Both test–retest reliability ($r = .61$ to $.90$) and interrater reliability ($r = .53$ to $.77$) are strong. Similarly, factorial, discriminant, criterion-related, and construct validity coefficients are all robust.

**Advantages and Limitations.**   Because teachers and parents are the individuals who most frequently identify a child as maladjusted (Kazdin, 1987; Rogers, Forehand, & Griest, 1981), their perceptions constitute a particularly valuable source of information. Adult ratings of student social behaviors are also efficient to collect, with rating scales typically completed in 20 to 45 minutes—considerably less time than required for other measures discussed in this chapter.

Like peer ratings, teacher and parent ratings of social competence reflect the respondent's perceptions, which may and often do differ from students' actual behaviors. Teachers, for instance, tend to exhibit bias in identifying students with social adjustment problems. In general, they tend to refer aggressive but not withdrawn children for help (Strain & Kerr, 1981). Parents, on the other hand, tend to underestimate their child's externalizing problems (Hinshaw, Han, Erhardt, & Huber, 1992).

Although teacher rating of children's social competence is an efficient measurement strategy, even more efficient is simply asking teachers to rank students in their class according to frequency of peer interaction. Using this approach, preschool teachers were able to identify accurately the least socially responsive student in their class (Greenwood, Walker, Todd, & Hops, 1979). Teachers in 20 preschools were asked to rank order their students on the basis of peer verbal interaction frequency during the day. Teacher rankings correlated highly with direct observation measures and showed high test–retest reliability. In contrast, peer nomination of preferred playing partners neither correlated highly with direct observation of children's play patterns, nor was reliable at retest. The authors concluded that, combined with observational measures to confirm the accuracy of selection, the use of teacher ranking is a cost-effective assessment procedure.

## Naturalistic Observation

Another method of measuring students' social competence is the use of trained observers to code children's social behaviors in such natural settings as classrooms and playgrounds. Two major methodological considerations exist in undertaking naturalistic observation of students' social behaviors. The first is the selection and definition of social behaviors to be coded. For instance, the rate at which children interact with peers is an index of neither current nor future maladjustment (La Greca & Stark, 1986). Low rates of playing with others is also not associated with low social status (Kupersmidt, Coie, & Dodge, 1990; McConnell & Odom, 1986).

Rather than frequency of interaction, La Greca and Stark (1986) suggested that one should measure the quality of children's social behaviors. Typically, this is achieved by coding a child's behavior into clearly defined response categories. Response categories of children's social interaction are usually tailored to the particular purposes of data collection. As illustration, one of the earliest behavior coding systems for scoring preschoolers' social behaviors, still in use, was developed by Parten (1932), who proposed a developmental sequence of play categories through which children would typically progress:

1. Unoccupied behavior

2. Solitary independent play

3. Onlooker activity

4. Parallel activity

5. Associative play

6. Cooperation or organized supplementary play

A coding system for recording behavior may be elaborate, such as the one developed by Krehbiel (1984) and used by Coie and Dodge (1988) to code behaviors of first- and third-grade boys both in the classroom and during other times of the day (e.g., in the lunchroom). This coding system, shown in Table 10.2, rated a total of 19 behavior categories, organized into five domains.

One of the simplest systems for coding children's playground behavior was described by Ollendick, Greene, Francis, and Brown (1991). All student behaviors were coded into one of three mutually exclusive options: positive social interaction (e.g., smiling, sharing, cooperating); negative social interaction (e.g., pushing, making offensive comments); or solitary play (e.g., interaction that is neither positive nor negative).

A second methodological issue in conducting naturalistic observation concerns the design of the observation system by which behaviors are recorded. A number of recording procedures are available, each differing in the schedule for observing behaviors and/or the unit of behavior observed (see Mash & Terdal, 1988, for a fuller description of behavior observation methodologies). Four of the more commonly used behavior recording procedures, described below, are compared in Table 10.3.

In event recording, a coder continuously tracks a child, recording every occurrence of a target behavior. For example, Coie and Dodge

---

**TABLE 10.2.  Social Behavior Codes Developed by Krehbiel (1984)**

*Solitary Play*
- On-task
- Off-task, nondisruptive
- Off-task, disruptive

*Peer Group Entry Attempt*
- Hovering
- Instrumental approach
- Direct approach
- Attention-seeking approach
- Group-centered approach
- Disruptive approach

*Approach to the Subject by Another*
- Positive approach
- Neutral approach
- Negative approach

*Interactive Behavior*
- Prosocial interactions
- Instrumental behaviors
- Rough play
- Bullying (or proactive) aggression
- Reactive (angry) aggression

*Teacher-Initiated Interaction*
- Positive interactions
- Negative interactions

Based on *School-Setting Behavior of Academic Achievement-Based Subtypes of Rejected Children* by G. Krehbiel, 1984, unpublished doctoral dissertation, Duke University, Durham, NC.

TABLE 10.3. A Comparison of Behavior Recording Procedures

| RECORDING PROCEDURE | OBSERVATION SCHEDULE | BEHAVIOR COUNTED |
|---|---|---|
| Event | Continuous | Every occurrence |
| Interval | Series of regular time intervals (e.g., 10 sec) | Occurrence for entire time interval |
| Partial interval | Series of regular time intervals (e.g., 10 sec) | Occurrence for part of a time interval |
| Momentary time sampling | Series of regular moments in time | Occurrence at a predetermined moment |

Based on *Behavioral Assessment of Childhood Disorders* (2nd ed.) by E. J. Mash and L. G. Terdal, 1988, New York: Guilford.

(1988) arranged for coders to observe the school behavior of individual boys for 12 separate 5-minute sessions. Coders recorded each new occurrence of a behavior by a key-press on a hand-held microprocessor, which stored both the frequency and the duration of behaviors in each category.

Ollendick et al. (1991) used both interval and partial interval recording methods to measure students' behavior during 3-minute time periods, on 3 separate days. Each time period was divided into 10-second observation intervals, followed by a 5-second interval for coders to record the results of their observation. Categories of positive social interaction and solitary play were recorded only if either occurred without interruption throughout a 10-second interval. Negative social interaction was recorded on a partial interval basis (i.e., if it occurred at any point during a 10-second interval). This particular composition of interval and partial interval recording procedures is especially sensitive in identifying occurrences of negative social interaction.

An example of momentary time sampling can be found in Hundert, Mahoney, and Hopkins (1993). They observed the peer interactions of each of 35 children with disabilities in 19 preschool classes, during five consecutive 30-minute indoor play periods. Audiotape sound signals via earphones were used to cue coders of the passage of 10 seconds. During each consecutive observation, coders observed a different participant in the study (i.e., a child, the classroom teacher, or the resource teacher), tallying observations of as many as four individuals in each class each minute, depending upon the number of participants. These behavior codes are shown in Table 10.4. Coders recorded the results of their observations on a data sheet, tallied the results at the end of the observation session, and

## TABLE 10.4.  Child and Teacher Behavior Codes Definitions

| CODE | ABBREVIATION | DEFINITION |
|---|---|---|
| *Child Codes* | | |
| Isolated/occupied play | (IO) | The child was engaged in a play activity (e.g., pushing a toy truck, coloring), but was more than 2 meters (m) away from any other child. |
| Proximity play | (PP) | The child was engaged in a play activity within 2 m of at least one other child, but not interacting either verbally or nonverbally with another child. |
| Interactive play | (IP) | The child was engaged in a play activity within 2 m of at least one other child, and was interacting with another child, either verbally (e.g., talking about a play activity) or nonverbally (e.g., allowing another child to take turns playing with a toy, listening when another child is talking specifically to him/her). |
| Negative play | (NP) | The child exhibited an aggressive, hostile, or rejecting verbal (e.g., yelling) or nonverbal (e.g., pushing, sticking out tongue, threatening to hit) behavior toward another child. |
| Teacher interaction | (TI) | The child displayed a verbal (e.g., talking) or nonverbal (e.g., sitting on lap) behavior directed toward a teacher or other adult in the classroom. |
| No play | (NO) | The child was not engaged in any play activity (e.g., watching other children). |
| Out | (OUT) | The child was physically out of the room, absent, or out of sight at the time of observation. |
| *Teacher Codes* | | |
| Individual child with disabilities | (I+) | The teacher was located within 3 m of one child with disabilities (who may have been in a group or isolated) and her verbal or nonverbal behavior was directed exclusively toward that child. |
| Individual child without disabilities | (I–) | The teacher was located within 3 m of one child without disabilities (who may have been in a group or isolated) and her verbal and nonverbal behavior was directed exclusively toward that child. |
| Group with one or more children with disabilities | (G+) | The teacher's verbal or nonverbal behavior was directed to a group that included one or more children with disabilities (e.g., asking the class to put away their toys). |
| Group without a child with disabilities | (G–) | The teacher's verbal or nonverbal behavior was directed toward a group that did not include a child with disabilities (e.g., distributing aprons to a group of children without disabilities who were about to play with water toys). |
| Other teacher | (OT) | This code was recorded when one teacher directed her behavior toward the other teacher. |
| No response | (NR) | No response was recorded when the teacher made no observable response directed to another individual or group (e.g., looking at a child). |

From "The Relationship Between the Peer Interaction of Children with Disabilities in Integrated Preschools and Resource and Classroom Teacher Behaviors" by J. Hundert, W. Mahoney, and B. Hopkins, 1993, *Topics in Early Childhood Special Education, 13*, p. 333. Copyright 1993 by PRO-ED. Reprinted by permission.

converted these sums into percentage scores. The group mean percentage of each behavior code is shown in Figure 10.1.

The accuracy of naturalistic observation depends directly on how well coders are able to measure behaviors reliably. To check interrater reliability, a second coder independently, but simultaneously, codes behaviors with the first coder. An agreement between coders is recorded whenever both agree on the occurrence of a behavior. The total number of agreements is divided by the total number of agreements plus disagreements, multiplied by 100 to produce a percentage score. Using agreement on behavior occurrences to calculate interrater reliability avoids the inflation of agreement estimates

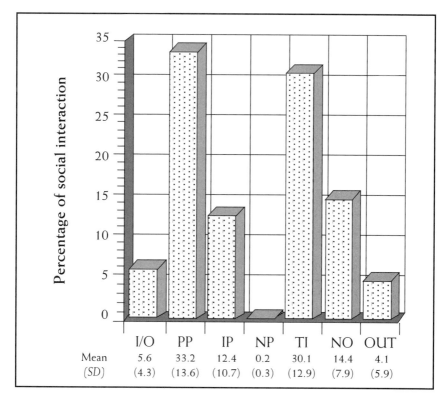

|  | I/O | PP | IP | NP | TI | NO | OUT |
|---|---|---|---|---|---|---|---|
| Mean | 5.6 | 33.2 | 12.4 | 0.2 | 30.1 | 14.4 | 4.1 |
| (SD) | (4.3) | (13.6) | (10.7) | (0.3) | (12.9) | (7.9) | (5.9) |

**FIGURE 10.1.** Mean and standard deviation of each play behavior of children with disabilities during indoor play periods. Key: I/O = isolated/occupied play; PP = proximity play; IP = interactive play; NP = negative play; TI = teacher interaction; NO = no play; OUT = out.

From "The Relationship Between the Peer Interaction of Children with Disabilities in Integrated Preschools and Resource and Classroom Teacher Behaviors" by J. Hundert, W. Mahoney, and B. Hopkins, 1993, *Topics in Early Childhood Special Education, 13,* p. 336. Copyright 1993 by PRO-ED. Reprinted by permission.

associated with using agreements on both occurrences and nonoccurrences (Hawkins & Dotson, 1975). Reliability coefficients of at least 75% agreement constitute acceptable scores. Alternatively, one can calculate a Kappan statistic (Cohen, 1960) to control for chance agreements.

Another threat to the accuracy of data collection is observer drift and bias (Kazdin, 1977). Once in the field, coders may shift their coding criteria from the original response definitions (O'Leary & Kent, 1973). To control for observer drift, coders are usually kept naive to the purpose of this study for which they are collecting data and are rotated to different sites.

**Advantages and Limitations.** Because the data can be interpreted with minimal inferences, naturalistic observations are considered to have high face validity (Asher & Hymel, 1981). Naturalistic observation is also sensitive to the effects of social competency building interventions (La Greca & Stark, 1986) and can be used repeatedly to track changes in children's social adjustment over time.

A significant limitation of naturalistic observation is the high time involvement of personnel required to conduct the observations (Asher & Hymel, 1981; La Greca & Stark, 1986). Collecting data on student social behavior can take weeks or months, entailing extensive preliminary training and subsequent deployment of a coder. In contrast, teacher or parent ratings of student social behaviors usually take minutes. Moreover, observation data typically provide neither normative information about behavior categories nor illumination of the nature of social difficulties experienced by particular children (La Greca & Stark, 1986).

Another limitation of naturalistic observation is that children and teachers may behave atypically during the observation period. When observed, children may curtail their aggressive behavior more than at other times. This type of reactivity to observation can be minimized if coders are gradually eased into the setting (Kazdin, 1977). Despite its limitations, however, naturalistic observation is one of the key measures taken in the assessment of a child's social adjustment.

## Peer Rating

An important outcome of children's social competence is the ability to make friends and be accepted by others. Therefore, peer ratings of a child's acceptance or status constitute an important indicator of his or her social competence. Typically, two methods of sociometric assessment—peer nomination and peer rating—are used, either separately or in combination.

In peer nomination, peers are asked to indicate the children in their class who best match a given description (e.g., "Who in your class would you like to play with the most?"). Children may be requested to select from either a fixed choice of specific children or an unlimited choice of classmates. McConnell and Odom (1986) suggested that providing children with fixed choices may direct them to nominate different classmates than they would otherwise.

When originally implemented, peer nomination procedures include both positive and negative categories (e.g., "Name three classmates you don't like very much") to estimate both peer acceptance and peer rejection. The results from a combination of negative and positive nominations are used to determine a child's social status in one of five subgroups, first proposed by Perry (1979) and later refined by Coie, Dodge, and Coppitelli (1982). Based on both the total number of nominations and the difference between positive and negative nominations, each student's score is standardized for the class. Table 10.5 illustrates the method used to categorize these results into social status subgroups.

Concerns have been expressed about the use of negative peer nominations, first that the procedure and results may upset less liked children in a class, and second that it may either sanctify criticizing others or diminish students' opinions of one another (Kupersmidt et al., 1990). Yet, little or no empirical evidence substantiates these concerns. Hayvren and

TABLE 10.5.  Method of Calculating Children's Social Status from Sociometric Results

| SOCIAL STATUS CATEGORY | SOCIOMETRIC RESULT | | | |
|---|---|---|---|---|
| | SOCIAL PREFERENCE[a] | SOCIAL IMPORTANCE[b] | ACCEPTED | REJECTED |
| Popular | High | | High | Low |
| Rejected | Low | | Low | High |
| Neglected | | Low | Low | Low |
| Controversial | | High | High | High |
| Average | Average | Average | | |

a. Standard score of negative nominations subtracted from positive nominations.
b. Standard score of negative nominations and positive nominations.

Based on "Dimensions and Types of Social Status: A Cross-Age Perspective" by J. D. Coie, K. A. Dodge, and H. Coppitelli, 1982, *Developmental Psychology, 18,* pp. 557–570.

Hymel (1984) observed that, following a session of positive and negative peer nominations, preschool children discussed whom they liked best, but not whom they disliked. Nor did children alter the way in which they interacted with one another after completing the peer nominations.

An all-positive approach to determining social status, developed by Asher and Dodge (1986), draws upon results of asking each student in a class to rate each other student on a 5-point scale of how much they like to play with that individual. This procedure is also referred to as the roster and ranking method (Roistacher, 1974). Students are provided with a list of their classmates' names and asked to rate the extent to which a presented statement (e.g., "like to work with," "like to play with," "like to sit next to") applies to each individual. Student scores are derived from the mean rating ascribed by peers.

A variation of the peer rating system has been used with kindergarten and first-grade students who may neither be able to read the names of the classmates, nor understand the nature of the rating task without additional assistance. Students are withdrawn from class individually to complete a peer rating and nomination procedure for his or her classmates (Asher, Singleton, Tinsley, & Hymel, 1979). Students are asked to sort pictures of their classmates, according to three categories depicted by representations of a smiling, neutral, or frowning face, indicating how much the child would like to play with the particular classmate. Conducting sociometric assessment in this manner is extremely time-consuming, and also requires prior parental and school permission to take photographs of the children (Bierman, 1987). Yet, without the use of photographs and time-consuming individual assistance, peer ratings of young children tend to be unreliable (Asher et al., 1979).

There is indication that peer rating and peer nomination procedures do not measure the same aspects of a child's social adjustment (Asher, 1985). Peer nomination seems to reflect how many peers regard the child as a friend, whereas peer rating is associated with the child's general acceptance within a group. In addition, peer rating is more sensitive to changes in status, and has a higher test–retest reliability (Putallaz & Gottman, 1983). It is probably wise to consider using both peer-rating procedures in combination to provide the richest depiction of a child's social adjustment.

**Advantages and Limitations.** Sociometric procedures tend to be reliable and valid measures of students' social competence. Children's social acceptance in kindergarten predicts teacher rating of their adjustment a year later (Ironsmith & Poteat, 1990). However, a number of limitations exist, particularly regarding sociometric measures completed by younger students. In addition to the high time demand and ethical concerns already discussed, there is a tendency for young students, as well as children with cognitive delays, to rate all of their classmates the same (McConnell & Odom, 1986). This limitation prompted Strain and Kohler (1988) to recommend that sociometric assessment not be conducted with preschool children.

Another limitation is that sociometric assessment does not lend itself to repeated measurement (Hymel & Rubin, 1985). As previously described, a child's social status is determined by converting nomination raw scores into standard scores for the class. Gains in a specific child's social adjustment would be overlooked if all students in a class increased their positive peer nominations, resulting in no change in the relative position of any individual, despite improvement in social functioning. Similarly, variations in class size would restrict comparing sociometric measurement from one school year to the next, and from one class to the next (Foster & Ritchey, 1979).

Another peer measure of social competence is referred to as peer assessment. In contrast to sociometric assessment, in which peers express their feelings toward classmates, in peer assessment students provide judgments about a peer's behavior (McConnell & Strain, 1986). *Class Play* (Bower, 1960), the *Shapiro Sociometric Role Assignment Test* (Shapiro & Sobel, 1981), and the *Pupil Evaluation Inventory* (Pekarik, Prinz, Liebert, Weintrub, & Neale, 1976) are examples of peer assessment measures.

## Self-Rating

Another measure of students' social competence can be obtained by asking children to rate their own social adjustment. A number of instruments have been designed to measure children's perceptions of their relationship to others. For instance, a commonly used self-rating measure is the *Perceived Competence Scale for Children* (Harter, 1982), on which third- to sixth-grade students rate the extent to which each of 40 statements applies to their own cognitive, social, and physical adjustment. This measure has been found to have adequate internal consistency reliability ($r = .73$ to $.86$) and test–retest reliability ($r = .69$ to $.87$). A separate version, using pictorial cues, has been developed for preschool and kindergarten students, with lower levels of reliability reported (Harter & Pike, 1984).

Another example of a self-report measure is the *Loneliness and Social Dissatisfaction Scale* (Asher & Wheeler, 1985). Children aged 8 to 12 years rate their endorsement of 24 self-descriptions of feelings of loneliness and social dissatisfaction. Items probe students' perceptions of loneliness, their current peer situation, their social competence, and their social adequacy. This measure has been found to be technically sound, with high internal consistency (Asher, Parkhurst, Hymel, & Williams, 1990). Recently, the *Loneliness and Social Dissatisfaction Scale* has been adapted for students in kindergarten and Grade 1 by changing the response format from a 5-point Likert scale to a yes–no–sometimes format (Cassidy & Asher, 1992).

# Intermeasure Agreement

One may expect that different measures of children's social competence should agree with one another. In other words, children who are rated as socially maladjusted by teachers should also be rejected by peers, perceive themselves to have social problems, and display behavior difficulties when observed. However, agreement among measures of social competence is more the exception than the rule.

## Teacher–Parent Rating Agreement

Adults in either the same house or the same classroom (e.g., teacher and teacher aide) tend to agree on their rating of children's behavioral adjustment. Achenbach, McConaughy, and Howell (1987) found that the average correlation coefficient among similar informants (teacher–teacher aide, mother–father) was approximately .60. In contrast, however, the average teacher–parent agreement was considerably lower, at .27. The authors assigned this difference in agreement levels to divergent perspectives of dissimilar informants, coupled with differential setting expectations, rather than as evidence of test unreliability.

Hinshaw et al. (1992) found that teacher ratings were more predictive of preschoolers' externalizing behaviors in school than were parents' ratings. On the other hand, based on direct observation measures, parents were more accurate than teachers in identifying socially isolated children.

## Teacher–Peer Rating Agreement

Another area of interest is agreement between teacher and peer ratings of student adjustment, which tends to be positive, although modest (Parker & Asher, 1987). For example, the correlation between teacher and peer ratings of both positive and negative peer nominations was reported as .50 and −.59

respectively (Landau, Milich, & Whitten, 1984). This result indicates considerable disagreement between peer and teacher judgment of students' social competence. The difference in perspective is understandable, given that teachers and peers are likely to hold dissimilar expectations of acceptable behaviors, and also have access to different contexts for observing children's behaviors.

Because of the high cost of sociometric peer assessment, it would be a great advantage to find a teacher measure of peer acceptance that could substitute for peer ratings. For instance, some investigators have identified socially rejected children by asking teachers to nominate them from their classes (Green, Foreman, Beck, & Vosk, 1980; Ollendick, Oswald, & Francis, 1989). In the Ollendick et al. (1989) study, teachers nominated popular, aggressive, or withdrawn fourth-grade students. Members of the resulting three groups of children were shown to differ on self-reports, peer sociometric nominations, and behavior observation, supporting claims for the accuracy of this cost-effective way of identifying children with social adjustment problems.

Ledingham, Younger, Schwartzman, and Bergeron (1982) took the comparison between peer and teacher ratings one step further to include self-ratings in the analysis. Groups of Grade 1, 4, and 7 students were rated on the *Pupil Evaluation Inventory* (Pekarik et al., 1976), by themselves, by their teachers, and by their classmates. Interrater agreement was consistently higher between peer and teacher ratings than between self-ratings and either of the other two measures.

# Conclusion

## IMPLICATIONS FOR BEST PRACTICE

■ Because of the divergence of measures, assessment information of students' social competence should be obtained from multiple sources, settings, and domains of social functioning.

■ Asking teachers to nominate the least socially active students is a reliable and more practical alternative to teacher rating measures.

■ Naturalistic observation, although time-intensive, is sensitive to tracking changes in students' social adjustment.

■ The use of sociometric measures may not be practical for use in kindergarten and first-grade classes.

■ In conducting sociometric assessment, both peer nomination and peer rating procedures should be used.

- ■ Social competence–enhancing interventions targeting classwide improvements should be evaluated by the collection of indicators of changes in the social functioning of the entire class.

- ■ Single-subject and single-classroom changes can be evaluated by a within-subject design.

- ■ The *Goal Attainment Scale* (Kiresuk & Lund, 1976) may be one of the most practical tools to evaluate changes in the social adjustment of students.

Information provided by different measures of students' social competence appears to tap different domains of children's functioning. Social competence is not a unitary concept, but one composed of multiple dimensions that may best be assessed by a combination of measures, including adult rating, sociometric rating, self-rating, and direct observation. Because of the divergence of these measures, assessment of social competence is most accurately assessed in a multimethod, multiagent approach (Walker, Irvin, Noell, & Singer, 1992). As illustrated in Figure 10.2, measures should be taken from a variety of settings and sources to provide a complete picture of a child's social competence.

Bagnato and Neisworth (1991) described a "convergent assessment model" for evaluating early intervention practices. They stated, "Convergent assessment refers to the synthesis of information gathered from several sources, instruments, settings, and occasions to produce the most valid appraisal of developmental status" (p. 57). Although this definition was used to describe early intervention measurement issues, it applies equally well to the measurement of children's social competence.

It is important to capture a complete picture of a child's social competence in different situations. Multiple domains of social competence need to be assessed, including aspects of a child's behavior, affect, and cognitive abilities. Multiple sources of information need to be tapped, including teachers, parents, peers, and the children themselves. Finally, assessment should be conducted across a variety of settings. Children's social behaviors may differ from the classroom to the playground, and from there to other environments.

## Assessing Class Social Competence

So far, the discussion has focused on measurement of social competence in individual children. Providing an intervention that targets enhanced social competence within entire classes of students might necessitate a change in the unit of assessment from single students to classes of students. In such a situation, measuring the social competence of every individual class member would be impractical.

One strategy for measuring class social competence is to sample the social functioning of a few students as indicators of the performance of the class as a whole. Using selected students to represent both the range and the mean of the class was a procedure instituted to estimate class functioning when considering the readiness of a child with disabilities for integration (Hundert, 1982; Salend, 1984). Within designated areas of functioning, teachers were asked to nominate the most competent student, the least competent student, and an average student. Assessment of the functioning of these three students was used to determine the range and mean of class functioning in the areas selected. It is important to note that this approach provides only a rough indication of class functioning.

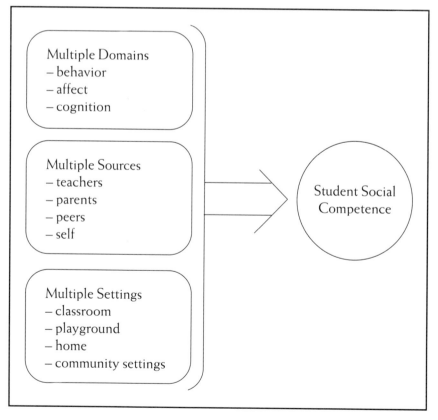

FIGURE 10.2. Multiple factors needed to assess student social competence.

Errors may certainly occur in teacher nominations. Even accurate nominations provide no information about the overall class distribution around the mean and within the provided range.

Another method of assessing class functioning involves asking the teacher to complete a social skills rating measure on the class as a whole. The teacher assesses the extent to which items on the measure apply to the class in general, rather than to any individual student. Results are used to generate a class profile of social functioning. Postintervention reassessment determines whether the teacher has perceived a change in classwide social functioning. Again in this case, because teacher rating instruments have been developed for the purpose of evaluating individual students, their use in measuring the competence of entire classes provides only a general indication rather than a detailed description.

## Evaluating the Effectiveness of an Intervention

Another assessment issue is how to measure the effects on students of a social competence–enhancing intervention. Addressing whether gains have occurred because of the introduction of a program rests on making two inferences from available information. The first is that positive change occurred in the social competence of children who received the intervention. The second is that this improvement can be attributed directly, at least in part, to the intervention administered. The first inference calls for quantifiable measures of students' social competence both before and after the intervention. Measures with the most promise for revealing changes in children's social competence over time are naturalistic observations and adult rating scales. As previously mentioned, sociometric assessment does not lend itself to repeated measures. Repeated observation of student behavior is also suited to single- or within-subject research designs. For a fuller explanation of this issue, the reader is directed to Odom's (1988) discussion of within-subject research design methodologies.

Within-subject designs, although rich in the information they provide, typically require the collection of reliable data repeatedly over a period of time, often based on naturalistic observation of student behaviors. For this reason, evaluation of intervention gains by direct measures of student behavior may not be feasible within the restraints of school-based evaluations.

Another option, consistent with the call by Kazdin (1993b) for practical evaluative procedures in applied settings, is the use of the *Goal Attainment Scale* (GAS), developed by Kiresuk and Lund (1976). The GAS has been used to evaluate outcomes of early intervention programs (Bailey & Simeonsson, 1988a; Simeonsson, Huntington, & Short, 1982). Before an intervention, a teacher (likely with others) would establish a few outcome goals, specifying five levels of possible attainment for each one, scaled along a continuum from least (−2) to most (+2) favorable outcome. An example of a hypothetical goal attainment scale for evaluating the impact of a social skills program on an entire class is illustrated in Table 10.6.

Using the GAS, teachers develop a progression scale based on their ideas of the important outcomes of an intervention, as well as attainment expectations. The class or an individual student's performance is rated both before and at various points after the intervention. Differential weightings can be attached to different goals, to reflect their relative contribution in the perception of overall success. In the hypothetical example shown in Table 10.6, the aggression goal was assigned a weighting of five, while the cooperation goal was assigned a weighting of three. Attained outcomes would be modified by the weightings to derive a global score of goal attainment. A standard score for the GAS can be calculated using a formula described by Kiresuk and Lund (1976) that would allow for the comparison of GAS scores across children, classes, or programs.

TABLE 10.6. Hypothetical Goal Attainment Scale for Class Outcome from a Social Skills Program

| SCALE ATTAINMENT LEVELS | SCALE 1: AGGRESSION (WEIGHTING = 5) | SCALE 2: COOPERATION (WEIGHTING = 3) |
|---|---|---|
| −2 Most unfavorable outcome likely | Aggressive act occurs five or more times each day | There are no examples of students cooperating during a week |
| −1 Less than expected | Aggressive act occurs three to five times each day | There are one or two examples of students cooperating during a week |
| 0 Expected level of success | Aggressive act occurs once or twice a day | There are three or four examples of students cooperating during a week |
| +1 More than expected success | Aggressive act occurs one or two times a week | There are one or two examples of students cooperating each day |
| +2 Best anticipated outcome | Aggressive act occurs three or fewer times a month | There are three or more examples of students cooperating each day |

The GAS may be one of the most useful teacher tools to evaluate the success of social competence–enhancing interventions. Because of the central involvement of teachers and others in defining not only the goals of an intervention but also the expected levels of attainment, the results may be likely to be understood and used.

Measurement of student social competence is still developing. The field needs assessment approaches that are practical for teachers to conduct while providing reliable information that influences program decisions. Time, costs, and technical complexities associated with the majority of assessment methods discussed in this chapter may exceed those that can be typically managed in classrooms. The *Goal Attainment Scale* is an approach within the reach of teachers that has the promise to pull together convergent information needed to understand students' social competence and to track the progress of children and classes.

# chapter 11

# Implementing Social Skills Interventions with Teachers

## ISSUES IN PRACTICE

- ■ What factors affect teachers' implementation of an intervention?
- ■ What types of implementation errors can be made?
- ■ What factors affect the likelihood that a teacher will adopt an intervention?
- ■ What factors affect the likelihood that a teacher will implement an intervention correctly?
- ■ What factors affect the likelihood that a teacher will persist with an intervention?
- ■ How do school administrative structures affect teacher implementation of an intervention?
- ■ How should a social competence–enhancing intervention be disseminated in schools?

Much of the research on the promotion of social competence in children has focused on ways to increase the effectiveness of therapeutic interventions. Although the effectiveness of an intervention is critical, it is insufficient by itself to ensure that the program has an impact on children's adjustment. An impeccably designed program for students' school behaviors will have no impact unless it is first put into practice by school staff, and second is implemented in a manner consistent with its design. McConnell, McEvoy, and Odom (1992) suggested that the impact of an intervention on children's behaviors across a variety of community settings is the product of both the *effectiveness* of the intervention (the extent to which it produces reliable changes in children's behavior) and the *likelihood of implementation* (the extent to which the intervention is implemented as designed). They expressed this relationship by the following formula:

Impact = Effectiveness × Likelihood of implementation.

In most studies of social skills interventions, procedures have been implemented by either experimenters or individuals provided by the experimenters, who are already skilled in the intervention procedures (Furman, Giberson, White, Gavin, & Wehner, 1989; McEvoy, Twardosz, & Bishop, 1990). As a result of studying interventions under ideal conditions, the factors that affect teacher implementation of interventions under less controlled conditions, more typical of school settings, are not well understood. Teachers may not be seen as having sufficient time or motivation to be the primary agents for implementing school-based social skills programs (e.g., Coie, Underwood, & Lochman, 1991).

This chapter examines factors affecting teacher implementation of social competence–enhancing interventions. Considered in the text are variables that influence teacher initial acceptance of an intervention, variables that contribute to the fidelity with which teachers implement an intervention, and variables that affect teacher continuity of an intervention.

Certainly, problems can occur in the translation of a planned intervention into action. Three types of implementation errors seem possible. First, teachers may choose not to implement intervention at all, regardless of its effectiveness. For example, only about 5% of materials covered in teacher lecture-based workshops were reported to be transferred to teachers' behaviors in classrooms (Joyce & Showers, 1983). Even when programs were mandatory, about a quarter of a group of teachers never implemented the initiative, even after 2 or 3 years (Hord, Rutherford, Huling-Austin, & Hall, 1987).

A second implementation error consists of teachers' adoption of an intervention, but not at the frequency or in the form that adheres to its design. Teachers frequently tend to pick and choose aspects of a program they like to implement and ignore other components (Durlak & Jason, 1984). In their discussion of common implementation errors associated with a classwide peer tutoring program, Greenwood, Carta, and Maheady (1991) indicated the need to implement the program at least four times a week, with all components intact, for students to benefit from the experience. In one study, teachers were found to omit important components of the procedure over time, resulting in a decline in student performance (Greenwood et al., 1984). With the introduction of methods to correct this "teacher drift," student performance returned to previously high levels.

A third type of implementation error occurs when teachers adopt an intervention, implement it correctly, but abandon the procedures too early to have sufficient impact on children. Weissberg, Caplan, and Harwood

(1991) estimated that a total of 40 to 50 hours of program implementation is required for a class-based social competence program to produce lasting effects on students. Social skills programs implemented over shorter periods may result in little or no impact.

To summarize, successful implementation of an intervention consists of:

■ Initial adoption of the intervention

■ Implementation with fidelity to design

■ Perseverance over a sufficiently long period of time

## What Factors Affect the Likelihood of Implementation?

Clearly, the effectiveness of an intervention is not a sufficient condition for its adoption by teachers (Odom, McConnell, & Chandler, 1993). Kazdin (1981), for instance, found no relationship between therapeutic effectiveness and the acceptability of child treatment techniques. In another investigation, elementary teachers were asked to rate the acceptability of 57 possible classroom strategies for dealing with students with learning or behavior problems (Johnson & Pugach, 1990). Interventions supported by research literature tended to be rated by teachers as less acceptable than strategies with unproven effectiveness, such as sending troublesome students to the principal.

Similar to teachers, clinicians also select treatment procedures for clients based on factors other than the effectiveness of the regime (Shamsie, 1981). This tendency extends to decision making by clinical managers as well. Asked to rank order factors that influence their decisions about the types of mental health services to provide, a sample of clinic managers rated empirical information about service effectiveness lower in importance than other factors, such as staff concerns about ease of implementation (Bigelow, 1975).

Witt and Elliott (1985) proposed a four-element working model of factors that influence successful treatment implementation:

1. Treatment acceptability

2. Treatment use

3. Treatment integrity

4. Treatment effectiveness

They suggested that the relationship among these four elements is both sequential and reciprocal; that is, not only does each element appear to affect teacher implementation of an intervention in the sequence indicated, but also each element affects every other one. For example, the more a teacher perceives an intervention as acceptable, the greater the probability of that teacher's using the intervention, and the more a teacher uses an intervention, the more likely he or she will view it as acceptable. Although this model has been criticized for being circular as well as untested (Peterson & McConnell, 1993), it does provide a framework for thinking about factors that influence implementation.

Factors affecting teacher implementation of social competence–enhancing interventions are considered in the remainder of this chapter for each of the three areas in which implementation errors can occur: initial intervention adoption, implementation integrity, and intervention continuity. Some studies have examined the extent to which individual differences in teachers have contributed to their judgment of intervention acceptability. For instance, the likelihood that a teacher will find an intervention acceptable varies inversely with the number of years of teacher experience (Witt & Robbins, 1985). Although at a conceptual level individual teacher differences may suggest an interesting variable to consider in planning the implementation of an intervention, this factor may lack direct practical implication, when consulting staff must deal effectively with *all* teachers, regardless of individual differences that may contribute to their acceptance of a proposed intervention.

## Factors Affecting Intervention Adoption

With the demands of educating a class of students, teachers tend to prefer less time-consuming interventions (Elliott, Witt, & Kratochwill, 1991; Witt, 1986) that do not require the aid of a specialist (Martens, Peterson, Witt, & Cirone, 1986). Witt (1986) cited the *Program for Academic Survival Skills* (Greenwood, Hops, et al., 1979) as an example of an intervention that meets the highest standards of methodology and effectiveness, but that requires too much teacher time to be feasible in classrooms. To ensure teachers' general acceptance, it must be possible to implement social competence–enhancing interventions with the time and resources typically available to teachers. Many, if not most, of the social skills programs that were described in Chapters 5 and 6 may not meet this criterion of acceptability. For example, in the *Child Development Project*, teachers were required to attend not only a week-long summer workshop, but also two meetings per month during the school year.

Another factor contributing to teachers' initial adoption of an intervention is the degree to which teachers perceive its congruence with standards of acceptable educational practice (Stein & Wang, 1988). The relationship between teachers' pedagogical beliefs and acceptance of an intervention was illustrated in a study of two groups of teachers who were shown an identical demonstration videotape of a behavior strategy for an elementary school class (Woolfolk & Woolfolk, 1979). In one group, the videotape was referred to as an example of "humanistic education"; in the second group, it was labeled "behavior modification." The humanistic label resulted in a more positive acceptability rating of the procedure portrayed than the behavior modification label.

The way in which an intervention is packaged also contributes to its acceptability (Weissberg & Allen, 1986). Weissberg, Caplan, and Sivo (1989) suggested that written manuals for school-based programs should be easy to follow and free of jargon.

## Factors Influencing Implementation Integrity

The difference between the actual and the intended way a strategy is put into place is a reflection of implementation integrity. Lack of intervention integrity was one of the factors cited by Kazdin (1993b) as contributing to poor treatment outcome in the field of child psychopathology. Despite increased awareness of this topic, however, studies tend not to report measures of intervention integrity. A review of articles published in a number of clinical journals from 1980 through 1988 found that over half essentially ignored this issue (Peterson, Homer, & Wonderlich, 1992).

The integrity with which an intervention is implemented is assumed to affect its effectiveness (Witt & Elliott, 1985). At the same time, the extent to which absolute integrity is necessary to ensure intervention effectiveness is unclear (Peterson & McConnell, 1993).

The integrity of teacher implementation of an intervention may be enhanced by specific forms of teacher training. One-shot, didactic workshops tend to produce little transfer of the workshop content into the classroom (Furman et al., 1989). Joyce and Showers (1983) found that teacher training programs that included elements of theory, demonstration, practice, and feedback produced skill acquisition in 80% of participants during the training sessions, but resulted in actual implementation in fewer than 5% of their classrooms. Classroom application of teacher training increased substantially when additional coaching was provided after the initial implementation period (Joyce & Showers, 1983). This result suggests that teacher training, regardless of its format, should be continued until teachers meet a performance criterion in their classrooms, indicating their mastery of the intervention procedures. For instance, in conducting the *Classwide Peer Tutoring Program*, teachers continued training until they could implement 90% of the performance criteria during a tutoring session (Greenwood, Carta, & Maheady, 1991).

An alternative strategy is to provide direct on-site coaching to teachers in their classrooms (e.g., Hundert & Taylor, 1993; Weissberg et al., 1989). The presence of a "facilitator" working alongside the teacher in implementing a classroom intervention has a number of advantages. The provision of on-site coaching avoids the cost and inconvenience of freeing teachers from classroom responsibilities to attend a workshop. It also allows teachers to observe the procedures being demonstrated with their own students. Through the modeling, feedback, and discussions that would ensue, teachers acquire mastery of the intervention components being introduced. Moreover, teachers prefer the help of an on-site consultant over more traditional workshop formats (Myles & Simpson, 1989).

In the provision of on-site coaching, the distinction between teacher training and teacher consultation becomes blurred. Several models of teacher consultation have been described, each representing a different theoretical or knowledge base (e.g., Polsgrove & McNeil, 1989; Tindal, Shinn, & Rodden-Nord, 1990; West & Idol, 1987). Table 11.1 describes the most common consultative models. As shown, the behavioral, mental health, and organizational development models differ both in the nature of consultant–consultee relationships formed and in the knowledge base on which the consultation is approached.

A meta-analysis conducted on 54 controlled studies indicated that consultation had an effect size of 0.47 (Medway & Updyke, 1985). This result reveals that the average recipient of consultation showed changes greater than 68% of individuals not receiving consultation. None of the models shown in Table 11.1 demonstrated greater effects than any of the others.

In addition to its theoretical orientation, consultation can be categorized by the nature of the relationship between consultant and consultee. In an expert model of consultation, a hierarchical relationship exists between consultant and consultee, with advice flowing from the consultant to the consultee. The major responsibility for solving the problem rests with the consultant, while responsibility for implementing the consultant's solution rests with the consultee. In either a collegial (Phillips & McCullough, 1990) or collaborative (Graden, 1989) consultative model, the consultant and consultee share responsibility for solving the problem

TABLE 11.1. Comparison of Behavioral, Mental Health, and Organizational Development Consultation Models

| MODEL | THEORY FOR CONSULTATION RELATIONSHIP | KNOWLEDGE BASE |
|---|---|---|
| Behavioral | Assumes that knowledge of behavioral approaches will help solve problems | Behavioral programming, social learning theory, applied behavior analysis |
| Mental Health | Assumes that consultee has capacity to solve most problems. Emphasis on consultee's feelings | Psychodynamic, clinical skills, diagnosis, decision making |
| Organizational | Goal is the improved functioning of the organizational system | Organizational change, process, developing communication, problem solving |

Adapted from "School Consultation: Part I. An Interdisciplinary Perspective on Theory, Models, and Research" by J. F. West and L. Idol, 1987, *Journal of Learning Disabilities, 20*, pp. 388–408.

through a blending of expertise in an atmosphere of mutual trust and respect. The following is a definition that captures the collaborative nature of this exchange: "Consultation is usually a process based upon an equal relationship characterized by mutual trust and open communication, joint approaches to problem identification, the pooling of personal resources to identify and select strategies that will have some probability of solving the problem that has been identified, and shared responsibility in the implementation and evaluation of the program or strategy that has been initiated" (Brown, Wyne, Blackburn, & Powell, 1979, p. 8). Teachers prefer the collaborative consultative model most and the expert consultative model least (Babcock & Pryzwansky, 1983).

A collaborative consultation approach also has been used in training teachers to consult with one another on behavior and learning problems (Pugach & Johnson, 1990). In this "peer collaboration consultation," teachers are taught to ask clarifying questions to explore factors that may be contributing to any problem situation the initiating teacher faces. The "facilitator" teacher would ask the initiating teacher probing questions, typically beginning with the phrase, "What question can you ask yourself about . . . ?"

By encouraging the initiating teacher to engage in reflective behavior, the presenting problem is clarified. The next step is for teachers to summarize the insights that emerged in the previous clarification phase. Next, the initiating teacher generates interventions to address the identified variables contributing to the problem. Finally, the initiating teacher develops a plan for tracking the implementation of the plan.

Teachers who received peer collaboration training were successful in resolving 85% of the problems they raised, reduced their number of referrals to special services, and increased both their positive attitudes to school and their tolerance for children with cognitive deficits (Pugach & Johnson, 1990).

Having teachers involved in deriving their own solutions to problems increases their commitment to these plans (Idol & West, 1987; York & Vandercook, 1990). Moreover, a collaborative process ensures that teachers are in a position to fit the intervention to the ecology of their school setting (Weissberg et al., 1989). As described by Phillips and McCullough (1990), "Schools are more likely to adopt, implement and maintain a format that they perceive to be compatible with current infrastructure— existing building, routines, resources and philosophy—than a format which dramatically deviates from building norms" (p. 299).

The collaborative approaches described are all based on the premise that teachers possess competencies to solve student problems they face in class. Although the success of the collaborative approach testifies to the validity of this orientation, it does raise the question of why competent teachers need any consultation at all. One possibility is that teachers have good ideas for solving problems but lack support to implement them (Elliott et al., 1991). Pugach and Johnson (1990) stated that lack of teacher support may stem historically from consultation approaches that diminish the teacher's role in deriving solutions and minimize teachers' sense of problem ownership. If this is the case, it may be more helpful to assist teachers to identify and overcome these barriers than to focus energy on deriving solutions for children's presenting problems.

Another possibility is that teachers have both good and poor ideas, but cannot discriminate between the two. Planning structures may be needed to guide teachers in determining which of their programming ideas are more worthwhile than others. It is interesting that many collaborative approaches to teacher consultation (e.g., Hundert & Hopkins, 1992; Peck, Killen, & Baumgart, 1989; Pugach & Johnson, 1990) have included the use of written or verbal cues that elicit teacher programming ideas. These cues may guide teachers in selecting optimal ideas, without providing program solutions.

Maintaining the integrity of a teacher-implemented intervention may require a double-stranded process of (a) monitoring to ensure that it is implemented as designed and (b) providing teachers with feedback on their degree of program adherence (Stein & Wang, 1988; Wang & Zollers, 1990). In this way, monitoring not only documents the extent to which teachers meet established criteria for the frequency and accuracy of program use, but also provides information to correct implementation errors and strengthen adherence to program procedures. However, monitoring also raises issues of teacher tolerance for evaluative observation, as well as time demands on personnel assigned as monitors.

The monitoring process may take a number of forms. As an example, an observer may compare teacher implementation of a program to developed criteria and provide feedback on the results. For instance, preschool teachers implementing kindergarten survival skill interventions were observed by consultants who informed them of the percentage of program components correctly achieved (Peterson & McConnell, 1993). Additional training and consultation were provided until teachers reached a goal of 85% of components correctly implemented.

Another way to monitor teacher program implementation is for teachers themselves to track their adherence to an intervention plan. An example of the checklist used by teachers implementing the *Classwide Social Skills Program* (Hundert & Taylor, 1993) is shown in Table 11.2. Monitoring that relies on teachers' self-reporting may be more practical and acceptable, but less precise than consultant feedback.

Moncher and Prinz (1991) suggested that determining a method for monitoring treatment fidelity be based on consideration of three factors:

1. The implementer's comfort level regarding direct observation

2. The accuracy of the information needed

3. The resources available

Combining teachers' self-monitoring with periodic observation and feedback by a consultant may provide the optimal balance among these three factors.

On the surface, the documenting of implementation integrity may appear inconsistent with a collaborative perspective, which invites teachers to provide direct input to program design modifications. In theory, how can adherence be maintained to a program that may be evolving? Perhaps the answer lies in differentiating necessary program components that cannot be changed without jeopardizing the effectiveness of the intervention from less crucial components that may be modified without lessening its impact. Moncher and Prinz (1991) expressed this issue as the

TABLE 11.2. Teacher Checklist for Daily Implementation of the
*Classwide Social Skills Program*

| LESSON | YES | NO | THROUGHOUT THE SCHOOL DAY | YES | NO |
|---|---|---|---|---|---|
| Did you have all the material you needed ready? | ___ | ___ | Did you prompt individual children to practice the desired social skills? | ___ | ___ |
| Did you read at least two home notes? | ___ | ___ | Did you provide instruction to practice the skill during opportunities that arise in the day? | ___ | ___ |
| Did you review the previous lesson (skill and skill components) and solicit at least one example of a student's application of the skill at home or school? | ___ | ___ | Did you award rays of sunshine throughout the day, and explain to children why they earned the rays? | ___ | ___ |
| Did you introduce a new social skill using adult–adult puppet play? | ___ | ___ | Did you praise children's social skills when they occurred? | ___ | ___ |
| Did you solicit the skills components using cue cards? | ___ | ___ | When you praised, did you describe the behavior that was praiseworthy? | ___ | ___ |
| Did you have children practice identifying the skill components by an adult–adult inappropriate presentation of skill? | ___ | ___ | For mild behavior problems, did you use planned ignoring? | ___ | ___ |
| Did you have one or two child–adult role plays to practice the skill? | ___ | ___ | | | |
| Did you have one or two child–child role plays to practice the skill? | ___ | ___ | | | |
| Did you select about five children to wear badges? | ___ | ___ | | | |

need to reach a balance between the structure and the flexibility of an intervention. Sufficient flexibility is required so that teachers may adapt a program to their class ecology, while its basic structure must be protected to avoid compromising effectiveness. An analogy may be found in identifying the critical ingredients for baking bread. Although yeast, flour, and water may be necessary ingredients, a range of other components (e.g., cheese, caraway seeds, type of flour) can be added or modified to taste, without changing the product as bread.

Training, consulting, monitoring, and feedback may all contribute to teachers' increased sense of efficacy in implementing an intervention. Moreover, teachers' self-efficacy has been found to predict which teachers are most receptive to implementation of new instructional procedures (Guskey, 1988), most willing to refer students to special services (Meyer & Foster, 1988), and most likely to engage in particular instructional practices (Gibson & Dembo, 1984). Stein and Wang (1988) proposed that teacher perception of self-efficacy in implementing a new practice is an important factor that contributes to successful adoption of ideas.

## Factors Affecting Teachers' Continued Intervention Implementation

After teachers decide to adopt an intervention and do so in ways consistent with its design, another potential source of implementation error is their premature abandonment of the program. Maintaining a continued intervention focus is particularly challenging, given the competing demands on teachers' time and priorities. Continued implementation may depend on the availability of support from both administration and other teachers at the school.

**Administrative Support.** Although central administration at the board level may play a critical role in supporting an intervention, most references to the importance of administrative support have focused on the role of the school principal. For instance, both cooperation and support of principals were judged as essential to the implementation of the *Prereferral Intervention Project,* in which teachers received consultation from a school-based team on ways of dealing with children with learning or behavior problems (Graden, Casey, & Bonstrom, 1985). Likewise, the principal's support was viewed as critical in the implementation of an inservice training to school personnel on strategies to educate students with severe disabilities in integrated settings (Thousand, Nevin-Parta, & Fox, 1987).

Yet, when a principal's support is unavailable, or even provided tacitly, teachers may be unlikely to initiate, let alone continue, a new intervention (Polsgrove & McNeil, 1989). In one study, the most common reason teachers gave for rejecting a particular learning or behavior problem intervention was their perception that it was either discouraged by school administration or inconsistent with school rules (Johnson & Pugach, 1990).

Furman et al. (1989) detailed a failing attempt to introduce a strategy for enhancing student peer relationships in two schools. In one school, where teachers participated in workshops and received individual consultation on the intervention, all participating teachers implemented the program. In contrast, teachers from the second school immediately expressed opposition to the project, claiming the time commitment to be excessive. The authors assigned the failure of this implementation to the fact that the principal in the second school was not actively involved in the project.

Principals are in key positions to set the climate for interventions at a school. However, a principal's general endorsement of an idea will have little impact on teacher commitment unless it is accompanied by *active* and *visible* participation in aspects of the project (Stein & Wang, 1988). For example, Graden et al. (1985) reported difficulty implementing the *Prereferral Intervention Project* when principals verbalized their support but did not allocate sufficient time for consultants to provide required services. More specifically, Phillips and McCullough (1990) suggested that principals can influence the success of an intervention by "a) clear communication of program purpose, goals and expectations; b) promotion of a climate in which collaborative consultation is valued; and c) provision of leadership in management strategies which facilitate program implementation and maintenance" (p. 297).

**Teacher–Teacher Support.** Another potential source of teacher support can be derived from one another. Teachers may highly value the advice offered by other teachers, whom they would view as understanding the practical issues involved in implementing an intervention in their classes. Arranging opportunities for teachers to discuss implementation issues may not only encourage this support but also increase teacher agreement on ways to approach student behavior problems at the school.

Weissberg et al. (1989) arranged bimonthly meetings with teachers to discuss their reactions to implementing a social competence promotion program, as well as to present additional learning experiences. Teachers observed live modeling or videotapes of effective strategies, role-played lessons, and received feedback. Similar teacher–teacher discussion meetings were used by Hundert and Taylor (1993) in implementing the *Classwide Social Skills Program*. Although a series of ongoing meetings may be necessary for the teachers implementing an intervention, orientation of all school staff in the procedures would enlist support from others who may not be directly involved (Greenwood, Carta, & Maheady, 1991).

Encouraging teacher–teacher support does not lessen the importance of obtaining active principal support. In fact, both the quality and the quantity of teacher–teacher support that is fostered in any particular school may depend in turn on the support of the principal. Berman and

McLaughlin (1976) showed evidence that teachers who felt supported by their principal were better able to support one another.

# Conclusion

## IMPLICATIONS FOR BEST PRACTICE

■ At least as much effort should be devoted to understanding and optimizing factors that affect teacher implementation of an intervention as is devoted to understanding and optimizing factors affecting program effectiveness.

■ An intervention must be able to be implemented with the time and resources typically available to a teacher.

■ An intervention must be perceived as congruent with a teacher's views of acceptable educational practices.

■ An intervention should be "packaged" to be easy to follow and jargon-free.

■ Teacher instruction in an intervention should involve on-site modeling, coaching, and feedback.

■ Teacher consultation should be collaborative and encourage teacher input into the program design.

■ Teachers should self-monitor their implementation of an intervention against provided criteria and receive periodic feedback from a consultant.

■ Teachers should be informed of which components of an intervention can and cannot be modified.

■ The active and visual support of principals for an intervention must be encouraged.

■ Interventions should be presented as prototypes that should be adapted by teachers within given parameters.

■ School system policies, procedures, and positions of responsibility need to be developed for longer term continuation of an intervention.

Any intervention, no matter how well conceived, will have little impact unless it is implemented at least with minimal precision. The initial adoption of a social skills intervention, the integrity of its implementation, and its continuation over time are all affected by a number of factors, summarized in a decision flowchart shown in Figure 11.1. In general, factors that influence teacher implementation of an intervention can be collapsed into

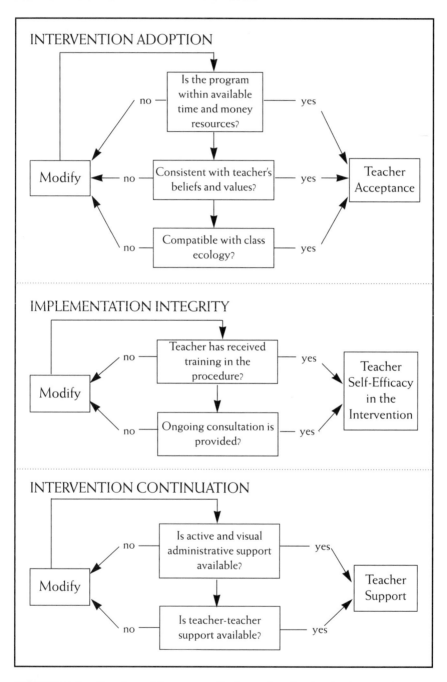

**FIGURE 11.1.** Flowchart of factors contributing to the adoption, implementation integrity, and continuation of an intervention.

three major variables: (a) teacher perceptions of the acceptability of an intervention, (b) teacher self-efficacy in implementing the intervention, and (c) supports available for continued teacher implementation of an intervention.

School consultants tend to provide special services to high caseloads of students with identified learning and/or behavior problems. Helping teachers implement a social skills program may require consultants to spend more time in classrooms, modeling and coaching teachers in the intervention procedures. This shift in consultant duties requires administrative support, lack of which was identified as a key barrier in the shift of consultants' role in implementing a prereferral system (Graden et al., 1985; Idol-Maestas & Ritter, 1985).

Another barrier to changing the role of school consultants is the historic separation between special and general education. Consultation resources tend to be allocated to a discrete and separate special education system and are typically not available for early intervention projects in general education streams. The dichotomy of special and general education services has prompted a call for their unification (Stainback & Stainback, 1984).

A major implication of focusing on factors influencing teacher implementation of interventions is the importance of treating teachers as prime change agents and central figures in the change effort (Graden, 1989; Greer, 1989). The goal of consultation should be to enable teachers to deal effectively with an increased range of student problems without having to rely on specialists. This type of relationship between teacher and consultant is consistent with Albee's (1968) dictum that psychology needs to give its knowledge away to others.

Finally, consultants will need to conceptualize ways of involving staff at all levels in the planning and decision-making process (Phillips & McCullough, 1990). Issues of initial acceptance of an intervention, logistics of implementation, and resource allocation are ones that affect teachers, principals, and central administrators alike. Weissberg et al. (1989) recommended that, before implementing a new school-based program, developers "obtain information about: a) the school system and local community for potential resources and supports as well as barriers and resistance to a proposed innovation; b) receptivity to and concerns about involvement with the effort; c) ensure that top-level district officials in the system are aware of and support the innovation and its goals; and d) identify personnel in the system to serve as within-system advocates of the innovation" (p. 287).

This last point may be particularly important. With the mobility of school personnel, the continuation of an intervention may rest upon its embeddedness in the administrative structures of the organization. It may be necessary to identify a specific individual in the system to guide the implementation of the project. Similarly, policies regarding who should use the intervention under what conditions may need to be developed in order to clarify responsibilities and expectations of all concerned (Graden et al., 1985).

A number of research results have demonstrated the effectiveness of various social skills interventions that may never find their way into common classroom practices. This fact prompted the following statement from McConnell et al. (1992): "results presented here would suggest that without some change in research dissemination, or service delivery systems, this empirical work will have little practical effect on intervention programs" (p. 299).

One difficulty may be the process by which interventions are disseminated. Traditionally, interventions are developed with primary consideration to the specific treatment variables that render the program effective. An intervention may be tested under controlled and optimal conditions. Dissemination often consists of providing information to potential consumers about the product in its final form.

The program product dissemination approach, described in Table 11.3, has two major drawbacks. First, the intervention is initially designed and tested without consideration of factors affecting its general acceptability, and therefore the likelihood of its adoption in the field. This strategy leaves consumers out of the process of program development. Exactly this situation was described as a problem for the "marketing" of behavior analysis. Bailey (1991), for instance, contended that behavior analysis has failed to consider consumer input in the development of its approaches and therefore has not had high impact in the field. He stated, "First, we did not do the front-end analysis with potential consumers to discover exactly what they were looking for, what form it should take, how it should be packaged and delivered and so forth" (p. 446).

A second drawback to traditional intervention dissemination procedures is that potential consumers (teachers, in this case) are asked to implement a program presented in its final form. Even with features that are known to be generally acceptable, compatibility of the intervention to all possible school settings is unlikely unless the intervention invites opportunities for adaptation. Teachers need the control necessary to fit an intervention to the specific circumstances or their own classrooms.

TABLE 11.3. Comparison of Program Product and Program Prototype
Dissemination Strategies

| DEVELOPMENT | TESTING | DISSEMINATION |
|---|---|---|
| PROGRAM PRODUCT DISSEMINATION | | |
| A program is designed from variables that enhance the likelihood of program effectiveness. | The product is tested under optimal conditions. | Potential consumers are invited to adopt the program as a final product. |
| PROGRAM PROTOTYPE DISSEMINATION | | |
| A prototype of a program is designed from variables that enhance the likelihood of program effectiveness *and* acceptability. | The prototype is tested under natural conditions. | Potential consumers are invited to modify then adopt the prototype. |

A more effective intervention dissemination process may be similar to both the "translative research model" described by Odom (1988) and the social marketing approach articulated by Winett, Moore, and Anderson (1991). In translative research, research and theoretical findings are converted to practical intervention techniques and tested in classroom settings before being exposed to consumers. In social marketing, one invites potential consumers of a product to test an "early facsimile" of the intervention being developed (Winett et al., 1991). In both processes, intervention development and testing take into consideration factors that influence consumer acceptance of the project. Only interventions demonstrated to have a high likelihood of being implemented are evaluated, and the evaluation is conducted under natural conditions in community settings.

Despite care in designing interventions to fit the needs of potential consumers, there still must be a mechanism for adapting the intervention to individual classroom needs. Even if extensively tested and refined, a program should be presented as a *prototypic* intervention, rather than a final product, with teachers invited to make modifications within specified parameters. For example, in the *Classwide Social Skills Program* (Hundert & Taylor, 1993), we felt that a system to both cue students of the target social skill and prompt teachers to provide feedback was a critical ingredient to the intervention. In our "prototype," we translated this feature into "sunshine badges," which students wore throughout the school day. Teachers were asked to praise all students who were using social skills and to place a "ray of sunshine" (made with a yellow marker) on the badge.

Teachers who felt uncomfortable with this procedure were invited to use a different reinforcement system, as long as it met the specified criteria of including visual cues to promote use of target social skills and potent teacher reinforcement. This approach to developing and disseminating an intervention prototype is described in Table 11.3.

A strategy to influence successful teacher implementation of a social skill intervention may need to draw upon a combination of ideas presented in this chapter. Factors influencing teacher adoption, intervention integrity, and continuation of intervention are interconnected (Witt & Elliott, 1985). For instance, one may provide consultation to assist teachers initially to implement an intervention, but the continuation of the intervention may depend on such administrative structures as intervention policies and consultative support provided on an ongoing basis.

# chapter 12

# Schools, Prevention, and Change

## ISSUES IN PRACTICE

■ What is the rationale for shifting services to promotion of social competence in all children?

■ How are schools suitable locales for social competence–building programs?

■ What factors are associated with successful attempts at the promotion of social competence in schools?

■ What conditions assist schools in delivering social competence–enhancing programs?

■ What are barriers to school adoption of these programs?

■ What factors affect schools' responses to change efforts?

■ How can change come about in schools to assist the adoption of social competence interventions?

Concerns about childhood violence are consuming a great deal of society's attention, usually at a point well after its effects have taken their toll. There is no sign that aggression in childhood is lessening—in fact, it appears to be increasing. In the United States, arrests of youths under 18 for murder and non-negligent manslaughter have increased by an astounding 60% from 1981 to 1990, compared with a 5.2% increase in arrest rates for individuals over 18 during this same time period (Federal Bureau of Investigation, 1991). More and more, juveniles are becoming responsible for a disproportionate number of the crimes committed in today's society (Farrington, 1986).

Although a relatively small percentage of children and youth are arrested for criminal behavior, many more struggle to adjust in society. An estimated half of the child population has been deemed at some degree of risk for unemployment, violence, school failure, and substance abuse (Task Force on Education of Young Adolescents, 1989). Society seems to be producing a generation of children who lack the academic, social, and coping skills to fulfill the demands of employment, develop meaningful relationships, and achieve personal contentment. The problem of so many maladjusted children consuming so many resources and causing so much grief to others may elude society's efforts at resolution, if it continues unabated. Society needs to judge how best to approach the issue of childhood maladjustment, not only in dealing with troubled individuals, but also in preventing maladjustment in others.

There is little reason to expect that clinic-based treatment alone will lessen maladjustment in the child population. The vast majority of children with behavior and emotional problems do not access mental health clinics (Offord et al., 1987). Even if more children were referred for treatment, insufficient numbers of professionals are available to provide individual therapy to all of those in need (Weissberg, Caplan, & Harwood, 1991). Moreover, although individual treatment may be beneficial for some children, many others either drop out of therapy prematurely or do not benefit greatly from the help. As expressed by Weissberg et al. (1991), "one could argue that a major proportion of our scarce mental health resources is being devoted too late and in a cost-inefficient manner toward a small segment of people who may show few benefits" (p. 831). Hopes of dealing with maladjustment in the child population seem to lie in either removing its causes or blocking its effects before they impair children's healthy growth (Consortium on the School-Based Promotion of Social Competence, 1991; Mulvey, Arthur, & Reppucci, 1993; Yoshikawa, 1994; Zigler, Taussig, & Black, 1992).

Yoshikawa (1994) suggested two developmental pathways leading to long-term prevention of antisocial and delinquent behaviors. One path is through strengthening parent–child relationships and family functioning; the other is through promoting children's cognitive and social competence in settings such as schools. The choice of schools as desirable settings for primary prevention and intervention is shared by others in the field (Kazdin, 1993b; Weissberg, 1990). In fact, a group of prominent authorities on the topic have formed a consortium to advocate for school-based social competence–building interventions (Consortium on School-Based Promotion, 1991). They suggest four themes to guide school's efforts in this area:

1. "Comprehensive social competence promotion should be an integral part of school curricula."

2. "For best results, curriculum efforts must be complemented by efforts at the school and community levels."

3. "There is a prevention technology and there are outcome data. When selecting programs, look for both."

4. "Implementation is a complex process. Educators need
   to collaborate with preventionists through preservice,
   inservice, and other professional development programs."
   (pp. 302, 303)

This chapter will consider the advantages of working with schools to promote social competence in children and the features of successful school effects in this endeavor. Also considered are factors that support and hinder adoption of social competence–enhancing interventions by schools. Finally, there is a discussion of school change efforts.

# School-Based Promotion of Social Competence

The remainder of this chapter describes the ways in which schools may be able to provide interventions to promote social competence in students. Not only is it important to explore how such interventions can be designed, but it is also critical to consider factors that affect the adoption of those interventions. There are significant challenges to school adoption and implementation of social competence–enhancing interventions, some that may call for substantial changes in the organization of schools. The following sections describe some of these challenges.

## Schools as Settings to Promote Social Competence

Schools offer a number of advantages as settings in which to promote social competence. First, they constitute one of the few locations with access to the majority of children 5 years of age and up. In any given year, about 9 out of every 10 children in society can be found in school (Coie et al., 1993). A second advantage of schools is that student academic and cognitive competence may be targeted alongside social competence (Johnson, Jason, & Betts, 1990; Yoshikawa, 1994). Academic deficits and school failure have been identified as factors in the causal pathway toward childhood maladjustment (Loeber & Dishion, 1983; Robins, 1966). Low verbal and cognitive processing abilities place children at a disadvantage for both school and social success (Yoshikawa, 1994). Helping children with maladjustment may best come about by focusing on both social and academic development.

Finally, schools also provide an environment that can be structured to encourage and reinforce the use of newly acquired social skills (Weissberg & Allen, 1986). The importance of meaningful opportunities for children to practice new skills has been identified as an important component of any successful social skills program (Bierman, 1986; Hawkins & Weis, 1985).

## Promotion of Social Competence in Schools

Given that schools may be a logical setting in which to provide social competence–enhancing programs, how should these strategies be designed? Most school-based prevention efforts have consisted of brief, single-component interventions, which may produce short-term behavior gains but are unlikely to result in lasting benefits (Weissberg et al., 1991). In contrast, successful strategies for the prevention of children's maladjustment seem to have in common the features discussed in the following paragraphs.

**Broad base.** Because children's behaviors unfold in multiple contexts (e.g., school, home, community), each of which may be associated with specific risk factors leading to maladjustment, prevention efforts may need to involve multiple socializing agents in multiple settings (Coie et al., 1993; Mulvey et al., 1993; Weissberg et al., 1991; Yoshikawa, 1994). Prevention programs should not only equip children with new social competence, but also help to structure environments to support children's use of these skills.

**Early start.** Risk factors accumulate to increase the trajectory toward childhood maladjustment (Coie et al., 1993; Mulvey et al., 1993). Therefore, it is important to begin prevention programs at a point early enough in a child's development to prevent multiple risk factors from interacting.

The first 5 years of a child's life have been identified as particularly sensitive in the establishment of a positive parent–child relationship (Yoshikawa, 1994). Programs that can strengthen a family's capacity to enhance the healthy development of young children are suggested as worthwhile prevention strategies (Rutter, 1980).

However, recognition of the importance of early intervention does not negate the need for both prevention and intervention efforts during school-age years (Kazdin, 1987). A comprehensive prevention strategy that targets parent–child relationships before the child enters school and continues to address positive peer relationships in school may have greater impact than either focus alone.

**Combined universal and high-risk prevention programs.** One prevention strategy is to expose virtually all children to an intervention that reduces the risk for maladjustment (Kazdin, 1993a). For instance, the class-wide and schoolwide social skills programs described in Chapter 6, delivered to all students in hopes of increasing their resilience to later life stressors, are examples of universal programs. Other prevention programs specifically target only those children at high risk of maladjustment by virtue of their exposure to severe or multiple risk factors. For instance, specific prevention programs have targeted children in inner-city schools, children experiencing stressful life events such as divorce of their parents (Pedro-Carroll, Cowen, Hightower, & Guare, 1986), and children in transition from elementary to middle school (Felner, Ginter, & Primavera, 1982). A combination of the two prevention strategies—universal and specifically targeted—may hold out the best promise for addressing childhood maladjustment.

A program that is universally delivered to all children may serve as a "safety net" to catch maladjusted children missed by targeted interventions. Moreover, the prior implementation of a universal program may help the generalization of targeted interventions to the classroom. Furthermore, a universal program alone may not be sufficiently potent to help those children at highest risk for maladjustment who may need the more intensive programming available through a targeted intervention.

## Conditions Necessary for School Adoption of Social Competence–Enhancing Interventions

The introduction of a social competence–building intervention over multiple years would be a significant undertaking that may exceed the capacities of many schools. Such a venture would require significant adjustments in how many schools are prepared to deal with student behaviors. For instance, it has been suggested that social competence promotion be included in school curricula (Consortium on School-Based Promotion, 1991). This suggestion would entail the development and adoption of new curricular materials to be used by teachers. Moreover, teacher time constraints would demand this new material to either displace or be integrated with existing curriculum. Introduction of new instructional content would need to be offset by a corresponding reduction in other instructional areas.

A second factor affecting school-based adoption of social competence intervention is the existence of policies and procedures that identify what is expected of teachers. Educators must know how much time to devote to social skills, what curriculum guidelines to follow, and how to evaluate student achievement. Without active administrative direction, it is unlikely that social skills curriculum would be implemented in the classroom (Hord, Rutherford, Huling-Austin, & Hall, 1987).

Accompanying the need for administrative direction is the provision of teacher consultation and training in the implementation of new classroom procedures. Chapter 11 provided an overview of the types of teacher supports deemed necessary to assist in initial program acceptance, correct implementation, and intervention maintenance.

Interventions should also allow teachers to adjust programs to fit their particular classroom situations. A balance must to be struck between ensuring fidelity to critical program ingredients and providing latitude to teachers in modifying the program within provided parameters to fit the characteristics of the classroom.

## Barriers to School Adoption of Social Competence–Enhancing Interventions

A number of factors challenge the adoption of school-based interventions to promote social competence in students. The most common barriers are summarized under headings of legitimacy of focus, ethic of intrinsic goodness, administrative impediments, and overfocus on individuals in need.

**Legitimacy of focus.** The prevention of social-emotional problems in students may not be seen as a priority for education, or at least may be considered of secondary importance to academic and cognitive development. In fact, the majority of curriculum innovations have been directed at cognitive and academic goals, to the neglect of goals for personal or social development (Fullan, 1982).

Forecasts of skills needed to prepare students for the 21st century have included getting along with others, behaving ethically, and developing long-term interpersonal relationships (Consortium on School-Based Promotion, 1991). In fact, the National Mental Health Association (1986) recommended that curricula from preschool through high school should include social competence–building programs. Nonetheless, helping students acquire enhanced social competence may be a goal that has not yet been fully embraced by schools. As long as meeting the social-emotional needs of children is viewed primarily as a matter for social and mental health agencies, rather than schools, educators will be reluctant to devote the attention warranted by the extent of this problem.

**Ethic of intrinsic goodness.** Carter (1983) described "the ethic of intrinsic goodness" as a tendency to judge an organization's commitment to a social cause by the size of its expenditure, regardless of how well those resources translate into effective solutions. Judging the value of a school's attempts to deal with childhood maladjustment by the size rather than the impact of the effort makes projects very vulnerable to be driven by political whims. Education has been criticized for its susceptibility to premature and excessive adoption of questionable educational programs on the one hand, and its neglect of sound programs on the other (Sarason, 1990).

**Administrative impediments.** In the upper regions of school system administration, where financial decisions are made, there may be little direct appreciation of the social and emotional issues facing students (Marcus & Olley, 1988). In one study, Alberta school superintendents reported that they spent only about 7% of their time with teachers, and 1% in classrooms observing students (Duigan, 1979). The majority of their time is divided between meetings and dealing with such administrative matters as policies and finances.

Not only are administrators distanced from the students, but they are also highly affected by administrative structure (Fullan, 1982). Some ideas in organizations are raised more easily than others (Sarason, 1990). Organizations tend to promote a collective and uniform understanding of issues, with dissenting views discouraged (Morgan, 1986; Sitkin, 1992). Attempts to introduce innovations in schools, especially those that may be perceived as unconventional or costly, are not likely to be supported unless they show compatibility with a political agenda (Fullan, 1982).

**Overfocus on individuals in need.** The service delivery system for children with maladjustment has been accused of spending scarce resources too late and of focusing attention on too few children, who may not even benefit from treatment (Weissberg, 1990). By narrowing the focus of services mainly to those who have already succumbed to disorders, professionals may not adequately meet the needs of the broader child population, many of whom are at risk but have not yet developed maladjustment.

From an epidemiological perspective (Winett, Moore, & Anderson, 1991), treatment providers need to search for interventions that have sufficient impact on the social and emotional development of children, to lessen the incidence of maladjustment in the child population. Of assistance in this search is a determination of the incidence of a disorder, the strength of association between risk factors and morbidity, and the proportion of the target population affected by individual risk factors (population-attributable risk) (Jeffrey, 1989).

In the case of childhood maladjustment, population-focused interventions often try to insulate large groups of children from the effects of risk factors that may promote maladjustment. Responding one-by-one to individuals already in need will not produce sufficient impact to lower the rate of maladjustment in the child population, for the reasons discussed earlier in this book.

The idea of needing to expose a sufficient proportion of the general child population to effects of risk factors provides an additional element to the formula proposed by McConnell, McEvoy, and Odom (1992), in identifying factors that determine whether a program has an impact. They argued that intervention impact is a product of two elements: effectiveness and likelihood of implementation. They also suggested that factors affecting program implementation (e.g., ease of use, implementers' proficiency in the procedures) differ from factors determining program effectiveness.

In practice, intervention impact would be achieved not only by procedural effectiveness and the likelihood of procedural implementation, but also by sufficient exposure of the child population to its effects. The factor of sufficient exposure expands the formula for impact suggested by McConnell et al. (1992) to read:

Impact of population-focused interventions = Effectiveness × Likelihood of implementation × Sufficiency of exposure.

Moving a service delivery system for children from reacting to the needs of the few, often at a point of crisis, to providing proactive services to a larger number of children constitutes a major challenge. Arguing that some resources should be reserved for the prevention of anticipated problems may not compete with the clamor for services from those already suffering the effects of childhood maladjustment.

## Schools and Change

Systemic school-based implementation of a large-scale, social competence–enhancing intervention is likely to be slow in coming. Schools are not known as organizations that readily adopt innovations. Owens (1970) suggested that the general acceptance of educational practices takes approximately 50 years—a much slower adoption rate than in fields such as agriculture or medicine.

Factors leading to educational change are multifaceted, interconnected, and complex (Fullan, 1993; Senge, 1990), a thorough discussion of which exceeds the scope of this chapter. However, one key factor hampering school change may be the lack of consensus among educators about either the purpose of education or the measurement of outcomes (Gardner, 1991). Fullan (1982) contended, "One of the most fundamental problems in education today is that people do not have a clear, coherent sense of *meaning* about what educational change is for, what it is, and how it proceeds" (p. 4). Without agreement that schools should be targeting social competence, and without understanding of how to measure gains in social adjustment, social competence–enhancing interventions would most likely not be adopted, or if adopted, not evaluated. As a result, the knowledge base from which to decide which interventions work would be slow in development. In fields such as medicine or agriculture, generally accepted protocols and standards exist for evaluating and disseminating new knowledge (Owens, 1970).

Even when educational innovations are developed, schools have little incentive for adopting new ways of operating (Owens, 1970). Without agreed-upon purposes of education, outcomes for these purposes, methods for evaluating those outcomes, or incentives for improved student achievement, school performance is unlikely to change.

A third key factor contributing to school resistance to change seems to be the mechanistic organization of schools (Morgan, 1986). Mintzberg (1989) suggested that mechanistic organizations emphasize standardized and uniform rules, policies, and regulations; clear hierarchical grids of authority; maintenance of control and smooth operating procedures; and insulation from external influences. A mechanical organizational structure tends not to respond to change as readily as an "organic control organization" (Gardner, 1992), a holographic organization (Morgan, 1986), or a "from-the-child-out" (Greer, 1989) model. In a mechanistic organizational structure, the adoption of change in classroom strategies may first require a modification of the decision-making structures in schools (e.g., Cauce, Comer, & Schwartz, 1987; Greer, 1989; Louis & Miles, 1991) or be initiated by forces external to those structures (Fullan, 1982).

## School Change Efforts

An account of a recent effort to restructure schools may illustrate some of the points raised above. In 1981, Bell described the foundation and activities of the National Commission on Excellence in Education. About 2 years later, the Commission released a report describing serious inadequacies in the American educational system. This report prompted a number of reform efforts, which primarily addressed improvements to educational practices and procedures.

Recently, Bell (1993) reflected on what had been accomplished in the decade following the release of the Commission's report. Believing the dissemination of reform recommendations to be disappointing, he commented, "And so we soon learned that gains in student achievement, decline in dropout rate, and other desirable outcomes cannot be attained simply by changing standards and mandating procedures and practices" (p. 594). In effect, Bell (1993) suggested that educational reform does not occur as a result of changes in educational practice alone.

Watzlawick, Weakland, and Fisch (1974) differentiated between first- and second-order changes in systems. First-order change focuses corrective action on the behavior or mechanics of a system, without changing the system itself. Implementing policies of student suspension and increased individual counseling to deal with child maladjustment in schools is an example of a first-order change effort. Second-order change proposes altering the rules that govern a system. A second-order educational change would be a modification in the pattern of school governance, such as decentralized decision making at the school level (Brown, 1990; Caldwell, 1993; Caldwell & Spinks, 1988). Although there is some question whether school flexibility stimulates innovation, the movement toward decentralization in schools reflects an attempt to make schools both more flexible in response to student needs and more accountable to community "stakeholders" (Mitchell & Beach, 1993).

Increased parents' choice of school attended by their children represents another second-order educational change. In 1991, President Bush released a document suggesting changes to the American public education system by the year 2000, with increased parental choice as an important component (Doyle, 1991).

Increased parent choice and control are rationales for the voucher plan (Weiler, 1974). The voucher plan proposes a system whereby parents redeem vouchers toward the cost of their children's education at any school of their choosing. The voucher plan introduces marketplace forces to the education system, representing a second-order change that has been identified as one possible scenario in the future of education (Caldwell, 1993).

## Sources of Change

In general, change efforts can be initiated from two different sources—those existing within the school system and those outside. Most educational changes, at least at the level of classroom practice, have been initiated by forces inside school systems. A 3-year study of federal and state dissemination programs indicated that in almost all instances of school change, efforts were initiated by central administration (Fullan, 1982). Louis (1994) suggested that, within limits, change can be "managed" from inside schools through the leadership of key individuals. Louis and Miles (1991) studied this process in the implementation of effective school procedures in urban high schools. They found that the rate of successful change was determined by the school's ability to cope with problems, which in turn was related to the existence of a change management group, empowered by stakeholders to facilitate the change process. This and other examples of successful internally driven change efforts (e.g., Prestine, 1993) tend to be restricted to first-order change examples (e.g., curriculum reform, improved instructional practices).

Second-order change in schools seems most likely to be initiated by forces external to the system. Such was the case in the introduction of the mainstream movement for children with disabilities (Guralnick, 1990; Strain & Kerr, 1981). In this instance, court litigation, the human rights movement, and parent lobbying groups resulted in legislation that mandated how children with special needs were to be educated. Similarly, many of the initial projects to introduce conflict mediation in schools were originated by the lobbying of other community organizations (Davis & Porter, 1985).

Even with these forces for educational change, interventions to promote student social competence may not be adopted by schools. Peck, Furman, and Helmstetter (1993) described the process of educational change as largely determined by sociopolitical factors of the organization. In attempting to implement any change with schools, one is dealing with an organization with a strong history of beliefs, values, and contextual constraints that can pose significant impediments. The process of school adoption of change may be one of mutual adaptation of the intervention (to fit into the school context) and of the school (to accommodate the intervention) (Firestone & Corbett, 1987).

Peck et al. (1993) proposed three principles for consideration in efforts to implement change efforts:

1. Change efforts must entail careful consideration of the role that local sociopolitical conditions play in implementation of new policies . . .

2. The change process begins where people are—ideologically, conceptually, and practically . . .

3. The implementation process is deeply affected by the congruency of the values implicit in the policy with those held by local stake holders in the educational system. (pp. 189, 190)

The process for initiating change in schools may best consist of mobilizing parents, mental health practitioners, and others who have a stake in school-based programs but are external to schools. These individuals could work collaboratively with schools once the momentum for change has been initiated, examining how to operationalize programs at a school level.

# Conclusion

## IMPLICATIONS FOR BEST PRACTICE

■ Reduction of maladjustment in the child population depends upon removing risk factors or blocking their effect.

■ Because of access to large numbers of children, the ability to target cognitive as well as social goals, and the presence of a natural peer group, schools hold promise as settings for programs to promote social competence in all students.

■ School programs to promote social competence in students should be broad based and combine targeted and universal approaches.

■ Social skills programs should be built into school curriculum, with accompanying school policies on its utilization.

■ School adoption of social competence–building interventions may need organizational and system changes to support that activity. Such a change may come about by external lobbying forces collaborating with leadership from the school system.

Large-scale adoption of population-focused social competence promotion in schools requires substantial changes in the way schools view their services. Facilitating the necessary changes in schools to support these interventions may need to involve such external forces as parent advocacy groups, universities, mental health centers, and government. Weissberg, Caplan, and Sivo (1989) suggested that the dissemination of social competence programs in schools is also dependent on the establishment of within-system advocates, system structures, and policies that support innovative programs.

In addition, the success of social competence–enhancing programs in schools depends on a number of other factors that have been discussed in this book, as summarized in the following paragraphs.

*Use of multiple components implemented by multiple socializing agents, in multiple settings.* It is not realistic to expect that one relatively short-term program offered during school hours will be enough to prevent or treat childhood maladjustment. Successful programs need to target a number of risk factors that add to the increased likelihood of children developing maladjustment. Professionals need to apply what is known about the risk of dysfunction to early interventions.

Moreover, generalization of the effects of social competence–enhancing interventions across settings and situations, as well as over time, will depend not only on equipping students with new social skills, but also on promoting school, peer, and home environments to reinforce their use.

*Early and sustained effort.* There seems to be a critical time in child development when youngsters are more susceptible to the effects of particular interventions (Yoshikawa, 1994). Interventions need to target parent–child relationships, starting well before children enter school, and be combined with school-based interventions that provide instruction in social cognitive processing to help children cope with academic and social tasks. These interventions must be provided continuously within the curriculum of preschools and elementary and secondary schools.

*Population-focused interventions.* Children's mental health problems must be conceptualized more broadly than thinking about children one at a time. Considering the relatively large number of children who are at risk for maladjustment, this is an issue facing a significant proportion of the child population, not merely those few who are identified at any one point in time. The population, not the individual, is the appropriate unit of analysis. Providing mental health services to the child population within communities will require (a) social competence programs that are universally available to all children; (b) more intensive programs delivered to children at increased risk of maladjustment; and (c) treatment and rehabilitation programs for children with fully developed behavior and emotional disorders.

*Integration into existing curriculum.* If a social competence–enhancing curriculum is to be introduced in the schools, how would it fit within the curriculum already in place? Given the level of competition for crowded classroom time, the addition of a social competence perspective may need to be integrated into existing curriculum areas (e.g., health education, guidance, "Man and Society") or replace existing curriculum areas, rather than be added to an already full school day.

*Systematic planning of program implementation.* The effectiveness of an intervention is not sufficient to ensure that teachers will adopt its procedures. In introducing social competence intervention in schools, one needs to develop an implementation process that increases the probability of a teacher's adoption, correct implementation, and persistence with the intervention. A key ingredient is the active involvement of teachers in modifying program prototypes to fit the needs of their classes.

*Need for system changes.* The ultimate success of school-based programs to promote social competence in children may rely on the overall health of schools as organizational structures. Energies need to be invested in understanding how school systems function and change so that leadership and organizational structures supporting healthy school climates may be encouraged. Also needing to be researched is the process by which collaborative relationships are formed and maintained between schools and external organizations in working toward change.

# Conclusion

This section combined an examination of assessment and implementation issues. An understanding of deficits in children's social skills and of existing competence, added to an understanding of the impact of environmental variables on the social behavior of those children, would be necessary for successful intervention. Likewise, the effectiveness of an intervention is not sufficient for it to have impact on children's adjustment. Efforts to maximize the likelihood that teachers will initially accept, correctly implement, and continue with an intervention are also important. Similarly, an understanding of schools and school change process is critical for broad-based adoption of social competence–enhancing interventions in schools.

# Concluding Comments

When I was an early teenager, my parents took my two younger brothers and me on a camping trip to a large provincial park. A couple of days after we arrived, they dropped us off to go horseback riding, instructing us to walk along the main road to return to the campsite once we were finished. We, however, decided to follow a path through the woods that we thought was a shorter route. As we found ourselves deeper and deeper in the woods, we realized that we were lost. We began to argue vehemently about ways of getting out of the woods. I wanted to retrace our steps and return to the main road. One brother suggested that we should continue the way we were going. My youngest brother argued that we should find a stream and follow it back to the campsite. Each held to his own solution, convinced that he was right. Finally, I decided to start back on my own. One brother opted to join me. Just as defiantly, my youngest brother refused to come with us and went off to find the stream. My brother and I managed to find our way back, but my youngest brother was lost for many hours, upsetting my parents and involving the park rangers in a search.

Looking back at this incident, I now perceive an issue that was of no importance at the time. My brothers and I had each argued why our particular course of action was correct. The issue, however, was not that there was one correct answer. Probably any one of the directions would have eventually taken us where we wanted to go. The real issue was this: We should have established *one* direction, and then we should have stayed together. This lesson has served me well in thinking about how professionals work with schools to build social competence in children. There may not be one correct way to enhance student's social competence, but those involved must be committed to finding a common way together.

# References

Abidin, R. R., Jenkins, C. L., & McGaughey, M. D. (1992). The relationship of early family variables to children's subsequent behavioral adjustment. *Journal of Clinical Child Psychology, 21*, 60–69.

Achenbach, T. M., & Edelbrock, C. (1983). *Manual for the Child Behavior Checklist and Revised Child Behavior Profile.* Burlington: Department of Psychiatry, University of Vermont.

Achenbach, T. M., McConaughy, S. H., & Howell, C. T. (1987). Child/adolescent behavioral and emotional problems: Implications of cross-informant correlations for situational specificity. *Psychological Bulletin, 101*, 213–232.

Adelman, H. S., & Taylor, L. (1991). Early school adjustment problems: Some perspectives and project report. *American Journal of Orthopsychiatry, 6*, 468–474.

Akhtar, N., & Bradley, E. J. (1991). Social information processing deficits of aggressive children: Present findings and implications for social skills training. *Clinical Psychology Review, 11*, 621–644.

Albee, G. W. (1968). Conceptual models and manpower requirements in psychology. *American Psychologist, 23*, 317–320.

Algozzine, B., Morsink, C. V., & Algozzine, K. M. (1988). What's happening in self-contained special education classrooms? *Exceptional Children, 55*, 259–265.

Anson, A. R., Cook, T. D., Habib, R., Grady, M. K., Haynes, N., & Comer, J. P. (1991). The Comer School Development Program. *Urban Education, 26*, 56–82.

Asher, S. R. (1985). An evolving paradigm in social skill training research with children. In B. H. Schneider, K. H. Rubin, & J. E. Ledingham (Eds.), *Children's peer relations: Issues in assessment and intervention* (pp. 157–174). New York: Springer-Verlag.

Asher, S. R., & Dodge, K. A. (1986). Identifying children who are rejected by their peers. *Developmental Psychology, 22*, 444–449.

Asher, S. R., & Hymel, S. (1981). Children's social competence in peer relations: Sociometric and behavioral assessment. In J. D. Wine & M. D. Smye (Eds.), *Social competence* (pp. 125–157). New York: Guilford.

Asher, S. R., Parkhurst, J. T., Hymel, S., & Williams, G. A. (1990). Peer rejection and loneliness in childhood. In S. R. Asher & J. D. Coie (Eds.), *Peer rejection in childhood* (pp. 253–273). New York: Cambridge University Press.

Asher, S. R., Singleton, L., Tinsley, B., & Hymel, S. (1979). A reliable sociometric measure for preschool children. *Developmental Psychology, 15*, 443–444.

Asher, S. R., & Wheeler, V. A. (1985). Children's loneliness: A comparison of rejected and neglected peer status. *Journal of Consulting and Clinical Psychology, 53*, 500–505.

Atwater, J. B., Carta, J. J., & Schwartz, I. S. (1989). *Assessment code/checklist for the evaluation of survival skills: ACCESS.* Kansas City: Juniper Gardens Children's Project, Bureau of Child Research, University of Kansas.

Babcock, N. L., & Pryzwansky, W. B. (1983). Models of consultation: Preferences of educational professionals at five stages of service. *Journal of School Psychology, 21*, 359–366.

Baer, R. A., Williams, J. A., Osnes, P. G., & Stokes, T. F. (1984). Delayed reinforcement as an indiscriminable contingency in verbal/nonverbal corresponding training. *Journal of Applied Behavior Analysis, 17,* 429–440.

Bagnato, S. J., & Neisworth, J. T. (1991). *Assessment for early intervention: Best practices for professionals.* New York: Guilford.

Bailey, D. B., Jr., Harms, T., & Clifford, R. M. (1983). Matching changes in preschool environments to desired changes in child behavior. *Journal of the Division for Early Childhood, 7,* 61–68.

Bailey, D. B., Jr., & McWilliam, R. A. (1990). Normalizing early intervention. *Topics in Early Childhood Special Education, 10,* 33–47.

Bailey, D. B., Jr., & Simeonsson, R. J. (1988a). *Family assessment in early intervention.* Columbus, OH: Merrill.

Bailey, D. B., Jr. , & Simeonsson, R. J. (1988b). Investigation of use of goal attainment scaling to evaluate individual progress of clients with severe and profound mental retardation. *Mental Retardation, 26,* 289–295.

Bailey, D. B., Jr., & Wolery, M. (1984). *Teaching infants and preschoolers with handicaps.* Columbus, OH: Merrill.

Bailey, J. S. (1991). Marketing behavior analysis requires different talk. *Journal of Applied Behavior Analysis, 24,* 445–448.

Barnett, W. S. (1993). Benefit–cost analysis of preschool education: Finding from a 25-year follow-up. *American Journal of Orthopsychiatry, 63*(4), 500–508.

Barton, L. E., & Johnson, H. A. (1990). Observational technology: An update. In S. R. Schroeder (Ed.), *Ecobehavioral analysis and developmental disabilities* (pp. 201–227). New York: Springer-Verlag.

Bates, J. E., Maslin, C. A., & Frankel, K. A. (1985). Attachment security, mother–infant interaction and temperament as predictors of behavior problems ratings at three years. In I. Bretherton & E. Waters (Eds.), *Growing points of attachment theory and research: Monographs of the Society for Research in Child Development* (Serial No. 209) (pp. 167–193). Chicago: Society for Research in Child Development.

Battistich, V., Solomon, D., Watson, M., Solomon, J., & Schaps, E. (1989). Effects of an elementary school program to enhance prosocial behavior on children's cognitive-social problem-solving skills and strategies. *Journal of Applied Developmental Psychology, 10,* 147–169.

Bauch, J. (1989). The transparent school model: New technology for parent involvement. *Educational Leadership, 47*(2), 32–34.

Baum, D. D., Duffelmeyer, F., & Geelan, M. (1988). Resource teacher perceptions of the prevalence of social dysfunction among students with learning disabilities. *Journal of Learning Disabilities, 21,* 380–381.

Becker, W. C. (1971). Teaching concepts and operations, or how to make kids smart. In W. C. Becker (Ed.), *An empirical basis for change in education* (pp. 36–51). Chicago: Science Research Press.

Beckoff, A. R., & Bender, W. N. (1989). Programming for mainstream kindergarten success in preschool: Teachers' perceptions of necessary prerequisite skills. *Journal of Early Intervention, 13,* 269–280.

Bell, T. H. (1993). Reflections one decade after *A Nation at Risk. Phi Delta Kappan, 74*(8), 592–597.

Berler, E. S., Gross, A. M., & Drabman, R. S. (1982). Social skills training with children: Proceed with caution. *Journal of Applied Behavior Analysis, 15,* 41–53.

Berman, P., & McLaughlin, M. W. (1976). Implementation of educational innovation. *Educational Forum, 40,* 345–370.

Bernal, M. E., Delfini, L. F., North, J. A., & Kreutzer, S. L. (1976). Comparison of boys' behaviors in homes and classrooms. In E. J. Mash, L. A. Hamerlynck, & L. C. Handy (Eds.), *Behavior modification and families* (pp. 204–227). New York: Brunner/Mazel.

Berry, P., & Marshal, B. (1978). Social interaction and communication patterns in mentally retarded children. *American Journal of Mental Deficiency, 83,* 44–51.

Bierman, K. L. (1986). The relation between social aggression and peer rejection in middle childhood. *Advances in Behavioral Assessment of Children and Families, 2,* 151–178.

Bierman, K. L. (1987). The clinical significance and assessment of poor peer relations: Peer neglect versus peer rejection. *Developmental and Behavioral Pediatrics, 8,* 233–240.

Bierman, K. L. (1989). Improving the peer relationships of rejected children. In B. B. Lachey & A. E. Kazdin (Eds.), *Advances in clinical child psychology* (pp. 53–84). New York: Plenum.

Bierman, K. L., & Furman, W. (1984). The effects of social skills training and peer involvement on the social adjustment of preadolescents. *Child Development, 55,* 151–162.

Bierman, K. L., Miller, C. L., & Stabb, S. D. (1987). Improving the social behavior and peer acceptance of rejected boys: Effects of social skills training with instructions and prohibitions. *Journal of Consulting and Clinical Psychology, 16,* 9–18.

Bigelow, D. A. (1975). The impact of therapeutic effectiveness data on community mental health centre management: The systems evaluation project. *Community Mental Health Journal, 11,* 64–73.

Billings, A. G., & Moos, R. H. (1983). Comparisons of children of depressed and non-depressed parents: A social-environmental perspective. *Journal of Abnormal Child Psychology, 11,* 463–486.

Blechman, E. A. (1984). Competent parents, competent children: Behavioral objectives of parent training. In R. F. Dangle & R. A. Polster (Eds.), *Parent training* (pp. 34–63). New York: Guilford.

Blechman, E. A. (1987). *Solving child behavior problems at home and at school.* Champaign, IL: Research Press.

Blechman, E. A., Taylor, C. J., & Schrader, S. M. (1981). Family problem solving versus home notes as early intervention with high-risk children. *Journal of Consulting and Clinical Psychology, 49,* 919–926.

Bodiford McNeil, C., Eyberg, S., Hembree Eisenstadt, T., Newcomb, K., & Funderburk, B. (1991). Parent–child interaction therapy with behavior problem children: Generalization of treatment effects to the school setting. *Journal of Consulting and Clinical Psychology, 20,* 140–151.

Boldizar, J. P., Perry, D. G., & Perry, L. C. (1989). Outcome values and aggression. *Child Development, 60,* 571–579.

Boothe, J. W., Bradley, L. H., Flick, T. M., Keough, K. E., & Kirk, S. P. (1993). The violence at your door. *The Executive Educator, 15*(1), 16–22.

Borduin, C. M., Henggeler, S. W., Blaske, D. M., & Stein, R. (1990). Multisystemic treatment of adolescent sexual offenders. *International Journal of Offender Therapy and Comparative Criminology, 34,* 105–113.

Bower, E. M. (1960). *Early identification of emotionally handicapped children in school.* Springfield, IL: Thomas.

Boyle, M. H., & Offord, D. R. (1990). Primary prevention of conduct disorder: Issues and prospects. *American Academy of Child and Adolescent Psychiatry, 29,* 227–233.

Boyle, M. H., Offord, D. R., Hofmann, H. G., Catlin, G. P., Byles, J. A., Cadman, D. T., Crawford, J. W., Links, P. S., Rae-Grant, N. I., & Szatmari, P. (1987). Ontario child health study: I. Methodology. *Archives of General Psychiatry, 44,* 826–831.

Breiner, J., & Forehand, R. (1981). An assessment of the effects of parent training on clinic-referred children's school behavior. *Behavioral Assessment, 3,* 31–42.

Bronfenbrenner, U. (1979). *The ecology of human development: Experiments by nature and design.* Cambridge, MA: Harvard University Press.

Brown, D., Wyne, M. D., Blackburn, J. E., & Powell, W. C. (1979). *Consultation: Strategy for improving education.* Boston: Allyn & Bacon.

Brown, D. J. (1990). *Decentralization and school-based management.* Lewes, England: Falmer.

Brown, W. H., Fox, J. J., & Brady, M. P. (1987). Effects of spatial density on three and four-year-old children's socially directed behavior during free-play: An investigation of a setting factor. *Education and Treatment of Children, 10,* 247–258.

Brown, W. H., & Odom, S. L. (1994). Strategies and tactic for promoting generalization and maintenance of young children's social behavior. *Research on Developmental Disabilities, 15,* 99–118.

Bruininks, R. H. (1991). Presidential address 1991 mental retardation: New realities, new challenges. *Mental Retardation, 29,* 239–251.

Brunk, M., Henggeler, S. W., & Whelan, J. P. (1987). Comparison of multisystemic therapy and parent training in the brief treatment of child abuse and neglect. *Journal of Consulting and Clinical Psychology, 55,* 171–178.

Bryan, T. H. (1974). Peer popularity of learning disabled children. *Journal of Learning Disabilities, 7,* 31–47.

Budd, K. S., Leibowitz, J. M., Riner, L. S., Mindell, C., & Goldfarb, A. L. (1981). Home-based treatment of severe disruptive behaviors: A reinforcement package for preschool and kindergarten children. *Behavior Modification, 5,* 273–298.

Buell, J., Stoddard, P., Harris, F. R., & Baer, D. M. (1968). Collateral social development accompanying reinforcement of outdoor play in a preschool child. *Journal of Applied Behavior Analysis, 1,* 167–173.

Burstein, N. D. (1986). The effects of classroom organization on mainstreaming preschool children. *Exceptional Children, 52,* 425–434.

Cahoon, P. (1988). Mediator magic. *Educational Leadership, 45,* 92–94.

Caldwell, B., & Spinks, J. M. (1988). *One self-managing school.* Lewes, England: Falmer.

Caldwell, B. J. (1993). The changing role of the school principal. In C. Dimmock (Ed.), *School-based management and school effectiveness* (pp. 165–184). New York: Routledge.

Camp, B. W., & Bash, M. S. (1985). *Think aloud: Increasing social and cognitive skills—A problem-solving program for children.* Champaign, IL: Research Press.

Campbell, S. B., Breaux, A. M., Ewing, L. J., & Szumowski, E. K. (1986). Correlates and predictors of hyperactivity and aggression: A longitudinal study of parent-referred problem preschoolers. *Journal of Abnormal Child Psychology, 14,* 217–234.

Caplan, M., Weissberg, R. P., Grober, J. S., Sivo, P. J., Grady, K., & Jacoby, C. (1992). Social competence promotion with inner-city and suburban young adolescents: Effects on social adjustment and alcohol use. *Journal of Consulting and Clinical Psychology, 60,* 56–63.

Carr, E. G., & Durand, M. (1985). Reducing behavior problems through functional communication training. *Journal of Applied Behavior Analysis, 18,* 111–126.

Carta, J. J., Atwater, J. B., Schwartz, I. S., & Miller, P. A. (1990). Applications of ecobehavioral analysis to the study of transitions across early education settings. *Education and Treatment of Children, 13,* 298–315.

Carta, J. J., Greenwood, C. R., & Atwater, J. (1985). *Ecobehavioral System for the Complex Assessment of Preschool Environments: ESCAPE.* Kansas City: Juniper Gardens Children's Project, Bureau of Child Research, University of Kansas.

Carta, J. J., Greenwood, C. R., & Robinson, S. L. (1987). Application of an ecobehavioral approach to the evaluation of early intervention programs. *Advances in Behavioral Assessment of Children and Families, 3,* 123–155.

Carta, J. J., Sainato, D. M., & Greenwood, C. R. (1988). Advances in the ecological assessment of classroom instruction for young children with handicaps. In S. L. Odom & M. B. Karnes (Eds.), *Early intervention for infants and children with handicaps* (pp. 217–239) Baltimore: Brookes.

Carter, R. K. (1983). *The accountable agency.* Newbury Park, CA: Sage.

Casey, R. J., & Berman, J. S. (1985). The outcome of psychotherapy with children. *Psychological Bulletin, 98,* 388–400.

Cassidy, J., & Asher, S. R. (1992). Loneliness and peer relations. *Child Development, 63,* 350–365.

Cauce, A. M., Comer, J. P., & Schwartz, D. (1987). Long term effects of a systems-oriented school prevention program. *American Journal of Orthopsychiatry, 57,* 127–131.

Chandler, C. L. (1991). Strategies to promote physical, social, and academic integration in a mainstream kindergarten. In G. Stoner, M. R. Shinn, & H. M. Walker (Eds.), *Interventions for achievement and behavior problems* (pp. 305–331). Silver Spring, MD: National Association of School Psychologists.

Chandler, L. K., Lubeck, R. C., & Fowler, S. A. (1992). The generalization and maintenance of preschool children's social skills: A critical review and analysis. *Journal of Applied Behavior Analysis, 25,* 415–428.

Christiansen, K. O. (1977). A preliminary study of criminality among twins. In S. A. Mednick & K. O. Christiansen (Eds.), *Biosocial issues of criminal behavior* (pp. 89–108). New York: Gardner.

Clark, D. B., & Baker, B. L. (1983). Brief reports: Predicting outcome in parent training. *Journal of Consulting and Clinical Psychology, 51,* 309–311.

Coddington, R. D. (1972). The significance of life events as etiologic factors in the diseases of children: II. A study of a normal population. *Journal of Psychosomatic Research, 16,* 205–213.

Cohen, J. (1960). A coefficient of agreement for nominal scales. *Educational and Psychological Measurement, 20,* 37–46.

Coie, J. D., & Dodge, K. A. (1983). Continuities and changes in children's social status: A five-year longitudinal study. *Merrill-Palmer Quarterly, 29,* 261–282.

Coie, J. D., & Dodge, K. A. (1988). Multiple sources of data on social behavior and social status in the school: A cross-age comparison. *Child Development, 59,* 815–829.

Coie, J. D., Dodge, K. A., & Coppitelli, H. (1982). Dimensions and types of social status: A cross-age perspective. *Developmental Psychology, 18,* 557–570.

Coie, J. D., & Krehbiel, G. (1984). Effects of academic tutoring on the social status of low-achieving, socially rejected children. *Child Development, 55,* 1465–1478.

Coie, J. D., & Kupersmidt, J. B. (1983). A behavioral analysis of emerging social status in boys' groups. *Child Development, 54,* 1400–1416.

Coie, J. D., Lochman, J. E., Terry, R., & Hyman, C. (1992). Predicting early adolescent disorder from childhood aggression and peer rejection. *Journal of Consulting and Clinical Psychology, 60*, 783–792.

Coie, J. D., Rabiner, D. L., & Lochman, J. E. (1989). Promoting peer relations in a school setting. In L. A. Bond & B. E. Compas (Eds.), *Primary prevention and promotion in the schools* (pp. 207–234). Newbury Park, CA: Sage.

Coie, J. D., Underwood, M., & Lochman, J. E. (1991). Programmatic intervention with aggressive children in the school setting. In D. J. Pepler & K. H. Rubin (Eds.), *The development and treatment of childhood aggression* (pp. 389–410). Hillsdale, NJ: Erlbaum.

Coie, J. D., Watt, N. F., West, S. G., Hawkins, J. D., Asarnow, J. R., Markman, H. J., Ramey, S. L., Shure, M. B., & Long, B. (1993). The science of prevention: A conceptual framework and some directions for a national research program. *American Psychologist, 48*(10), 1013–1022.

Coleman, J. M., & Minnett, A. M. (1992). Learning disabilities and social competence: A social ecological perspective. *Exceptional Children, 59*, 234–246.

Coleman, R. G. (1973). A procedure for fading from experimenter-school–based to parent-home–based control of classroom behavior. *Journal of School Psychology, 11*, 71–79.

Comer, J. P. (1980). *School power.* New York: Free Press.

Compas, B. E. (1987). Coping with stress during childhood and adolescence. *Psychological Bulletin, 101*, 393–403.

Cone J. D., & Hoier, T. S. (1986). Assessing children: The radical behavioral perspective. In R. J. Prinz (Ed.), *Advances in behavioral assessment of children and families* (pp. 1–27). New York: JAI Press.

Connell, H. M., Irvine, L., & Rodney, J. (1982). Psychiatric disorder in Queensland primary school children. *Australian Pediatric Journal, 18*, 177–188.

Consortium on the School-Based Promotion of Social Competence. (1991). Preparing students for the twenty-first century: Contributions of the prevention and social competence promotion fields. *Teachers College Record, 93*(2), 297–305.

Cowen, E. L. (1991). In pursuit of wellness. *American Psychologist, 46*, 404–408.

Cowen, E. L., & Gesten, L. (1978). Community approaches to intervention. In B. B. Wolman, J. Egan, & O. A. Ross (Eds.), *Handbook of treatment of mental disorders in childhood and adolescence* (pp. 102–125). Englewood Cliffs, NJ: Prentice-Hall.

Cowen, E. L., Pederson, A., Babigian, H., Izzo, L. D., & Trost, M. A. (1973). Long-term follow-up of early detected vulnerable children. *Journal of Consulting and Clinical Psychology, 41*, 438–446.

Crick, N. R., & Dodge, K. A. (1994). A review and reformulation of social information-processing mechanisms in children's social adjustment. *Psychological Bulletin, 115*, 47–101.

Crick, N. R., & Grotpeter, J. K. (in press). Relational aggression, gender, and social-psychological adjustment. *Child Development.*

Cunningham, C. E., Bremner, R., & Secord-Gilbert, M. (1993). Increasing the availability, accessibility, and cost efficacy of services for families of ADHD children: A school-based systems-oriented parenting course. *Canadian Journal of School Psychology, 9*(1), 1–15.

Dadds, M. R., & McHugh, T. A. (1992). Social support and treatment outcome in behavioral family therapy for child conduct problems. *Journal of Consulting and Clinical Psychology, 60*, 252–259.

Dangle, R. F., & Polster, R. A. (1984). *Parent training.* New York: Guilford.

Davis, A., & Porter, K. (1985). Tales of schoolyard mediation. *Update on Law-Related Education, 9*(1), 20–28.

DeKlyen, M., & Odom, S. L. (1989). Activity structure and social interactions with peers in developmentally integrated play groups. *Journal of Early Intervention, 13,* 342–352.

Deutsch, M. (1993, May). Educating for a peaceful world. *American Psychologist, 48*(5), 510–517.

Dodge, K. A. (1983). Behavioral antecedents of peer social status. *Child Development, 54,* 1386–1399.

Dodge, K. A. (1993). Social cognitive mechanisms in the development of conduct disorder and depression. *Annual Review of Psychology, 44,* 559–584.

Dodge, K. A., Coie, J. D., & Brakke, N. P. (1982). Behavior patterns of socially rejected and neglected preadolescents: The roles of social approach and aggression. *Journal of Abnormal Child Psychology, 10,* 389–410.

Dodge, K. A., & Feldman, E. (1990). Issues in social cognition and sociometric status. In S. R. Asher & J. D. Coie (Eds.), *Peer rejection in childhood* (pp. 119–156). New York: Cambridge University Press.

Dodge, K. A., & Frame, C. L. (1982). Social cognitive biases and deficits in aggressive boys. *Child Development, 53,* 620–635.

Dodge, K. A., Pettit, G. S., McClaskey, C. L., & Brown, M. M. (1986). Social competence in children. *Monographs of the Society for Research in Child Development, 51,* 1–85.

Dodge, K. A., Schlundt, D. G., Schockern, I., & Delugach, J. D. (1983). Social competence and children's sociometric status: The role of peer group entry strategies. *Merrill-Palmer Quarterly, 29,* 309–336.

Doke, L. A., & Risley, T. R. (1972). The organization of day-care environments: Required vs. optional activities. *Journal of Applied Behavior Analysis, 5,* 405–420.

Dougherty, E. H., & Dougherty, A. (1977). The daily report card: A simplified and flexible package for classroom behavior management. *Psychology in the Schools, 14,* 191–195.

Doyle, D. (1991, November). America 2000. *Phi Delta Kappan,* pp. 185–218.

Dubow, E. F., Tisak, J., Causey, D., Hryshko, A., & Reid, G. (1991). A two-year longitudinal study of stressful life events, social support, and social problem-solving skills: Contributions to children's behavioral and academic adjustment. *Child Development, 62,* 583–599.

Duigan, P. (1979, November). The pressures of the superintendency: Too many deadlines, not enough time. *The Executive Educator,* pp. 34–35.

Dumas, J. E. (1984). Child, adult-interactional, and socioeconomic setting events as predictors of parent training outcome. *Education and Treatment of Children, 7*(4), 351–364.

Dumas, J. E. (1989a). Let's not forget the context in behavioral assessment. *Behavioral Assessment, 11,* 231–247.

Dumas, J. E. (1989b). Treating antisocial behavior in children: Child and family approaches. *Clinical Psychology Review, 9,* 197–222.

Dunst, C. J. (1993). Implications of risk and opportunity factors for assessment and intervention practices. *Topics in Early Childhood Special Education, 13*(2), 143–153.

Dunst, C., Trivette, C., & Deal, A. (1988). *Enabling and empowering families.* Cambridge, MA: Brookline.

Durand, V. M. (1990). *Severe behavior problems: A functional communication training approach.* New York: Guilford.

Durand, V. M., & Carr, E. G. (1991). Functional communication training to reduce challenging behavior: Maintenance and application in new settings. *Journal of Applied
Behavior Analysis, 24,* 251–264.

Durand, V. M., & Crimmins, C. B. (1988). Identifying the variables maintaining self-
injurious behavior. *Journal of Autism and Developmental Disorder, 18,* 99–117.

Durlak, J. A., & Jason, L. A. (1984). Preventative programs for adolescents. In M. C.
Roberts & L. Peterson (Eds.), *Prevention of problems in childhood: Psychological research and
applications* (pp.103–132). New York: Wiley.

Dush, D. M., Hirt, M. L., & Schroeder, H. E. (1989). Self-statement modification in the
treatment of child behavior disorders: A meta-analysis. *Psychological Bulletin, 106,*
97–106.

Elias, M. J., & Allen, G. J. (1992). A comparison of instructional methods for delivering
social competence/social decision making program to at risk, average, and competent
students. *School Psychology Quarterly, 6,* 257–272.

Elias, M. J., & Clabby, J. F. (1992). *Building social problem-solving skills.* San Francisco: Jossey-
Bass.

Elias, M. J., Gara, M., Ubriaco, M., Rothbaum, P. A., Clabby, J. F., & Schuyler, T. (1986).
Impact of a preventive social problem solving intervention on children's coping with
middle-school stressors. *American Journal of Community Psychology, 14,* 259–275.

Elias, M. J., & Weissberg, R. P. (1990). School-based social competence promotion as a primary prevention strategy: A tale of two projects. *Prevention in Human Services, 7,*
177–200.

Elliott, S. N., & Gresham, F. M. (1991). *Social skills intervention guide: Practical strategies for social
skills training.* Circle Pines, MN: American Guidance Service.

Elliott, S. N., Witt, J. C., & Kratochwill, T. R. (1991). Selecting, implementing, and evaluating classroom interventions. In G. Stoner, M. R. Shinn, & H. M. Walker (Eds.), *Interventions for achievement and behavior problems* (pp. 99–135). Silver Spring, MD: National
Association of School Psychologists.

Emery, R. E., Fincham, F. D., & Cummings, E. M. (1992). Parenting in context: Systemic
thinking about parental conflict and its influence on children. *Journal of Consulting and
Clinical Psychology, 60,* 909–912.

Esser, G., Schmidt, M. H., & Woerner, W. (1990). Epidemiology and course of psychiatric
disorders in school-age children: Results of a longitudinal study. *Journal of Child Psychology and Psychiatry, 31,* 243–263.

Eyberg, S. M., & Robinson, E. A. (1983). Conduct problem behavior: Standardization of a
behavioral rating scale with adolescents. *Journal of Clinical Child Psychology, 12,*
347–357.

Fagot, B. I. (1973). Influence of teacher behavior in the preschool. *Developmental Psychology,
9,* 198–206.

Farrington, D. P. (1986). Stepping stones to adult criminal careers. In D. Olweus, J. Block,
& M. Radke-Yarrow (Eds.), *Development of antisocial and prosocial behavior: Research, theories,
and issues* (pp. 359–384). New York: Academic Press.

Farrington, D. P. (1991). Childhood aggression and adult violence: Early precursors and
later-life outcomes. In D. J. Pepler & K. H. Rubin (Eds.), *The development and treatment of
childhood depression* (pp. 5–29). Hillsdale, NJ: Erlbaum.

Fauber, R. L., & Long, N. (1991). Children in context: The role of the family in child psychotherapy. *Journal of Consulting and Clinical Psychology, 59,* 813–820.

Feagans, L., & McKinney, J. D. (1981). The pattern of exceptionality across domains in learning disabled children. *Journal of Applied Developmental Psychology, 1,* 313–328.

Federal Bureau of Investigation. (1991). *Uniform crime reports for the United States: 1991.* Washington, DC: U.S. Government Printing Office.

Felner, R. D., Ginter, M., & Primavera, J. (1982). Primary prevention during school transitions: Social support and environmental structure. *American Journal of Community Psychology, 10,* 277–290.

Firestone, W. A., & Corbett, H. D. (1987). Planned organizational change. In N. Bogan (Ed.), *Handbook of research on educational administration* (pp. 321–340). New York: Longman.

Fischer, M., Rolf, J. E., Hasazi, J. E., & Cummings, L. (1984). Follow-up of a preschool epidemiological sample: Cross-age continuities and predictions of later adjustment with internalizing and externalizing dimensions of behavior. *Child Development, 55,* 137–150.

Fitt, S. (1974). The individual and his environment. *School Review, 8,* 617–620.

Forgatch, M. S., & Toobert, D. J. (1979). A cost-effective parent training program for use with normal preschool children. *Journal of Pediatric Psychology, 4,* 129–145.

Foster, S. L., & Ritchey, W. L. (1979). Issues in the assessment of social competence in children. *Journal of Applied Behavior Analysis, 12,* 625–638.

Fowler, S. A., Dougherty, B. S., Kirby, K. C., & Kohler, F. W. (1986). Role reversals: An analysis of therapeutic effects achieved with disruptive boys during their appointments as peer monitors. *Journal of Applied Behavior Analysis, 19,* 437–444.

Friedman, R. M., & Street, S. (1985). Admission and discharge criteria for children's mental health services: A review of the issues and options. *Journal of Clinical Child Psychology, 14,* 229–235.

Fullan, M. (1982). *The meaning of educational change.* Toronto: Ontario Institute in Studies of Education.

Fullan, M. (1993). *Change forces.* London: Falmer.

Furman, W., Giberson, R., White, A. S., Gavin, L. A., & Wehner, E. A. (1989). Enhancing peer relations in school systems. In B. H. Schneider, G. Attili, J. Nadel, & R. P. Weissberg (Eds.), *Social competence in developmental perspective* (pp. 355–369). Norwell, MA: Kluwer Academic Publishers.

Furman, W., Rahe, D. F., & Hartup, W. W. (1979). Rehabilitation of socially withdrawn preschool children through mixed-age and same-age socialization. *Child Development, 50,* 915–922.

Furman, W., & Robbins, P. (1985). What is the point? Issues in the selection of treatment objectives. In B. H. Schneider, K. E. Rubin, & J. E. Ledingham (Eds.), *Children's peer relations in assessment and intervention* (pp. 41–56). New York: Springer-Verlag.

Gallup, G. H. (1983). The 15th annual Gallup poll of the public's attitudes toward the public schools. *Phi Delta Kappan, 65,* 33–51.

Garber, H., & Heber, F. R. (1977). The Milwaukee Projects: Indications of the effectiveness of early intervention in preventing mental retardation. In P. Mittler (Ed.), *Research to practice in mental retardation* (Vol. 1, pp. 119–127). Baltimore: University Park Press.

Gardner, H. (1991). *The unschooled mind.* New York: Basic Books.

Gardner, J. F. (1992). Quality, organization design, and standards. *Mental Retardation, 30*(3), 173–177.

Garmezy, N., Masten, A. S., & Tellegen, A. (1984). The study of stress and competence in children: A building block for developmental psychopathology. *Child Development, 55,* 97–111.

Gersten, J. C., Langner, T. S., Eisenberg, J. G., & Simcha-Fagan, O. (1977). An evaluation of the etiological role of stressful life-events in psychological disorders. *Journal of Health and Social Behaviors, 18*, 228–244.

Gesten, E. L., Rains, M. H., Rapkin, B. D., Weissberg, R. P., de Apocada, R. F., Cowen, E. L., & Bowen, R. (1982). Training children in social problem-solving competencies: A first and second look. *American Journal of Community Psychology, 10*, 95–115.

Gewirtz, J. L. (1972). Some contextual determinants of stimulus potency. In R. D. Parke (Ed.), *Recent developments in social learning theory* (pp. 7–33). New York: Academic Press.

Gibson, S., & Dembo, M. H. (1984). Teacher efficacy: A construct validation. *Journal of Educational Psychology, 76*, 569–582.

Gillespie, J. F., Durlak, J., & Sherman, D. (1982). Relationship between kindergarten children's interpersonal problem solving skills and other indices of school adjustment: A cautionary note. *American Journal of Community Psychology, 10*, 149–153.

Goldstein, H., & Cisar, C. L. (1992). Promoting interaction during sociodramatic play: Teaching scripts to typical preschoolers and classmates with disabilities. *Journal of Applied Behavior Analysis, 25*, 265–280.

Goldstein, H., Wickstrom, S., Hoyson, M., Jamieson, B., & Odom, S. (1988). Effects of sociodramatic play on social and communication interaction. *Education and Treatment of Children, 11*, 97–117.

Graden, J. L. (1989). Redefining "prereferral" intervention as intervention assistance: Collaboration between general and special education. *Exceptional Children, 56*, 227–231.

Graden, J. L., Casey, A., & Bonstrom, O. (1985). Implementing a prereferral intervention system: Part II. The data. *Exceptional Children, 51*, 487–496.

Graham, P., Rutter, M., & George, S. (1973). Temperamental characteristics as predictors of behavioral disorders in children. *American Journal of Orthopsychiatry, 43*, 328–339.

Green, K., Foreman, R., Beck, S., & Vosk, B. (1980). An assessment of the relationship among measures of children's social competence and children's academic achievement. *Child Development, 51*, 1149–1156.

Greenwood, C. R., & Carta, J. J. (1987). An ecobehavioral interaction analysis of instruction within special education. *Focus on Exceptional Children, 19*, 1–12.

Greenwood, C. R., Carta, J. J., & Atwater, J. (1991). Ecobehavioral analysis in the classroom: Review and implications. *Journal of Behavioral Education, 1*, 59–77.

Greenwood, C. R., Carta, J. J., Kamps, D., & Arreaga-Mayer, C. (1990). Ecobehavioral analysis of classroom instruction. In S. R. Schroeder (Ed.), *Ecobehavioral analysis and developmental disabilities* (pp. 33–63). New York: Springer-Verlag.

Greenwood, C. R., Carta, J. J., & Maheady, L. (1991). Peer tutoring programs in the regular education classroom. In G. Stoner, M. R. Shinn, & H. M. Walker (Eds.), *Interventions for achievement and behavior problems* (pp. 179–200). Silver Spring, MD: National Association of School Psychologists.

Greenwood, C. R., Delquadri, J. C., Stanley, S. O., Terry, B., & Hall, R. V. (1985). Assessment of eco-behavioral interaction in school settings. *Behavioral Assessment, 7*, 331–347.

Greenwood, C. R., Dinwiddie, G., Terry, B., Wade, L., Thibadeau, S., & Delquadri, J. (1984). Teacher- vs. peer-mediated instruction. *Journal of Applied Behavior Analysis, 17*, 521–538.

Greenwood, C. R., Hops, H., Walker, H. M., Guild, J. J., Stokes, J., Young, K. R., Keleman, K. S., & Willardson, M. (1979). Standardized classroom management program: Social validation and replication studies in Utah and Oregon. *Journal of Applied Behavior Analysis, 12*, 235–253.

Greenwood, C. R., Walker, H. M., Todd, N. M., & Hops, H. (1979). Selecting a cost-effective screening measure for the assessment of preschool social withdrawal. *Journal of Applied Behavior Analysis, 12,* 639–652.

Greer, J. V. (1989). Another perspective and some immoderate proposals on "teacher empowerment." *Exceptional Children, 55,* 294–297.

Gresham, F. M. (1982). Misguided mainstreaming: The case for social skills training with handicapped children. *Exceptional Children, 48,* 422–433.

Gresham, F. M. (1986). Conceptual issues in the assessment of social competence in children. In P. S. Strain, M. J. Guralnick, & H. M. Walker (Eds.), *Children's social behavior* (pp. 143–179). Orlando, FL: Academic Press.

Gresham, F. M. (1988). Social competence and motivational characteristics of learning disabled students. In M. C. Wang, M. C. Reynolds, & H. J. Walberg (Eds.), *Handbook of special education, research, and practice* (Vol. 2, pp. 283–302). Oxford: Pergamon.

Gresham, F. M. (1993). School-based social skills training: Implications for students with mild disabilities. *Exceptionality Education Canada, 3,* 61–78.

Gresham, F. M., & Elliott, S. N. (1990). *Social Skills Rating System manual.* Circle Pines, MN: American Guidance Service.

Gresham, F. M., & Nagle, R. J. (1980). Social skills training with children: Responsiveness to modeling and coaching as orientation. *Journal of Consulting and Clinical Psychology, 48,* 718–729.

Griest, D. L., & Forehand, R. (1982). How can I get any parent training done with all these other problems going on? The role of family variables in child behavior therapy. *Child and Family Behavior Therapy, 4*(1), 73–80.

Griest, D. L., Forehand, R., Wells, K. C., & McMahon, R. J. (1980). An examination of differences between nonclinic and behavior problem clinic-referred children and their mothers. *Journal of Abnormal Psychology, 89,* 497–500.

Gronland, N. E., & Holmlund, W. S. (1958). The value of elementary sociometric status scores for predicting pupils' adjustment in high school. *Educational Administration Supervision, 44,* 225–260.

Guerra, N. G., & Slaby, R. G. (1989). Evaluative factors in social problem solving by aggressive boys. *Journal of Abnormal Child Psychology, 17,* 277–289.

Guralnick, M. J. (1981). The social behavior of preschool children at different developmental levels: Effects of group composition. *Journal of Experimental Child Psychology, 31,* 115–130.

Guralnick, M. J. (1990). Social competence and early intervention. *Journal of Early Intervention, 14,* 3–14.

Guralnick, M. J., & Groom, J. M. (1987). The peer relations of mildly handicapped preschool children in mainstreamed playgroups. *Child Development, 58,* 1556–1572.

Guralnick, M. J., & Groom, J. M. (1988). Peer interactions in mainstreamed and specialized classrooms: A comparative analysis. *Exceptional Children, 54,* 415–425.

Guralnick, M. J., & Weinhouse, E. M. (1984). Peer-related social interactions of developmentally delayed young children: Development and characteristics. *Developmental Psychology, 20,* 815–827.

Guskey, T. R. (1988). Teacher efficacy, self-concept, and attitudes toward the implementation of instructional innovation. *Teaching and Teacher Education, 4,* 63–69.

Hall, M. C. (1984). Responsive parenting: A large-scale training program for school districts, hospitals, and mental health centers. In R. F. Dangle & R. A. Polster (Eds.), *Parent training* (pp. 67–92). New York: Guilford.

Hamilton, V. J., & Gordon, D. A. (1978). Teacher–child interactions in preschool and task persistence. *American Educational Research Journal, 15,* 459–466.

Handen, B. L., Feldman, R. S., & Honigman, A. (1987). Comparison of parent and teacher assessments of developmentally delayed children's behavior. *Exceptional Children, 54,* 137–144.

Haring, T. G. (1992). The context of social competence: Relations, relationships, and generalization. In S. L. Odom, S. R. McConnell, & M. A. McEvoy (Eds.), *Social competence of young children with disabilities* (pp. 307–320). Baltimore: Brookes.

Harter, S. (1982). The perceived competence scale for children. *Child Development, 53,* 87–97.

Harter, S., & Pike, R. (1984). The pictorial scale of perceived competence and social acceptance for young children. *Child Development, 55,* 1969–1982.

Hauser-Cram, P., & Wyngaarden Krauss, M. (1991). Measuring change in children and families. *Journal of Early Intervention, 15,* 288–297.

Hawkins, J. D., & Dotson, V. A. (1975). Reliability scores that delude: An Alice in Wonderland trip through the misleading characteristics of inter observer agreement scores in interval recording. In E. Ramp & G. Semb (Eds.), *Behavioral analysis: Areas of research and application* (pp. 359–376). Englewood Cliffs, NJ: Prentice-Hall.

Hawkins, J. D., Von Cleve, E., & Catalano, R. F., Jr. (1991). Reducing early childhood aggression: Results of a primary prevention program. *Journal of the American Academy of Child and Adolescent Psychiatry, 30*(2), 208–217.

Hawkins, J. D., & Weis, J. G. (1985). The social developmental model: An integrated approach to delinquency prevention. *Journal of Primary Prevention, 6,* 73–97.

Hayvren, M., & Hymel, S. (1984). Ethical issues in sociometric testing: The impact of sociometric measures on interactive behavior. *Developmental Psychology, 20,* 844–849.

Hendrickson, J. M., Gardner, N., Kaiser, A., & Riley, A. (1993). Evaluation of a social interaction coaching program in an integrated day-care setting. *Journal of Applied Behavior Analysis, 26,* 213–225.

Hendrickson, J. M., Strain, P. S., Tremblay, A., & Shores, R. E. (1981). Relationship between toy and material use and the occurrence of social interactive behaviors by normally developing preschool children. *Psychology in the Schools, 18,* 500–504.

Henggeler, S. W., & Borduin, C. M. (1990). *Family therapy and beyond: A multisystemic approach to treating the behavior problems of children and adolescents.* Pacific Grove, CA: Brooks/Cole.

Henggeler, S. W., Rodick, J. D., Borduin, C. M., Hanson, C. L., Watson, S. M., & Urey, J. R. (1986). Multisystemic treatment of juvenile offenders: Effects on adolescent behavior and family interaction. *Developmental Psychology, 22,* 132–141.

Hett, C. A., & Krikorian, L. A. (1993). Fostering communication through school and home newsletters. In M. J. Elias (Ed.), *Social decision making and life skills development: Guidelines for middle school educators* (pp. 261–271). Gaithersburg, MD: Aspen.

Hill, R. (1958). Social stresses on the family. *Social Casework, 39,* 139–150.

Hinshaw, S. P. (1987). On the distinction between attentional deficits/hyperactivity and conduct problems/aggression in child psychopathology. *Psychological Bulletin, 101,* 443–463.

Hinshaw, S. P. (1992a). Academic underachievement, attention deficits, and aggression: Comorbidity and implications for intervention. *Journal of Consulting and Clinical Psychology, 60,* 893–903.

Hinshaw, S. P. (1992b). Externalizing behavior problems and academic underachievement in childhood and adolescence: Causal relationships and underlying mechanisms. *Psychological Bulletin, 111,* 127–155.

Hinshaw, S. P., Han, S. S., Erhardt, D., & Huber, A. (1992). Internalizing and externalizing behavior problems in preschool children: Correspondence among parent and teacher ratings and behavior observation. *Journal of Clinical Child Psychology, 21,* 143–150.

Hirschi, T., & Hindelang, M. J. (1977). Intelligence and delinquency: A revisionist review. *American Sociological Review, 42,* 571–587.

Honig, A. S., & McCarron, P. A. (1988). Prosocial behaviors of handicapped and typical peers in an integrated preschool. *Early Child Development and Care, 33,* 113–125.

Hord, S. M., Rutherford, W. L., Huling-Austin, L., & Hall, G. E. (1987). *Taking charge of change.* Alexandria, VA: Association for Supervision and Curriculum Development.

Howes, C. (1990). Social status and friendship from kindergarten to third grade. *Journal of Applied Developmental Psychology, 11,* 321–330.

Hughes, J. N., & Sullivan, K. A. (1988). Outcome assessment in social skills training with children. *Journal of School Psychology, 26,* 167–183.

Hundert, J. (1982). Some considerations of planning the integration of handicapped children into the mainstream. *Journal of Learning Disabilities, 15,* 73–80.

Hundert, J. (1994). The ecobehavioral relationship between teachers' and disabled preschoolers' behaviors before and after supervisor training. *Journal of Behavioral Education, 4,* 77–93.

Hundert, J., & Hopkins, B. (1992). Training supervisors in a collaborative team approach to promote peer interaction of children with disabilities in integrated preschools. *Journal of Applied Behavior Analysis, 25,* 385–400.

Hundert, J., & Houghton, A. (1992). Promoting social interaction of children with disabilities in integrated preschools: A failure to generalize. *Exceptional Children, 58,* 311–320.

Hundert, J., Mahoney, W., & Hopkins, B. (1993). The relationship between the peer interaction of children with disabilities in integrated preschools and resource and classroom teacher behaviors. *Topics in Early Childhood Special Education, 13,* 328–343.

Hundert, J., & Taylor, L. (1993). Classwide promotion of social competence in young students. *Exceptionality Education Canada, 3,* 79–101.

Hymel, S., & Rubin, K. H. (1985). Children with peer relationships and social skills problems: Conceptual, methodological, and developmental issues. In G. J. Whitehurst (Ed.), *Annals of Child Development* (Vol. 2, pp. 251–297). Greenwich, CT: JAI.

Hymel, S., Wagner, E., & Butler, L. J. (1990). Reputational bias: View from the peer group. In S. R. Asher & J. D. Coie (Eds.), *Peer rejection in childhood* (pp. 156–186). New York: Cambridge University Press.

Hymel, S., Zinck, B., & Ditner, E. (1993). Cooperation versus competition in the classroom. *Exceptionality Education Canada, 3,* 103–128.

Idol, L., & West, J. F. (1987). Consultation in special education (Part II): Training and practice. *Journal of Learning Disabilities, 20,* 474–493.

Idol-Maestas, L., & Ritter, S. (1985). A follow-up study of resource/consulting teachers. *Teacher Education and Special Education, 8,* 121–131.

Interagency Committee on Learning Disabilities. (1987). *Learning disabilities: A report to Congress.* Washington, DC: Author.

Ironsmith, M., & Poteat, G. M. (1990). Behavioral correlates of preschool sociometric status and the prediction of teacher ratings of behavior in kindergarten. *Journal of Clinical Child Psychology, 19,* 17–25.

Jackson, N. F., Jackson, D. A., & Monroe, C. (1983). *Getting along with others: Teaching social effectiveness to children*. Champaign, IL: Research Press.

Jason, L., & Rhodes, J. (1989). Children helping children: Implications for prevention. *Journal of Primary Prevention, 9*, 203–211.

Jastak, S., & Wilkinson, G. S. (1984). *Wide Range Achievement Test: Administration manual*. Wilmington, DE: Jastak Associates.

Jeffrey, R. W. (1989). Risk behavior and health: Contrasting individual and population perspectives. *American Psychologist, 44*, 1194–1202.

Jenkins, J. R., Odom, S. L., & Speltz, M. L. (1989). Effects of social integration on preschool children with handicaps. *Exceptional Children, 55*, 420–428.

Jenkins, J. R., Speltz, M. L., & Odom, S. L. (1985). Integrating normal and handicapped preschoolers: Effects on child development and social interaction. *Exceptional Children, 52*, 7–17.

Jenkins, J. R., & Heinen, A. (1989). Students' preferences for service delivery: Pull-out, in-class or integrated models. *Exceptional Children, 55*, 516–523.

Johnson, D. W., & Johnson, R. T. (1986). Mainstreaming and cooperative learning strategies. *Exceptional Children, 52*, 553–561.

Johnson, D. W., Johnson, R. T., & Maruyama, G. (1983). Interdependence and interpersonal attraction among heterogeneous and homogeneous individuals: A theoretical formulation and a meta-analysis of the research. *Review of Educational Research, 3*, 5–54.

Johnson, J. H., Jason, L. A., & Betts, D. M. (1990). Promoting social competencies through educational efforts. In T. P. Gullotta, G. R. Adams, & R. Montemayor (Eds.), *Developing social competency in adolescence: Advances in adolescent development* (pp.139–160). Newbury Park, CA: Sage.

Johnson, L. C., & Abramovitch, R. (1988). Paternal unemployment and family life. In A. R. Pence (Ed.), *Ecological research with children and families: From concepts to methodologies* (pp. 49–75). New York: Teachers College Press.

Johnson, L. J., & Pugach, M. C. (1990). Classroom teachers' views of intervention strategies for learning and behavior problems: Which are reasonable and how frequently are they used? *Journal of Special Education, 24*, 69–84.

Joyce, B., & Showers, B. (1982). The coaching of teachers. *Educational Leadership, 40*, 4–10.

Joyce, B., & Showers, B. (1983). *Power in staff development through research on training*. Alexandria, VA: Association for Supervision and Curriculum Development.

Kagan, J., & Snidman, N. (1991). Temperamental factors in human development. *American Psychologist, 46*, 856–862.

Kazdin, A. E. (1977). Artifact, bias and complexity of assessment: The ABC's of reliability. *Journal of Applied Behavior Analysis, 10*, 141–150.

Kazdin, A. E. (1981). Acceptability of child treatment techniques: The influence of treatment efficacy and adverse side effects. *Behavior Therapy, 12*, 493–506.

Kazdin, A. E. (1987). Treatment of antisocial behavior in children: Current status and future directions. *Psychological Bulletin, 102*, 187–203.

Kazdin, A. E. (1992). Child and adolescent dysfunction and paths toward maladjustment: Targets for intervention. *Clinical Psychology Review, 12*, 795–817.

Kazdin, A. E. (1993a). Adolescent mental health: Prevention and treatment programs. *American Psychologist, 48*, 127–144.

Kazdin, A. E. (1993b, June). Psychotherapy for children and adolescents: Current progress and future research directions. *American Psychologist, 48*(6), 644–657.

Kazdin, A. E., Bass, D., Siegel, T., & Thomas, C. (1989). Cognitive-behavioral therapy and relationship therapy in the treatment of children referred for antisocial behavior. *Journal of Consulting and Clinical Psychology, 57,* 522–535.

Kazdin, A. E., Mazurick, L., & Bass, D. (1993). Risk for attrition in treatment of antisocial children and families. *Journal of Clinical Child Psychology, 22,* 2–16.

Kazdin, A. E., Siegel, T. C., & Bass, D. (1992). Cognitive problem-solving skills training and parent management training in the treatment of antisocial behavior in children. *Journal of Consulting and Clinical Psychology, 60,* 733–747.

Kelley, M. L. (1990). *School–home notes: Promoting children's classroom success.* New York: Guilford.

Kendall, P. C., & Braswell, L. (1985). *Cognitive-behavioral therapy for impulsive children.* New York: Guilford.

Kennedy, C. H., & Itkonen, T. (1993). Effects of setting events on the problem behavior of students with severe disabilities. *Journal of Applied Behavior Analysis, 26,* 321–327.

Kern-Dunlap, L., Dunlap, G., Clarke, S., Childs, K. E., White, R. L., & Stewart, M. P. (1992). Effects of a videotape feedback package on the peer interaction of children with serious behavioral and emotional challenges. *Journal of Applied Behavior Analysis, 25,* 341–353.

Kettlewell, P. W., & Kausch, D. F. (1983). The generalization of the effects of a cognitive-behavioral treatment program for aggressive children. *Journal of Abnormal Child Psychology, 11,* 101–114.

King, C. A., & Kirschenbaum, D. S. (1990). An experimental evaluation of a school-based program for children at risk: Wisconsin Early Intervention. *Journal of Community Psychology, 18,* 167–177.

King, C. A., & Young, R. D. (1981). Peer popularity and peer communication patterns: Hyperactive versus active but normal boys. *Journal of Abnormal Child Psychology, 9,* 465–482.

Kiresuk, T., & Lund, S. (1976). Process and measurement using goal attainment scaling. In G. V. Glass (Ed.), *Evaluation studies review annual* (Vol. 1, pp. 383–399). Beverly Hills, CA: Sage.

Koegel, L. K., Koegel, R. L., Hurley, C., & Frea, W. D. (1992). Improving social skills and disruptive behavior in children with autism through self-management. *Journal of Applied Behavior Analysis, 25,* 341–353.

Kohn, M. (1977). *Social competence, symptoms and underachievement in childhood: A longitudinal perspective.* Washington, DC: Winston.

Kopp, C. B., Baker, B. L., & Brown, K. W. (1992). Social skills and their correlates: Preschoolers with developmental delays. *American Journal on Mental Retardation, 96,* 357–366.

Krantz, P. J., & McClannahan, L. E. (1993). Teaching children with autism to initiate to peers: Effects of script-fading procedure. *Journal of Applied Behavior Analysis, 26,* 121–132.

Krantz, P., & Risley, T. R. (1977). Behavioral ecology in the classroom. In K. D. O'Leary & S. G. O'Leary (Eds.), Classroom management: The successful use of behavior modification (2nd ed., pp. 349–367). New York: Pergamon.

Krehbiel, G. (1984). *School-setting behavior of academic achievement-based subtypes of rejected children.* Unpublished doctoral dissertation, Duke University, Durham, NC.

Krenz, D. (1991, October). Conflict management: A practical process. *The Reporter,* pp. 17–19.

Kupersmidt, J. B., Coie, J. D., & Dodge, K. A. (1990). The role of poor peer relationships in the development of disorder. In S. R. Asher & J. D. Coie (Eds.), *Peer rejection in childhood* (pp. 274–305). New York: Cambridge University Press.

Ladd, G. W. (1981). Effectiveness of a social learning method for enhancing children's social interaction and peer acceptance. *Child Development, 52,* 171–178.

Ladd, G. W. (1983). Social networks of popular, average, and rejected children in school settings. *Merrill-Palmer Quarterly, 29,* 283–307.

Ladd, G. W. (1985). Documenting the effects of social skills training with children: Process and outcome assessment. In B. H. Schneider, K. H. Rubin, & J. E. Ledingham (Eds.), *Children's peer relations: Issues in assessment and intervention* (pp. 243–269). New York: Springer-Verlag.

Ladd, G. W. (1989). Children's social competence and social supports: Precursors of early school adjustment? In B. H. Schneider, G. Attili, J. Nadel, & R. P. Weissberg, *Social competence in developmental perspective* (pp. 277–291). Kluwer Academic.

Ladd, G. W., & Mize, J. (1983). A cognitive-social learning model of social skill training. *Psychological Review, 90,* 127–157.

Ladd, G. W., Price, J. M., & Hart, C. H. (1988). Predicting preschoolers' peer status from their playground behaviours. *Child Development, 59,* 986–992.

La Greca, A. (1981). Social behavior and social perception in learning-disabled children: A review with implications for social skills training. *Journal of Pediatric Psychology, 6,* 395–416.

La Greca, A. M., & Stark, P. (1986). In P. S. Strain, M. J. Guralnick, & H. M. Alker (Eds.), *Children's social behavior* (pp. 181–213). Orlando, FL: Academic Press.

Landau, S., Milich, R., & Whitten, P. (1984). A comparison of teacher and peer assessment of social status. *Journal of Clinical Child Psychology, 13,* 44–49.

Landau, S., & Moore, L. A. (1991). Social skills deficits in children with attention-deficit hyperactivity disorder. *School Psychology Review, 20,* 235–251.

Lane, P. S., & McWhirter, J. J. (1992). A peer mediation model: Conflict resolution for elementary and middle school children. *Elementary School Guidance and Counseling, 27,* 15–23.

Larson, K. A. (1988). A research review and alternative hypothesis, explaining the link between learning disability and delinquency. *Journal of Learning Disability, 21,* 357–369.

Ledingham, J. E., Younger, A., Schwartzman, A., & Bergeron, G. (1982). Agreement among teacher, peer, and self-rating of children's aggression, withdrawal, and likability. *Journal of Abnormal Child Psychology, 10,* 363–372.

LeLaurin, K., & Risley, T. R. (1972). The organization of day care environments: "Zone" versus "man-to-man" staff assignments. *Journal of Applied Behavior Analysis, 5,* 225–232.

Levine, S., Elzey, F. F., & Lewis, M. (1969). *California Preschool Social Competency Scale.* Palo Alto, CA: Consulting Psychologists.

Lewine, R. J. (1981). Sex differences in schizophrenia: Timing or subtypes? *Psychological Bulletin, 70,* 681–693.

Lewis, R. J., Dlugokinski, E. L., Caputo, L. M., & Griffin, R. B. (1988). Children at risk for emotional disorders: Risk and resource dimensions. *Clinical Psychology Review, 8,* 417–440.

Lochman, J. E. (1992). Cognitive-behavioral intervention with aggressive boys: Three year follow-up and preventive effects. *Journal of Consulting and Clinical Psychology, 60,* 426–432.

Lochman, J. E., Birch, P. R., Curry, J. F., & Lampron, L. B. (1984). Treatment and generalization effects of cognitive-behavioral and goal setting interventions with aggressive boys. *Journal of Consulting and Clinical Psychology, 52,* 915–916.

Lochman, J. E., & Curry, J. F. (1986). Effects of social problem-solving training and self-instruction training with aggressive boys. *Journal of Clinical Child Psychology, 15,* 159–164.

Lochman, J. E., & Lampron, L. B. (1986). Situational social problem-solving skills and self-esteem of aggressive and nonaggressive boys. *Journal of Abnormal Child Psychology, 14,* 605–617.

Lochman, J. E., & Lenhart, L. A. (1993). Anger coping intervention for aggressive children: Conceptual models and outcome effects. *Clinical Psychology Review, 13,* 785–805.

Lochman, J. E., Wayland, K. K., & White, K. J. (1993). Social goals: Relationship to adolescent adjustment and to social problem solving. *Journal of Abnormal Child Psychology, 21,* 135–151.

Loeber, R. (1982). The stability of antisocial and delinquent child behavior: A review. *Child Development, 53,* 1431–1446.

Loeber, R. (1988). The natural histories of juvenile conduct problems, substance use and delinquency: Evidence for developmental progressions. In B. Lahey & A. E. Kazdin (Eds.), *Advances in Clinical Child Psychology: Vol. 11* (pp. 73–124). New York: Plenum.

Loeber, R. (1991). Antisocial behavior: More enduring than changeable? *Journal of the American Academy of Child and Adolescent Psychiatry, 30,* 393–397.

Loeber, R., & Dishion, T. J. (1983). Early predictors of male delinquency: A review. *Psychological Bulletin, 94,* 68–99.

Lore, R. K., & Schultz, L. A. (1993). Control of human aggression: A comparative perspective. *American Psychologist, 48,* 16–25.

Lougee, M. D., Grueneich, R., & Hartup, W. W. (1977). Social interaction in same- and mixed-age dyads of preschool children. *Child Development, 48,* 1353–1361.

Louis, K. S. (1994). Beyond "managed" change: Rethinking how schools improve. *School Effectiveness and School Improvement, 5*(1), 2–24.

Louis, K. S., & Miles, M. B. (1991). Managing reform: Lessons from urban high schools. *School Effectiveness and School Improvement, 2*(2), 75–96.

Lynam, D., Moffitt, T., & Stouthamer-Loeber, M. (1993). Explaining the relation between IQ and delinquency: Class, race, test motivation, school failure, or self-control? *Journal of Abnormal Psychology, 102,* 187–196.

Marcus, L. M., & Olley, J. G. (1988). Developing public school services for students with autism. In M. D. Powers (Ed.), *Expanding systems of service delivery for persons with developmental disabilities* (pp. 179–197). Baltimore: Brookes.

Martens, B. K., Peterson, R. L., Witt, J. C., & Cirone, S. (1986). Teacher perceptions of school-based interventions: Ratings of intervention effectiveness, ease of use, and frequency of use. *Exceptional Children, 53,* 213–223.

Martin, S. S., Brady, M. P., & Williams, R. E. (1991). Effects of toys on the social behavior of preschool children in integrated and nonintegrated groups: Investigation of a setting event. *Journal of Early Intervention, 15,* 153–161.

Mash, E. J., & Terdal, L. G. (1988). *Behavioral assessment of childhood disorders* (2nd ed.). New York: Guilford.

Matson, J. L., Fee, V. E., Coe, D. A., & Smith, D. (1991). A social skills program for developmentally delayed preschoolers. *Journal of Clinical Child Psychology, 20,* 428–433.

Maxwell, J. (1989). Mediation in the schools. *Mediation Quarterly, 7,* 149–154.

McAllister, J. R. (1991). Curriculum-based behavioral interventions for preschool children with handicaps. *Topics in Early Childhood Special Education, 11*, 48–58.

McConaughty, S. H., & Ritter, D. R. (1986). Social competence and behavioral problems of learning disabled boys aged 6–11. *Journal of Learning Disabilities, 19*, 39–45.

McConnell, S. R. (1987). Entrapment effects and the generalization and maintenance of social skills training for elementary school students with behavioral disorders. *Behavioral Disorders, 12*, 252–263.

McConnell, S. R., McEvoy, M. A., & Odom, S. L. (1992). Implementation of social competence interventions in early childhood special education classes. In S. L. Odom, S. R. McConnell, & M. A. McEvoy (Eds.), *Social competence of young children with disabilities: Issues and strategies for intervention* (pp. 277–306). Baltimore: Brookes.

McConnell, S. R., & Odom, S. L. (1986). Sociometrics: Peer-referenced measures and the assessment of social competence. In P. S. Strain, M. J. Guralnick, & H. M. Walker (Eds.), *Children's social behavior: Development, assessment and modification* (pp. 215–284). Orlando, FL: Academic Press.

McConnell, S. R., Sisson, L. A., Cort, C. A., & Strain, P. S. (1991). Effects of social skills training and contingency management on reciprocal interaction of preschool children with behavioral handicaps. *The Journal of Special Education, 24*, 473–495.

McConnell, S. R., Strain, P. S., Kerr, M. M., Stagg, V., Lenkner, D. A., & Lambert, D. L. (1984). An empirical definition of elementary school adjustment: Selection of target behaviors for a comprehensive treatment program. *Behavior Modification, 8*(4), 451–473.

McCord, J. (1979). Some child-rearing antecedents of criminal behavior in adult men. *Journal of Personality and Social Psychology, 9*, 1477–1486.

McCormick, M. (1988). *Mediation in the schools: An evaluation of the Wakefield Pilot Peer Mediation Program in Tucson, Arizona.* Washington, DC: American Bar Association.

McCubbin, H., & Patterson, J. (1983). The family stress process: The double ABCX model of family adjustment and adaptation. In H. McCubbin, M. Sussman, & J. Patterson (Eds.), *Advances and developments in family stress theory and research* (pp. 251–283). New York: Haworth.

McEvoy, M. A., Fox, J. J., & Rosenberg, M. S. (1991). Organizing preschool environments: Suggestions for enhancing the development/learning of preschool children with handicaps. *Topics in Early Childhood Special Education, 11*, 18–28.

McEvoy, M. A., Nordquist, V. M., Twardosz, S., Heckaman, K. A., Wehby, J. H., & Denny, R. K. (1988). Promoting autistic children's peer interaction in an integrated setting using affection activities. *Journal of Applied Behavior Analysis, 21*, 193–200.

McEvoy, M. A., Odom, S. L., & McConnell, S. R. (1992). Peer social competence intervention for young children with disabilities. In S. L. Odom, S. R. McConnell, & M. A. McEvoy (Eds.), *Social competence of young children with disabilities: Issues and strategies for intervention* (pp. 113–133). Baltimore: Brookes.

McEvoy, M. A., Shores, R. E., Wehby, J. F., Johnson, S. M., & Fox, J. J. (1990). Special education teachers' implementation procedures to promote social interaction among children in integrated settings. *Education and Training in Mental Retardation, 25*, 267–276.

McEvoy, M. A., Twardosz, S., & Bishop, N. (1990). Affection activities: Procedures for encouraging young children with handicaps to interact with their peers. *Education and Treatment of Children, 13*, 159–167.

McGinnis, E., & Goldstein, A. P. (1984). *Skill-streaming the elementary school child.* Champaign, IL: Research Press.

McIntosh, R., Vaughn, S., & Zaragoza, N. (1991). A review of social intervention for students with learning disabilities. *Journal of Learning Disabilities, 24,* 451–458.

McMahon, R. J., & Forehand, R. (1984). Parent training for the noncompliant child: Treatment outcome, generalization, and adjuctive therapy procedures. In R. F. Dangle & R. A. Polster (Eds.), *Parent training* (pp. 298–328).New York: Guilford.

McMahon, R. J., Forehand, R., Griest, D. L., & Wells, K. C. (1981). Who drops out of treatment during parent behavioral training? *Behavioral Counseling Quarterly, 1*(1), 79–85.

Meador, A. E., & Ollendick, T. H. (1984). Cognitive behavior therapy with children: An evaluation of its efficacy and clinical utility. *Child and Family Behavior Therapy, 6,* 25–44.

Mednick, S. A., Gabrielli, W. F., & Hutchings, B. (1984). Genetic influences in criminal convictions: Evidence from an adoption cohort. *Science, 224,* 891–894.

Medway, F. J., & Updyke, J. F. (1985). Meta-analysis of consultation outcomes studies. *American Journal of Community Psychology, 15,* 489–505.

Meichenbaum, D. (1977). *Cognitive-behavior modification: An integrative approach.* New York: Plenum.

Merrell, K. W. (1993). *School Social Behavior Scales: Test manual.* Brandon, VT: Clinical Psychology.

Meyer, C. J. W., & Foster, S. F. (1988). The effect of teacher self-efficacy on referral change. *Journal of Special Education, 22,* 378–391.

Meyer, L. H., Fox, A., Schermer, A., Ketelsen, D., Montan, N., Maley, K., & Cole, D. (1987). The effects of teacher intrusion on social play interactions between children with autism and their non-handicapped peers. *Journal of Autism and Developmental Disorders, 17,* 315–332.

Michelson, L., & Mannarino, A. (1986). Social skills training with children: Research and clinical application. In P. S. Strain, M. J. Guralnick, & H. M. Walker (Eds.), *Children's social behavior: Development, assessment and modification* (pp. 373–406). New York: Academic Press.

Miller, K. A. (1989). Enhancing early childhood mainstreaming through cooperative learning: A brief literature review. *Child Study Journal, 19,* 285–290.

Miller, G. E., & Prinz, R. J. (1990). Enhancement of social learning family interventions for childhood conduct disorder. *Psychological Bulletin, 108*(2), 291–307.

Milne, A. A. (1926). *Winnie-the-Pooh.* New York: E. P. Dutton.

Mintzberg, H. (1989). The machine organization. In H. Mintzberg (Ed.), *Mintzberg on management: Inside our strange world of organizations* (pp. 130–152). New York: Free Press.

Mitchell, D. E., & Beach, S. A. (1993). School restructuring: The superintendent's view. *Educational Administrator Quarterly, 29*(2), 249–274.

Mitchell, M. E. (1989). The relationship between social network variables and the utilization of mental health services. *Journal of Community Psychology, 17,* 258–266.

Mize, J., & Ladd, G. W. (1990). Toward the development of successful social skills training for preschool children. In S. R. Asher & J. D. Coie (Eds.), *Peer rejection in childhood* (pp. 338–361). Cambridge, England: Cambridge University Press.

Moncher, F. J., & Prinz, R. J. (1991). Treatment fidelity in outcome studies. *Clinical Psychology Review, 11,* 247–266.

Montes, R., & Risley, T. R. (1975). Evaluating traditional day care practices: An empirical approach. *Child Care Quarterly, 4,* 208–215.

Morgan, G. (1986). Chapter 4: Toward self-organization: Organization as brains. In *Images of organization* (pp. 77–109). Beverly Hills, CA: Sage.

Mulvey, E. P., Arthur, M. W., & Reppucci, N. D. (1993). The prevention and treatment of juvenile delinquency: A review of the research. *Clinical Psychology Review, 13,* 133–167.

Myles, B. W., & Simpson, R. L. (1989). Regular educators' modification preferences for mainstreaming mildly handicapped children. *Journal of Special Education, 22,* 479–491.

National Education Association. (1979). Teacher opinion poll. *Today's Education, 68,* 10.

National Mental Health Association. (1986). *Report of the National Mental Health Association Commission on the Prevention of Mental-Emotional Disabilities.* Alexandria, VA: Author.

Nordquist, V. M., Twardosz, S., & McEvoy, M. A. (1991). Effects of environmental reorganization in classrooms for children with autism. *Journal of Early Intervention, 15,* 135–152.

Novak, M. A., Olley, J. G., & Kearney, D. S. (1980). Social skills of children with special needs in integrated and separate preschools. In T. M. Field (Ed.), *High risk infant and children* (pp. 327–346). New York: Academic Press.

O'Connor, M. (1975). The nursery school environment. *Developmental Psychology, 11,* 556–561.

Odom, S. L. (1988). Research in early childhood special education. In S. L. Odom & M. B. Karnes (Eds.), *Early intervention for infants and children with handicaps: An empirical basis* (pp. 1–21). Baltimore: Brookes.

Odom, S. L., & Asher, S. R. (1977). Coaching children in social skills for friendship making. *Child Development, 48,* 495–506.

Odom, S. L., Bender, M. K., Stein, M. L., Doran, L. P., Houden, P. M., McInnes, M., Gilbert, M. M., Deklyen, M., Speltz, M. L., & Jenkins, J. R. (1988). *The integrated preschool curriculum.* Seattle: University of Washington Press.

Odom, S. L., & Brown, W. H. (1993). Social interaction skills interventions for young children with disabilities in integrated settings. In C. A. Peck, S. L. Odom, & D. D. Bricker (Eds.), *Integrating young children with disabilities into community programs* (pp. 39–64). Baltimore: Brookes.

Odom, S. L., Chandler, L. K., Ostrosky, M., McConnell, S. R., & Reaney, S. (1992). Fading teacher prompts from peer-initiation interventions for young children with disabilities. *Journal of Applied Behavior Analysis, 25,* 307–317.

Odom, S. L., Hoyson, M., Jamieson, B., & Strain, P. S. (1985). Increasing handicapped preschoolers' peer social interactions: Cross-setting and component analysis. *Journal of Applied Behavior Analysis, 18,* 3–16.

Odom, S. L., Jenkins, J. R., Speltz, M. L., & DeKlyen, M. (1982). Promoting social integration of young children at risk for learning disabilities. *Learning Disabilities Quarterly, 5,* 379–387.

Odom, S. L., McConnell, S. R., & Chandler, L. K. (1993). Acceptability and feasibility of classroom-based social interaction interventions for young children with disabilities. *Exceptional Children, 60,* 226–236.

Odom, S. L., & McEvoy, M. A. (1988). Integration of young children with handicaps and normally developing children. In S. L. Odom & M. B. Karnes (Eds.), *Early intervention for infants and children with handicaps* (pp. 241–267). Baltimore: Brookes.

Odom, S. L., Peterson, C., McConnell, S., & Ostrosky, M. (1990). Ecobehavioral analysis of early education/specialized classroom settings and peer social interaction. *Education and Treatment of Children, 13,* 316–330.

Odom, S. L., & Strain, P. S. (1984). Classroom-based social skills instruction for severely handicapped preschool children. *Topics in Early Childhood Special Education, 4,* 97–116.

Odom, S. L., & Strain, P. S. (1986). A comparison of peer-initiation and teacher-antecedent interventions for promoting reciprocal social interaction of autistic preschoolers. *Journal of Applied Behavior Analysis, 19*, 59–71.

Odom, S. L., & Watts, E. (1991). Reducing teacher prompts in peer-mediated interventions for young children with autism. *The Journal of Special Education, 25*, 26–43.

Office of Technology Assessment, U.S. Congress. (1986, December). *Children's mental health: Problems and services* (OTA Publication No. OTA-BP-H-33). Washington, DC: U.S. Government Printing Office.

Offord, D. R., Alder, R. J., & Boyle, M. H. (1986). Prevalence and sociodemographic correlates of conduct disorder. *American Journal of Social Psychiatry, 6*(4), 272–278.

Offord, D. R., Boyle, M. H., & Racine, Y. A. (1989). Ontario Child Health Study: Correlates of disorder. *Journal of the American Academy of Child and Adolescent Psychiatry, 28*, 856–860.

Offord, D. R., Boyle, M. H., & Racine, Y. A. (1991). The epidemiology of antisocial behavior in childhood and adolescence. In D. J. Pepler & K. H. Rubin (Eds.), *The development and treatment of childhood aggression* (pp. 31–54). Hillsdale, NJ: Erlbaum.

Offord, D. R., Boyle, M. H., Szatmari, P., Rae-Grant, N. I., Links, P. S., Cadman, D. T., Byles, J. A., Crawford, J. W., Munroe Blum, H., Byrne, C., Thomas, H., & Woodward, C. A. (1987). Ontario child health study: II. Six-month prevalence of disorder and rates of service utilization. *Archives of General Psychiatry, 44*, 832–836.

O'Leary, K. D., & Kent, R. (1973). Behavior modification for social action: Research tactics and problems. In L. A. Hamerlynck, L. C. Handy, & E. J. Mash (Eds.), *Behavior change: Methodology, concepts, and practice* (pp. 69–96). Champaign, IL: Research Press.

Oliva, A. H., & La Greca, A. M. (1988). Children with learning disabilities: Social goals and strategies. *Journal of Learning Disabilities, 21*, 301–306.

Ollendick, T. H., Greene, R. W., Francis, G., & Baum, C. G. (1991). Sociometric status: Its stability and validity among neglected, rejected and popular children. *Journal of Child Psychology and Psychiatry, 32*, 525–534.

Ollendick, T. H., Oswald, D. P., & Francis, G. (1989). Validity of teacher nominations in identifying aggressive, withdrawn, and popular children. *Journal of Clinical Child Psychology, 18*, 221–229.

Olweus, D. (1979). Stability of aggressive reaction patterns in males: A review. *Psychological Bulletin, 86*, 852–875.

Olweus, D. (1991). Bully/victim problems among school children: Basic facts and effects of a school based intervention program. In D. J. Pepler & K. H. Rubin (Eds.), *The development and treatment of childhood aggression* (pp. 411–448). Hillsdale, NJ: Erlbaum.

O'Neil, R. E., Horner, R. H., Albin, R. W., Storey, K., & Sprague, J. R. (1990). *Functional analysis of problem behavior: A practical assessment guide.* Sycamore, IL: Sycamore Press.

Osnes, P. G., Guevremont, D. C., & Stokes, T. F. (1986). If I say I'll talk more, then I will. *Behavior Modification, 10*, 287–299.

Owens, R. G. (1970). *Organizational behavior in schools.* Englewood Cliffs, NJ: Prentice-Hall.

Parke, R. D., & Slaby, R. G. (1983). The development of aggression. In E. M. Hetherington (Ed.), *Handbook of child psychology: Vol. 4. Socialization, personality, and social development* (pp. 557–641). New York: Wiley.

Parker, J. G., & Asher, S. R. (1987). Peer relations and later personal adjustment: Are low-accepted children at risk? *Psychological Bulletin, 102*, 257–389.

Parten, M. B. (1932). Social participation among preschool children. *Journal of Abnormal Social Psychology, 7*, 243–269.

Patterson, G. R. (1976). The aggressive child: Victim and architect of a coercive system. In E. J. Mash, L. A. Hamerlynck, & L. C. Handy (Eds.), *Behavior modification and families* (pp. 267–316). New York: Brunner/Mazel.

Patterson, G. R. (1986a). The contribution of siblings to training for fighting: A microsocial analysis. In D. Olweus (Ed.), *Development of antisocial and prosocial behavior* (pp. 235–261). New York: Academic Press.

Patterson, G. R. (1986b). Performance models for antisocial boys. *American Psychologist, 41,* 432–444.

Patterson, G. R., Capaldi, D., & Bank, L. (1991). An early starter model for predicting delinquency. In D. J. Pepler & K. H. Rubin (Eds.), *The development and treatment of childhood depression* (pp. 139–168). Hillsdale, NJ: Erlbaum.

Patterson, G. R., Chamberlain, P., & Reid, J. B. (1982). A comparative evaluation of a parent-training program. *Behavior Therapy, 13,* 638–650.

Patterson, G. R., & Dishion, T. J. (1985). Contributions of families and peers to delinquency. *Criminology, 23,* 63–79.

Patterson, G. R., Reid, J. B., Jones, R. R., & Conger, R. W. (1975). *A social learning approach to family intervention* (Vol. 1). Eugene, OR: Castalia.

Peck, C. A., Furman, G. C., & Helmstetter, E. (1993). Integrated early childhood programs: Research on the implementation of change in organizational contexts. In C. A. Peck, S. L. Odom, & D. D. Bricker (Eds.), *Integrating young children with disabilities into community programs* (pp. 187–205). Baltimore: Brookes.

Peck, C. A., Killen, C. C., & Baumgart, D. (1989). Increasing implementation of special education instruction in mainstream preschools: Direct and generalized effects of nondirective consultation. *Journal of Applied Behavior Analysis, 22,* 197–210.

Pedro-Carroll, J. L., Cowen, E. L., Hightower, D., & Guare, J. C. (1986). Preventive intervention with latency-aged children of divorce: A replication study. *American Journal of Community Psychology, 14,* 277–290.

Peed, S., Roberts, M., & Forehand, R. (1977). Evaluation of the effectiveness of a standardized parent training program in altering the interaction of mothers and their noncompliant children. *Behavior Modification, 1*(3), 323–350.

Pekarik, E. G., Prinz, R. J., Liebert, D. E., Weintrub, W., & Neale, J. M. (1976). The pupil evaluation inventory: A sociometric technique for assessing children's social behavior. *Journal of Abnormal Child Psychology, 4,* 83–97.

Pekarik, G., & Stephenson, L. A. (1988). Adult and child client differences in therapy dropout research. *Journal of Clinical Child Psychology, 17,* 316–321.

Pelham, W. E., & Bender, M. E. (1982). Peer relationships in hyperactive children: Description and treatment. In K. Gadow & I. Bailer (Eds.). *Advances in learning and behavioral disabilities* (Vol. 1). Greenwich, CT: JAI Press.

Pelham, W. E., & Milich, R. (1984). Peer relations in children with hyperactivity/attention deficit disorder. *Journal of Learning Disabilities, 17,* 560–567.

Pellegrini, D. S., & Urbain, E. S. (1985). An evaluation of interpersonal cognitive problem solving training with children. *Journal of Child Psychology and Psychiatry, 26,* 17–41.

Pentz, M. A., Dwyer, J. H., MacKinnon, D. P., Flay, B. R., Hansen, W. B., Wang, E. Y. I., & Johnson, C. A. (1989). A multi-community trial for primary prevention of adolescent drug abuse: Effects on drug use prevalence. *Journal of the American Medical Association, 261,* 3259–3266.

Pepler, D. J., & Craig, W. M. (1993). School-based social skills training with aggressive children: Necessary, but not sufficient? *Exceptionality Education Canada, 3,* 177–194.

Pepler, D. J., King, G., & Byrd, W. (1991). A social-cognitively based social skills training program for aggressive children. In D. J. Pepler & K. H. Rubin (Eds.), *The development and treatment of childhood aggression* (pp. 361–379). Hillsdale, NJ: Erlbaum.

Perry, J. C. (1979). Popular, amiable, isolated, rejected: A reconceptualization of sociometric status in preschool children. *Child Development, 50,* 1231–1234.

Peterson, C. A., & McConnell, S. R. (1993). Factors affecting the impact of social interaction skills interventions in early childhood special education. *Topics in Early Childhood Special Education, 13,* 38–56.

Peterson, L., Homer, A. L., & Wonderlich, S. A. (1992). The integrity of independent variables in behavior analysis. *Journal of Applied Behavior Analysis, 15,* 477–492.

Phillips, V., & McCullough, L. (1990). Consultation-based programming: Instituting the collaborative ethic in schools. *Exceptional Children, 56,* 291–303.

Pisterman, S., McGrath, P. J., Firestone, P., Goodman, J. T., Webster, I., & Mallory, R. (1989). Outcome of parent mediated treatment of preschoolers with attention deficit disorder with hyperactivity. *Journal of Consulting and Clinical Psychology, 57,* 636–643.

Polsgrove, L., & McNeil, M. (1989). The consultation process: Research and practice. *Remedial and Special Education, 10,* 6–13.

Porter, J., & Rourke, B. (1985). Socio-emotional functioning of learning disabled children: A subtypal analysis of personality patterns. In B. P. Rourke (Ed.), *Neuropsychology of learning disabilities: Essentials of subtype analysis* (pp. 257–279). New York: Guilford.

Powers, M. D. (1988). A systems approach to serving persons with severe developmental disabilities. In M. Powers (Eds.), *Expanding systems of service delivery for persons with developmental disabilities* (pp. 1–14). Baltimore: Brookes.

President's Commission on Mental Health. (1978). *Report to the President from the President's Commission of Mental Health.* Washington, DC: U.S. Government Printing Office.

Prestine, N. (1993). Feeling the ripples, riding the waves. In J. Murphy & P. Hallinger (Eds.), *Restructuring schools: Learning from ongoing efforts* (pp. 32–62). Newbury Park, CA: Corwin.

Prinz, R. J., Blechman, E. A., & Dumas, J. E. (1994). An evaluation of peer-coping-skills training for childhood aggression. *Journal of Clinical Child Psychology, 23,* 193–203.

Pryor-Brown, L., & Cowen, E. L. (1989). Stressful life events, support, and children's school adjustment. *Journal of Clinical Child Psychology, 18,* 214–220.

Pugach, M. C., & Johnson, L. J. (1990). Meeting diverse needs through professional peer collaboration. In W. Stainback & S. Stainback (Eds.), *Support networks for inclusive schooling* (pp. 123–137). Baltimore: Maple.

Putallaz, M., & Gottman, J. (1983). Social relationship problems in children: An approach to intervention. In B. B. Lahey & A. E. Kazdin (Eds.), *Advances in clinical child psychology* (Vol. 6, pp. 1–43). New York: Plenum.

Putnam, J. W., Rynders, J. E., Johnson, R. T., & Johnson, D. W. (1989). Collaborative skill instruction for promoting positive interactions between mentally handicapped and nonhandicapped children. *Exceptional Children, 55,* 550–557.

Quay, H. C., & Peterson, D. R. (1983). *Interim manual for the Revised Behavior Problem Checklist* (1st ed.). Unpublished manuscript, University of Miami, Coral Gables, FL.

Quilitch, H. R., & Risley, T. R. (1973). The effects of play materials on social play. *Journal of Applied Behavior Analysis, 6,* 573–578.

Reid, J. B., & Patterson, G. R. (1991). Early prevention and intervention with conduct problems: A social interaction model for the integration of research and practice. In G. Stoner, M. R. Shinn, & H. M. Walker (Eds.), *Interventions for achievement and behavior problems* (pp. 715–739). Silver Spring, MD: National Association of School Psychologists.

Renshaw, P. D., & Asher, S. R. (1982). Social competence and peer status: The distinction between goals and strategies. In K. H. Rubin & H. S. Ross (Eds.), *Peer relationships and social skills in childhood* (pp. 375–395). New York: Springer-Verlag.

Repp, A. C., Felce, D., & Barton, L. E. (1988). Basing the treatment of stereotypic and self-injurious behaviors on hypothesis of their causes. *Journal of Applied Behavior Analysis, 21,* 281–289.

Rickard, K. M., Graziano, W., & Forehand, R. (1984). Parental expectations and childhood deviance in clinic referred and non-clinic children. *Journal of Clinical Child Psychology, 13,* 179–186.

Rickel, A. U., & Burgio, J. C. (1982). Assessing social competencies in lower income preschool children. *American Journal of Community Psychology, 10,* 635–647.

Risley, T. R., Clark, H. B., & Cataldo, M. F. (1976). Behavioral technology for the normal middle-class family. In E. J. Mash, L. A. Hamerlynck, & L. C. Handy (Eds.), *Behavior modification and families* (pp. 34–60). New York: Brunner/Mazel.

Risley, T., & Hart, B. (1968). Developing correspondence between nonverbal and verbal behavior of pre-school children. *Journal of Applied Behavior Analysis, 1,* 267–281.

Roberts, C., Pratt, C., & Leach, D. (1985). Classroom and playground interaction of students with and without disabilities. *Exceptional Children, 32,* 212–224.

Robins, L. (1983). Continuities and discontinuities in psychiatric disorders of children. In D. E. Mechanic (Ed.), *Handbook of health care, and the health professions* (pp. 195–219). New York: Free Press.

Robins, L. N. (1966). *Deviant children grown up: A sociological and psychiatric study of sociopathic personality.* New York: Krieger.

Roderick, T. (1988). Johnny can learn to negotiate. *Educational Leadership, 45,* 86–90.

Rogers, T. R., Forehand, R., & Griest, D. L. (1981). The conduct disordered child: An analysis of family problems. *Clinical Psychology Review, 1,* 139–147.

Rogers-Warren, A. K. (1982). Behavioral ecology in classrooms for young, handicapped children. *Topics in Early Childhood Special Education, 2,* 21–32.

Rogers-Warren, A., Ruggles, L., Peterson, N., & Cooper, A. (1981). Playing and learning together: Patterns of social interaction in handicapped and non-handicapped children. *Journal of the Division for Early Childhood, 3,* 56–63.

Roistacher, R. C. (1974). A microeconomic model of sociometric choice. *Sociometry, 37,* 219–238.

Rolf, M. (1961). Childhood social interactions and young adult bad conduct. *Journal of Abnormal and Social Psychology, 63,* 333–337.

Rolf, M., Sells, S. B., & Golden, M. M. (1972). *Social adjustment and personality development in children.* Minneapolis: University of Minneapolis Press.

Rosenberg, M. S., & Baker, K. (1985). Instructional time and the teacher educator: Training preservice and beginning teachers to use time effectively. *Teacher Educator, 20,* 195–207.

Ross, J. A. (1988). Improving social-environmental studies of problem solving through cooperative learning. *American Educational Research Journal, 25,* 573–591.

Rotholz, D. A., Kamps, D. M., & Greenwood, C. R. (1989). Ecobehavioral assessment and analysis in special education settings for students with autism. *Journal of Special Education, 23,* 59–81.

Rourke, B. P. (1988). Socioemotional disturbances of learning disabled children. *Journal of Consulting and Clinical Psychology, 56,* 801–810.

Rubin, K. H., Bream, L. A., & Rose-Krasnor, L. (1991). Social problem solving and aggression in childhood. In D. J. Pepler & K. H. Rubin (Eds.), *The development and treatment of childhood aggression* (pp. 219–248). Hillsdale, NJ: Erlbaum.

Rubin, K. H., Le Mare, L. J., & Lollis, S. (1990). Social withdrawal in childhood: Developmental pathways to peer rejection. In S. R. Asher & J. D. Coie (Eds.), *Peer rejection in childhood* (pp. 217–249). New York: Cambridge University Press.

Rubin, K. H., & Rose-Krasnor, L. (1992). Interpersonal problem-solving and social competence in children. In V. B. van Hasselt & M. Hersen (Eds.), *Handbook of social development: A lifespan perspective* (pp. 283–323). New York: Plenum.

Rutter, M. (1980). *Changing youth in a changing society: Patterns of adolescent development and disorder.* Cambridge, MA: Harvard University Press.

Rutter, M. (1987). Temperament, personality and personality disorder. *British Journal of Psychiatry, 150,* 443–458.

Rutter, M., Cox, A., Tupling, C., Berger, M., & Yule, W. (1975). Attainment and adjustment in two geographical areas: I. The prevalence of psychiatric disorder. *British Journal of Psychiatry, 126,* 493–509.

Rutter, M., & Quinton, D. (1984). Parental psychiatric disorder: Effects on children. *Psychological Medicine, 14,* 853–880.

Rutter, M., Tizard, J., & Whitmore, K. (1970). *Education, health and behavior.* London: Longman.

Sainato, D. M., & Carta, J. J. (1992). Classroom influences on the development of social competence in young children with disabilities. In S. L. Odom, S. R. McConnell, & M. A. McEvoy (Eds.), *Social competence of young children with disabilities* (pp. 93–109). Baltimore: Brookes.

Salend, A. J. (1984). Factors contributing to the development of successful mainstreaming programs. *Exceptional Children, 50,* 409–415.

Salvia, J., & Ysseldyke, J. E. (1981). *Assessment in special and remedial education.* Dallas: Houghton Mifflin.

Salzberg, C. L., Lignugaris-Kraft, B., & McCuller, G. L. (1988). Reasons for job loss: A review of employment termination studies of mentally retarded workers. *Research in Developmental Disabilities, 9,* 153–170.

Sameroff, A. J., & Seifer, R. (1983). Familial risk and child competence. *Child Development, 54,* 1254–1268.

Sancilio, M. F. M. (1987). Peer interaction as a method of therapeutic intervention with children. *Clinical Psychology Review, 7,* 475–500.

Sarason, S. (1990). *The predictable failure of educational reform.* San Francisco: Jossey-Bass.

Sater, G. M., & French, D. C. (1989). A comparison of the social competencies of learning disabled and low achieving elementary-aged children. *Journal of Special Education, 23,* 29–42.

Schmidt, F., Friedman, A., & Marvel, J. (1992). *Mediation for kids.* Miami, FL: Grace Contrino Abrams Peace Education Foundation.

Schneider, B. H. (1992). Didactic methods for enhancing children's peer relations: A quantitative review. *Child Psychology Review, 12,* 363–382.

Schneider, B. H., & Byrne, B. M. (1985). Children's social skills training: A meta-analysis. In B. H. Schneider, K. H. Rubin, & J. E. Ledingham (Eds.), *Children's peer relations: Issues in assessment and interventions* (pp. 175–192). New York: Springer-Verlag.

Schneider, B. H., & Byrne, B. M. (1987). Individualizing social skills training for behavior disordered children. *Journal of Consulting and Clinical Psychology, 55,* 444–445.

Schneider, B. H., & Byrne, B. M. (1989). Parents rating children's social behavior: How focused the lens? *Journal of Clinical Child Psychology, 18*, 237–241.

Schrumpf, F., Crawford, D., & Usadel, H. C. (1991). *Peer mediation: Conflict resolution in schools, program guide* (2nd ed.). Champaign, IL: Research Press.

Schumaker, J. B., & Hazel, J. S. (1984). Social skills assessment and training for the learning disabled: Who's on first and what's on second? Part I. *Journal of Learning Disabilities, 17*, 422–431.

Schumaker, J. B., Hovell, M. F., & Sherman, J. A. (1977). An analysis of daily report cards and parent-managed privileges in the improvement of adolescents' classroom performance. *Journal of Applied Behavior Analysis, 10*, 449–464.

Scruggs, T. E., & Mastropieri, M. A. (1986). Academic characteristics of behaviorally disordered and learning disabled students. *Behavioral Disorders, 11*, 184–190.

Seeman, J. (1989). Toward a model of positive health. *American Psychologist, 44*, 1099–1109.

Self, H., Benning, A., Marston, D., & Magnusson, D. (1991). Cooperative teaching project: A model for students at risk. *Exceptional Children, 58*, 26–33.

Seligman, M., & Benjamin Darling, R. (1989). *Ordinary families, special children*. New York: Guilford.

Senge, P. (1990, Fall). The leader's new work: Building learning organizations. *Sloan Management Review*, pp. 7–23.

Shamsie, S. J. (1981). Anti-social adolescents: Our treatments do not work: Where do we go from here? *Canadian Journal of Psychiatry, 26*, 357–364.

Shapiro, S. B., & Sobel, M. (1981). Two multinominal random sociometric voting models. *Journal of Educational Statistics, 6*, 287–310.

Sheehan, R., & Day, D. (1975). Is open space just empty space? *Day Care and Early Education, 3*, 10–13.

Shure, M. B. (1992). *I can problem solve*. Champaign, IL: Research Press.

Shure, M. B., & Spivack, G. (1979). Interpersonal cognitive problem solving and primary prevention: Programming for preschool and kindergarten children. *Journal of Clinical Child Psychology, 8*, 89–94.

Simeonsson, R. J., Huntington, G., & Short, R. (1982). Individual differences and goals: An approach to the evaluation of child progress. *Topics in Early Childhood Special Education, 1*(4), 71–80.

Sitkin, S. B. (1992). Learning through failure: The strategy of small losses. *Research in Organizational Behavior, 14*, 231–266.

Slavin, R. (1990). *Cooperative learning: Theory, research, and practice*. Englewood Cliffs, NJ: Prentice-Hall.

Slavin, R. E., Stevens, R. J., & Madden, N. A. (1988). Accommodating student diversity in reading and writing instruction: A cooperative learning approach. *Remedial and Special Education, 9*, 60–66.

Smith, P. K., & Connolly, K. J. (1976). Social and aggressive behavior as a function of crowding. *Social Science Information, 16*, 601–620.

Soloman, D., Watson, M. W., Delucchi, K. L., Schaps, E., & Battistich, V. (1988). Enhancing children's prosocial behavior in the classroom. *American Educational Research Journal, 25*, 527–554.

Solomon, R. W., & Wahler, R. G. (1973). Peer reinforcement control of classroom problem behavior. *Journal of Applied Behavior Analysis, 6*, 49–56.

Speigel-McGill, P., Bambara, L. M., Shores, R. E., & Fox, J. J. (1984). The effects of proximity on socially oriented behaviors of severely multiply handicapped children. *Education and Treatment of Children, 7*, 365–378.

Spivack, G., Platt, J. J., & Shure, M. B. (1976). *The problem solving approach to adjustment.* San Francisco: Jossey-Bass.

Spivack, G., & Shure, M. B. (1974). *Social adjustment of young children.* San Francisco: Jossey-Bass.

Spivack, G., & Shure, M. B. (1982). Interpersonal cognitive problem solving and clinical theory. In B. B. Lahey & A. E. Kazdin (Eds.), *Advances in child psychology* (Vol 5, pp. 322–372). New York: Plenum.

Stainback, W., & Stainback, S. (1984). A rationale for the merger of special and regular education. *Exceptional Children, 51,* 102–111.

Stanley, S. O., & Greenwood, C. R. (1981). *Code for instructional structure and student academic response (CISSAR): Observer's manual.* Kansas City: Juniper Gardens Children's Project, Bureau of Child Research, University of Kansas.

Stanley, S. O., & Greenwood, C. R. (1983). Assessing opportunity to respond in classroom environments through direct observation: How much opportunity to respond does the minority, disadvantaged, student receive in school? *Exceptional Children, 49,* 370–373.

Stein, M. K., & Wang, M. C. (1988). Teacher development and school improvement: The process of teacher change. *Training and Teacher Education, 4,* 171–187.

Stephens, T. M. (1992). *Social skills in the classroom.* Odessa, FL: Psychological Assessment Resources.

Stephens, T. M., & Arnold, K. D. (1992). *Social Behavior Assessment Inventory.* Odessa, FL: Psychological Assessment Resources.

Stodolsky, S. S. (1974). How children find something to do in preschool. *Genetic Psychology Monographs, 90,* 245–303.

Stokes, T. F., & Baer, D. M. (1977). An implicit technology of generalization. *Journal of Applied Behavior Analysis, 10,* 349–367.

Stokes, P. S., & Osnes, P. G. (1986). Programming the generalization of children's social behavior. In P. S. Strain, M. J. Guralnick, & H. M. Walker (Eds.), *Children's social behavior* (pp. 407–443). New York: Academic Press.

Stone, W. L., & La Greca, A. M. (1990). The social status of children with learning disabilities: A re-examination. *Journal of Learning Disabilities, 23,* 32–37.

Strain, P. S., & Kerr, M. M. (1981). *Mainstreaming children in schools: Research and programmatic issues.* New York: Academic Press.

Strain, P. S., & Kohler, F. W. (1988). Social skill intervention with young children with handicaps: Some new conceptualizations and directions. In S. L. Odom & M. B. Karnes (Eds.), *Early intervention for infants and children with handicaps* (pp. 129–144) Baltimore: Brookes.

Strain, P. S., Lambert, D. L., Kerr, M. M., Stagg, V., & Lenkner, D. A. (1983). A naturalistic assessment of children's compliance to teachers' requests and consequences for compliance. *Journal of Applied Behavior Analysis, 16,* 243–249.

Strain, P. S., & Odom, S. L. (1986). Peer social initiations: Effective intervention for social skills development of exceptional children. *Exceptional Children, 52,* 543–551.

Strain, P. S., Odom, S. L., & McConnell, S. (1984). Promoting social reciprocity of exceptional children: Identification, target behavior selection, and intervention. *Remedial and Special Education, 5,* 21–28.

Strain, P. S., Shores, R. E., & Timm, M. (1977). Effects of peer social initiations on the behavior of withdrawn preschool children. *Journal of Applied Behavior Analysis, 10,* 289–298.

Strayhorn, J. M., & Strain, P. S. (1986). Social and language skills for preventive mental health: What, how, who, and when. In P. S. Strain, M. J. Guralnick, & H. M. Walker (Eds.), *Children's social behavior* (pp. 287–330). Orlando, FL: Academic Press.

Swanson, H. L., & Malone, S. (1992). Social skills and learning disabilities: A meta-analysis of the literature. *School Psychology Review, 21,* 427–443.

Swearingen, E. M., & Cohen, L. H. (1985). Life events and psychological distress: A perspective study of young adolescents. *Developmental Psychology, 21,* 1045–1054.

Task Force on Education of Young Adolescents. (1989). *Turning points: Preparing American youth for the 21st century.* Washington, DC: Carnegie Council on Adolescent Development.

Tateyama-Sniezek, K. M. (1990). Cooperative learning: Does it improve the academic achievement of students with handicaps? *Exceptional Children, 56,* 426–437.

Taylor, J., & Carr, E. G. (1993). Reciprocal social influences on the analysis and intervention of severe challenging behavior. In J. Reichle & D. P. Wacker (Eds.), *Communication alternatives to challenging behavior: Integrating functional assessment and intervention strategies* (pp. 63–82). Baltimore: Brookes.

Thomas, A., Chess, S., & Birch, H. G. (1968). *Temperament and behavior disorders in children.* New York: New York University.

Thousand, J., Nevin-Parta, A., & Fox, W. L. (1987). Inservice training to support the education of learners with severe handicaps in their local public schools. *Teacher Education and Special Education, 10,* 4–13.

Tindal, G., Shinn, M. R., & Rodden-Nord, K. (1990). Contextually based school consultation: Influential variables. *Exceptional Children, 56,* 324–336.

Topping, K. (1989, March). Peer tutoring and pair reading: Combining two powerful techniques. *The Reading Teacher,* pp. 11–19.

Tremblay, R. E., Loeber, R., Gagnon, C., Charlebois, P., Larivee, S., & LeBlanc, M. (1991). Disruptive boys with stable and unstable high fighting behavior patterns during elementary school. *Journal of Abnormal Child Psychology, 19,* 285–300.

Tremblay, R. E., Masse, B., Perron, D., Le Blanc, M., Schwartzman, A. E., & Ledingham, J. E. (1992). Early disruptive behavior, poor school achievement, delinquent behavior, and delinquent personality: Longitudinal analyses. *Journal of Consulting and Clinical Psychology, 60,* 64–72.

Tremblay, R. E., McCord, J., Boileau, H., Charlebois, P., Gagnon, C., Le Blanc, M., & Larievee, S. (1991). Can disruptive boys be helped to become competent? *Psychiatry, 54,* 148–161.

Tremblay, R. E., Vitaro, F., Bertrand, L., Beauchesne, H., Boileau, H., & David, L. (1992). Parent and child training to prevent early onset of delinquency: The Montreal longitudinal-experimental study. In J. McCord & R. E. Tremblay (Eds.), *Preventing antisocial behavior: Interventions from birth to adolescence* (pp. 117–195). New York: Guilford.

Tronick, E. Z., Ricks, M., & Cohn, J. F. (1982). Maternal and infant affective exchange: Patterns of adaptation. In T. Field & A. Fogel (Eds.), *Emotion and early interaction* (pp. 83–100). Hillsdale, NJ: Erlbaum.

Turnbull, A. P., & Turnbull III, H. R. (1986) *Families, professionals, and exceptionality: A special partnership.* Columbus, OH: Merrill.

Turnbull, A., & Winton, P. (1984). Parent involvement policy and practice: Current research and implications for families with young severely handicapped children. In J. Blacher (Ed.), *Severely handicapped young children and their families: Research in review* (pp. 377–397). New York: Academic Press.

Vaughn, S., Haager, D., Hogan, A., & Kouzekanani, K. (1992). Self-concept and peer acceptance in students with LD: A four to five year prospective study. *Journal of Educational Psychology, 84,* 43–50.

Wahler, R. G. (1980). The insular mother: Her problems in parent–child treatment. *Journal of Applied Behavior Analysis, 13,* 207–219.

Wahler, R. G., & Dumas, J. E. (1989). Attentional problems in dysfunctional mother–child interactions: An interbehavioral model. *Psychological Bulletin, 105,* 116–130.

Walker, H. M., Irvin, L. K., Noell, J., & Singer, G. H. (1992). A construct score approach to the assessment of social competence. *Behavior Modification, 16,* 448–474.

Walker, H. M., & McConnell, S. R. (1988). *The Walker–McConnell Scale of Social Competence and School Adjustment: A rating scale for teachers.* Austin, TX: PRO-ED.

Walker, H. M., McConnell, S., Holmes, D., Todis, B., Walker, J., & Golden, N. (1988). *The ACCEPTS Program: A curriculum for children's effective peer and teacher skills.* Austin, TX: PRO-ED.

Wallander, J. L., & Hubert, N. C. (1987). Peer social dysfunction in children with developmental disabilities: Empirical basis and a conceptual model. *Clinical Psychology Review, 7,* 205–221.

Wang, M. C., & Zollers, N. J. (1990). Adaptive instruction: An alternative service delivery approach. *Remedial and Special Education, 11,* 7–21.

Watzlawick, P., Weakland, J., & Fisch, R. (1974). *Change: Principles of problem formulation and problem resolution.* New York: Norton.

Webster-Stratton, C. (1989). Systematic comparison of consumer satisfaction of three cost effective programs of conduct problem children. *Behavior Therapy, 20,* 103–115.

Webster-Stratton, C., Hollinsworth, T., & Kolpacoff, M. (1989). The long-term effectiveness and clinical significance of three cost-effective training programs for families with conduct-problem children. *Journal of Consulting and Clinical Psychology, 57,* 550–553.

Weiler, D. (1974). *A public school voucher demonstration: The first year at Alum Rock* (Rand Report No. 1495). Santa Monica , CA: Rand Corporation.

Weissberg, R. P. (1990, August). Support for school-based social competence promotion. *American Psychologist,* pp. 986–988.

Weissberg, R. P., & Allen, J. P. (1986). Promoting children's social skills and adaptive interpersonal behavior. In B. A. Edelstein & L. Michelson (Eds.), *Handbook of prevention* (pp. 153–175). New York: Plenum.

Weissberg, R. P., Caplan, M., & Harwood, R. L. (1991). Promoting competent young people in competence-enhancing environments: A systems-based perspective on primary prevention. *Journal of Consulting and Clinical Psychology, 59,* 830–841.

Weissberg, R. P., Caplan, M. Z., & Sivo, P. J. (1989). A new conceptual framework for establishing school-based social competence promotion programs. In L. A. Bond & B. E. Compas (Eds.), *Primary prevention and promotion in the schools* (pp. 255–296). Newbury Park, CA: Sage.

Weissberg, R. P., Gesten, E. L., Rapkin, B. D., Cowen, E. L., Davidson, E., Flores de Apodaca, R., & McKim, B. J. (1981). Evaluation of a social-problem-solving training program for suburban and inner-city third-grade children. *Journal of Consulting and Clinical Psychology, 49,* 251–261.

Weissberg, R. P., Stroup Jackson, A., & Shriver, T. P. (1993). Promoting positive social development and health practices in young urban adolescents. In M. J. Elias (Ed.), *Social decision making and life skills development* (pp. 45–56). Gaithersburg, MD: Aspen.

Weist, M. D., Borden, M. C., Finney, J. W., & Ollendick, T. H. (1991). Social skills for children: Training empirically-derived target behaviors. *Behavior Change, 8,* 174–182.

Weist, M. D., Ollendick, T. H., & Finney, J. W. (1991). Toward the empirical validation of treatment targets in children. *Clinical Psychology Review, 11,* 515–538.

Weisz, J. R., Weiss, B., & Donenberg, G. R. (1992). The lab versus the clinic: Effects of child and adolescent psychotherapy. *American Psychologist, 47,* 1578–1585.

Wentzel, K. R. (1991). Relations between social competence and academic achievement in early adolescence. *Child Development, 62,* 1066–1078.

West, D. J., & Farrington, D. T. (1973). *Who becomes delinquent?* London: Heinemann.

West, D. J., & Farrington, D. T. (1977). *The delinquent way of life.* New York: Crance, Russak.

West, J. F., & Idol, L. (1987). School consultation: Part I. An interdisciplinary perspective on theory, models, and research. *Journal of Learning Disabilities, 20,* 388–408.

Whaley, K. T., & Bennett, T. C. (1991). Promoting engagement in early childhood education. *Teaching Exceptional Children, 23,* 51–54.

Wheeler, V. A., & Ladd, G. W. (1982). Assessment of children's self-efficacy for social interactions with peers. *Developmental Psychology, 18,* 795–805.

White, B. N. (1980). Mainstreaming in grade school and preschool: How the child with special needs interacts with peers. In I. M. Field (Ed.), *High risk infants and children* (pp. 347–371). New York: Academic Press.

White, M. A. (1975). Natural rates of teacher approval and disapproval in the classroom. *Journal of Applied Behavior Analysis, 8,* 367–372.

Willems, E. P. (1974). Behavioral technology and behavioral ecology. *Journal of Applied Behavior Analysis, 7,* 151–165.

Wilson, H. (1980). Parental supervision: A neglected aspect of delinquency. *British Journal of Criminology, 20,* 203–235.

Winett, R. A., Moore, J. F., & Anderson, E. S. (1991). Extending the concept of social validity: Behavior analysis for disease prevention and health promotion. *Journal of Applied Behavior Analysis, 24,* 215–230.

Winton, P. (1986). Effective strategies for involving families in intervention efforts. *Focus on Exceptional Children, 19*(2), 1–10.

Witt, J. C. (1986). Teachers' resistance to the use of school-based interventions. *Journal of School Psychology, 24,* 37–44.

Witt, J. C., & Elliott, S. N. (1985). Acceptability of classroom intervention strategies. In T. R. Kratochwill (Ed.), *Advances in school psychology* (pp. 251–288). Hillsdale, NJ: Erlbaum.

Witt, J. C., Miller, C. D., McIntyre, R. M., & Smith, D. (1984). Effects of variables on parental perceptions of staffings. *Exceptional Children, 51*(1), 27–32.

Witt, J. C., & Robbins, J. R. (1985). Acceptability of reductive interventions for the control of inappropriate child behavior. *Journal of Abnormal Child Psychology, 13,* 59–67.

Wolery, M., & Gast, D. L. (1984). Effective and efficient procedures for the transfer of stimulus control. *Topics in Early Childhood Special Education, 4,* 52–77.

Wolf, M. M. (1978). Social validity: The case for subjective measurement, or how applied behavior analysis is finding its heart. *Journal of Applied Behavior Analysis, 11,* 203–214.

Woolfolk, R. C., & Woolfolk, A. E. (1979). Modifying the effect of the behavior modification label. *Behavior Therapy, 10,* 575–578.

York, J., & Vandercook, T. (1990). Strategies for achieving an integrated education for middle school students with severe disabilities. *Remedial and Special Education, 11,* 6–16.

Yoshikawa, H. (1994). Prevention as cumulative protection: Effects of early family support and education on chronic delinquency and its risks. *Psychological Bulletin, 115,* 28–54.

Yule, W. (1981). The epidemiology of child psychopathology. In B. B. Lahey & A. E. Kazdin (Eds.), *Advances in clinical child psychology* (Vol. 4, pp. 1–51). New York: Plenum.

Zahn, G. L., Kagan, S., & Widaman, K. F. (1986). Cooperative learning and classroom climate. *Journal of School Psychology, 24,* 351–362.

Zangwill, W. M. (1984). An evaluation of a parent training program. *Child & Family Behavior Therapy, 5*(4), 1–16.

Zaragoza, N., Vaughn, S., & McIntosh, R. (1991). Social skills interventions and children with behavior problems: A review. *Behavioral Disorders, 16,* 260–275.

Zigler, E., Taussig, C., & Black, K. (1992). Early childhood intervention: A promising preventative for juvenile delinquency. *American Psychologist, 47,* 997–1006.

# Author Index

# Subject Index

# About the Author

Joel Hundert, Ph.D., is a child psychologist, director of *Behavior Therapy Consultation Services* at Chedoke–McMaster Hospitals, and associate professor of psychiatry at McMaster University, Hamilton, Ontario. His research interests include school and preschool interventions to promote social competence and integration of preschoolers with disabilities. He has numerous scholarly publications and is on the editorial board of several journals.